the masterpiece

GOD'S UNFOLDING REVELATION

Sacha Stella Jannirs
Blessings
Joseph R Chambers

JOSEPH CHAMBERS

21ST CENTURY PRESS

PUBLISHING WITH PURPOSE

www.21STCENTURYPRESS.COM

THE MASTERPIECE
The Church in the Book Of Revelation
By Joe Chambers
Copyright © 2007

Published by 21st Century Press

21st Century Press
2131 W. Republic Rd.
PMB 41
Springfield, MO 65807

ISBN-13: 978-0-9779535-0-9

Cover: Keith Locke
Book Design: Terry White

Visit our web-site at: www.21stcenturypress.com

21ST CENTURY
PRESS
PUBLISHING WITH PURPOSE
WWW.21STCENTURYPRESS.COM

Dedication

This book is dedicated to great Senior Adults in Charlotte, NC, that have been a strength to this pastor.

Special mentions include:

Dorcas & Frances Ballard
Juanita Ballard
Sylvia Beasley
Marlon Clark
Eddie & Mary Cobb
James & Rose Lindsey
Nona Lindsey
Bill & Teen McCall
Mickie Morrison
Ann Milligan
Lucielle Mumford
Bill Osborn
Flonnie Pressley
Ida Mae Seawright
Jim & Cora Spell
Kenneth & Sandie Wilkinson
Eugene & Ruby Williams
Aundra Wright

The Masterpiece

The Church in the Book Of Revelation

PREFACE

The Book of Revelation is a storybook. It takes the reader from the scene of Christ's glory as the Father's High Priest in His heavenly temple to the final temple called "New Jerusalem" where His Bride will dwell eternally with Him. The Book of Revelation is the "masterpiece" of all Biblical stories. It begins with His glory and ends with His saints' glory. At the beginning of this story, He walks in the midst of His church, but in the end, His church walks in the midst of New Jerusalem, the most spectacular city ever dreamed of. This storybook is the "Revelation of Jesus Christ," the complete unveiling of all His glory. The very first chapter gives forty-one references to the Son of God.

Revelation chapter one is a word portrait of the "Only Begotten Son." In the first eight verses there are twenty-three redemptive titles or descriptive words that the angel gives John concerning Jesus Christ. All of these terms or titles relate to His life, His ministry, and His accomplishments and promises. The second half of the first chapter is the portrait of Him as the High Priest in the Father's heavenly temple. There are eighteen titles or descriptions of Him in His roles as our Advocate and Intercessor. Stephen got a little view of this great truth of His intercession, just before he was ushered up into heaven, when he saw Him *"standing at the Father's right hand"* (Acts 7:56).

From this picture of His glorious person, the storybook takes us through all the great end-times events until we walk down the streets of gold in the matchless city He has prepared for His Bride. The story is not all pretty, but it's all true and will unfold in the order in which it is told. The great thing about the Book of Revelation is that God wants you to be prepared and to be in heaven, not on earth as the story unfolds its dark scenes. Nobody that reads The Revelation before the Rapture should have to endure the hellish events that will occur on earth. If there is one reason above all others that He gave us this "Book of Revelation," it is to educate as to what we can do to be on the right side as the story transpires.

Do not let anyone make you think that the devil or his Antichrist and false prophets are the main characters of this book. They are not! The Son of God is the heart of Revelation. His unveiling is so that we might see Him from His resurrection glory to His eternal presence in the new heaven and the new earth. This is the theme of this book. His presence is the life of the story. While He is the life of Revelation, He is always in the very presence of His Father that gave Him as the sacrifice. He is called a Lamb more than any other of His great titles because His death makes the whole story possible.

The dark parts of Revelation are never meant to scare you but to show the end of sin. This story will excite you to know that when God finally says *"there shall be no more curse"* (Revelation 22:3a), and puts an end to sin once and for all, the results will truly be heaven on earth. The Son of God directs every scene of horror because sin must be seen in its right character. While sin reveals all its ugliness, the rainbow over the Father's throne keeps sending a message of mercy. Not one time in this book are sinners left without the opportunity to call on the "God of all mercies." The story of Revelation gives us an honest look at sin, but in the presence of a *"Lamb as it had been slain"* (Revelation 5:9).

What a story this "masterpiece" of all God's literature repre-sents. This great Book of Revelation makes the whole Bible become a different book. Our God and His Son are at the center revealing their great love. God's Bible is not a narrow book as some may accuse. It is factual, so factual that no science has ever proven it to be false. The archeologists have searched the crust of the earth and have found much evidence of past history, but each new finding only proves that history is "His-story."

Read this book like a story and revel in its great revelations. Believe in the Lord Jesus Christ with a total surrender to Him; for He lives in this great Book of Revelation, and you will be on the winning side, for you will know the end of the story.

The grace of our Lord be with you all. Amen.
—Revelation 22:21

The End Times Model

"Every End Time prophecy in the Bible was ordained by God to fit the model in the Book of Revelation."

The Beginning
- "In the beginning ..." (Genesis 1:1)
- "In the beginning was the Word ..." (John 1:1)
- "Yet, it pleased the Lord to bruise Him." (Isaiah 53:10)
- "Who being the brightness of His glory ..." (Hebrews 1:3)
- "Behold, I come quickly." (Revelation 22:7)
  - "One like unto the Son of man ..." (Revelation 1:13)
    - "I am He that liveth." (Revelation 1:18)

THE FAMILY OF GOD

- "Noah found grace ..." (Genesis 6:8)
- "Come thou and all thy house (family) ..." (Genesis 7:1)
- "... church in the wilderness." (Acts 7:38)
- "The remnant of my people ..." (Zephaniah 2:9)
- "... I will build my church." (Matthew 16:18)
- "... that He might present it to Himself a glorious church." (Ephesians 5:27)
- "Unto the angel of the church ..." (Rev. 2:1)

THE RAPTURE OF HIS SAINTS

- "Come ... into the ark." (Genesis 7:1)
- "Enoch ... was not; for God took him." (Genesis 5:24)
- "Elijah went up by a whirlwind." (II Kings 2:11)
- "Come ... enter thou into thy chambers." (Isaiah 26:20)
- "They shall be Mine ... when I make up My jewels." (Malachi 3:17)
- "... shall be caught up." (I Thessalonians 4:17)
- "I will come again, and receive you unto my-self." (John 14:3)
- And they sang, "And hast made us unto our God kings and priests." (Revelation 5:10)

The Great Tribulation

Four Creatures
- "Four living creatures" (Ezekiel 1:5)
- "And four great beasts" (Daniel 7:3)
- "One of the four beasts" (Revelation 6:1)

Seven-Sealed Book (Seven Trumpets/Seven Thunders)
- A book ... "therein lamentations....woe" (Ezekiel 2:10)
- "A book that is sealed" (Isaiah 29:11)
- "And He came and took the book." (Revelation 5:7)
- "The Lamb opened one of the seals." (Revelation 6:1)

The Latter Rain
- "The sun shall be turned into darkness" (Joel 2:31)
- "Whosoever shall call ... shall be saved." (Acts 2:21)
- "Came out of great tribulation, and have washed their robes" (Revelation 7:14)

Joel's Army (Spirits Out of Hell) Tormenting Men
- "... the appearance of horses" (Joel 2:4)
- "Like unto horses ... hair of women" (Revelation 9:7-8)

Ten study booklets, one covering each section in this model, are available!

Chap. 1 | 21 - 22 | 20 | 19 | 18 | 17 | 6-11 | 12-16 | 2-3 | 4-5

The Book of Revelation

"The Revelation of Jesus Christ, which God gave unto him, to shew unto his servants things which must shortly come to pass." "Write the things which thou hast seen, and the things which are, and the things which shall be hereafter." (Revelation 1:1,19)

New Jerusalem
- "Behold, I create new heavens and a new earth." (Isaiah 65:17)
- "Jesus said, "I go to prepare a place..." (John 14:2)
- "And I saw a new heaven and a new earth." (Revelation 21:1)
- "... prepared as a bride for her husband" (Revelation 21:2)
- "... saved shall walk in the light of it." (Revelation 21:24)
- "They shall reign for ever." (Revelation 22:5)

The White Throne
Jesus Christ is your only escape!
- "Judgment cometh from the Lord." (Proverbs 29:26)
- "Judgment also will I lay to the line." (Isaiah 28:17)
- "Reserved unto fire ... judgment" (II Peter 3:7)
- "And I saw a great white throne." (Revelation 20:11)
- "Not ... in the book ... cast into the lake of fire." (Rev. 20:15)

The Marriage Supper
- "... out of the ivory palaces" (Psalm 45:8)
- "Come ... enter thou into thy chambers." (Isaiah 26:20)
- Abraham "looked for a city which hath foundations." (Hebrews 11:10)
- "... present it to Himself a glorious church" (Eph 5:27)
- We shall reign on the earth. (Revelation 5:10)
- "Blessed ... called unto the Marriage Supper." (Rev. 19:9)

Babylon Rebuilt
- "Babylon hath been a golden cup." (Jeremiah 51:7)
- "Babylon is fallen, is fallen." (Isaiah 21:9)
- "Babylon is fallen, is fallen." (Revelation 14:8)
- Antichrist slain in the entrance of Nimrod. (Micah 5:6)
- "Babylon, that mighty city ..." (Revelation 18:10)

Mystery Babylon, One World Religion
- "Neither shall he regard the God of his fathers." (Daniel 11:37)
- "... multitude "corrupt by flatteries." (Daniel 11:32)
  - A worldwide multitude that has lost all Biblical discernment and cannot be saved after the Rapture.
  - "God shall send them strong delusion." (II Thessalonians 2:11)
    - "The Great Whore that sitteth" (Revelation 17:1)

The Unholy Trinity

Satan
- "Thou shalt be brought down to hell." (Isaiah 14:15)
- "I beheld Satan as lightning fall from heaven." (Luke 10:18)
- "And the great dragon was cast out." (Revelation 12:9)

Antichrist
- "A ... beast, dreadful and terrible" (Daniel 7:7)
- "... A beast rise up out of the sea" (Revelation 13:1)

Anti-Spirit (False Anointing)
- "Arise false Christs, and false prophets." (Matthew 24:24)
- "... beheld another beast" (Revelation 13:11)

Seven Plaques (Seven Vials)
- "When thy judgments are in the earth" (Isaiah 26:9)
- "... in His hand a sharp sickle" (Revelation 14:14)

All Israel Shall Be Saved
- "... a time of trouble, such as never was" (Daniel 12:1)
- "I will pour upon (Israel) ... grace" (Zechariah 12:10)
- "I will bring the third part through the fire." (Zechariah 13:9)
- "And so all Israel shall be saved." (Romans 11:26)

Seven Years Seen From Heaven	Same Seven Years Seen From Earth
Jesus said, "Then shall be great tribulation ..." (Matthew 24:21)	"Such as was not since the beginning..." (Matthew 24:21)

THE MASTERPIECE OF LITERATURE

Introduction One

Without the Book of Revelation, the other sixty-five books of the Bible— Genesis to Jude—do not present a clear outline of end-time prophecy. Each writer gives us a beautiful part of the whole, but these parts were never meant to finish the story. The Bible must be rightly divided, with every book and every writer set together in harmony to finish the whole. The glorified Son of God chose John the apostle to be His writer and then gave John the revelation in precise order to put the whole of end-time truth in an exact outline just as it will occur. This book is God's model of perfect fulfillment as the Lord Himself has ordered. Any Bible student that ignores this book and its order will be helpless to teach or preach prophecy.

There is a masterpiece of order in this Book of Revelation. The flow of each chapter follows a design that makes the book easy to understand, but only if you follow the pattern. To move at random in reading or studying it will confuse you completely. Our God is an orderly Creator and His revelations are pure and precise. It is evident that His Holy Spirit and His angels that assisted in this great revelation were acting at His command. The whole twenty-two chapters give us an unparalleled masterpiece of literature. The text itself sets the perfect moment when future revelations begin. John writes, *"After this I looked, and, behold, a door was opened in heaven: and the first voice which I heard was as it were of a trumpet talking with me; which said, Come up hither,*

11

and I *will shew thee things which must be hereafter*" (Revelation 4:1). From this point forward, nothing can be interpreted as historic or occurring prior to the church in heaven at the Rapture.

The order of the names ascribed to His saints truly documents the flow of the story. A description of the Son of God and the names given in each revelation follow a beautiful pattern. We will look at these two facts after we view a model of the entire book. First, let's look at that model of the book and set the outline for us to follow. This model will clear up a lot of confusion and help you get a broad picture to be used in your study time. (See model page 10) Let's review each of the ten sections in this pattern and build a plan to illustrate this great book of the Bible. Understanding The Revelation will make the entire Bible come alive for you. Remember, it is a story that Jesus is conveying to us. Fixing the chronological sequence is important if you intend to enjoy this great Revelation story. We start with Christ after He was crucified, resurrected and glorified. He is altogether lovely and glorious in chapter one of the Book of Revelation. As you view the section of the "end-time model," the progression becomes very simple. From the glory of His resurrection we move carefully to the story of His eternal city named, New Jerusalem. You will be ecstatic when you reach that star-studded city that John saw "coming down" from heaven to earth (Revelation 21:2).

Revelation One
The Beginning
- "In the beginning ..." (Genesis 1:1)
- "In the beginning was the Word ..." (John 1:1)
- "Yet, it pleased the Lord to bruise Him." (Isaiah 53:10)
- "Who being the brightness of His glory ..." (Hebrews 1:3)
- "Behold, I come quickly." (Revelation 22:7)
- "One like unto the Son of man ..." (Revelation 1:13)

12

- "I am He that liveth." (Revelation 1:18)

This is the introduction to the whole book and gives us a breathtaking description of the Son of God. There are forty-one different titles or descriptive word pictures of Him given in this first chapter. The different descriptions of Jesus Christ in His glory are repeated in the seven letters to the churches. Each church letter only includes a part of that vision so that all seven letters become a complete repeat of Him as seen in chapter one.

Revelation Two and Three
The Family of God
- "Noah found grace ..." (Genesis 6:8)
- "Come thou and all thy house (family) ..." (Genesis 7:1)
- "... church in the wilderness." (Acts 7:38)
- "The remnant of my people ..." (Zephaniah 2:9)
- "... I will build my church." (Matthew 16:18)
- "... that He might present it to Himself a glorious church." (Ephesians 5:27)
- "Unto the angel of the church ..." (Rev. 2:1)

The seven letters to the seven churches in Asia were never meant to be limited to those seven churches. These are letters for the churches universal until the church is caught up to the throne. The seven churches all existed in John's day, and models of each exist today. The seven historical time periods will be described in chapters two and three with all the contents of each of the seven churches and periods.

These letters are the last love letters and warnings from Jesus Christ to the body of Christ. They should be read, studied, and preached with vigor and joy. The church was commended because they did not tolerate false teachers and exposed them with great dedication. The call to holiness and separation was dynamic. The church, true to the meaning of the word, is a called-out company, set in authority to conduct the business of the Lord. Revelation chapters two and three reveal the beautiful story of the church, both its strength and promises and its weaknesses and failure. His love for the church is in itself a divine love story.

Revelation Four and Five
The Rapture of His Saints

- "Come ... into the ark." (Genesis 7:1)
- "Enoch ... was not; for God took him." (Genesis 5:24)
- "Elijah went up by a whirlwind." (II Kings 2:11)
- "Come ... enter thou into thy chambers." (Isaiah 26:20)
- "They shall be Mine ... when I make up My jewels." (Malachi 3:17)
- "... shall be caught up." (I Thessalonians 4:17)
- "I will come again, and receive you unto myself." (John 14:3)
- And they sang, "And hast made us unto our God kings and priests." (Revelation 5:10)

The church is only called "the church" one time after Revelation 4:1. This is a warning intended to speak to us before the actual beginning of events that occur after chapter four or as we read and study this great revelation. The saints are immediately given a new title as this chapter is presented. We will be His elders and are called elders in every instance from Revelation four to Revelation nineteen and verse fourteen. This is absolute proof that the saints will be caught up in the Rapture in fulfillment of this vision in chapters four and five and before chapter six opens.

We are called elders because we will be His elders in the transactions of the succeeding chapters. We will not just be His saints watching the opening of His seals and the transaction of His judgments, we will be a part of the scene. "Elder" is a marvelous title to describe our activities with the Lord of the church. The fact that we are seated on thrones while this vision is unveiled multiplies our involvement with the coming events of the Great Tribulation. The taking of the seven-sealed book in chapter five is the preparation for the Tribulation to begin in chapter six. This book is the title deed of the earth and it is the document that will determine the rest of this "Masterpiece" of God's full redemption story.

Revelation Six to Eleven: Seven Years Seen From Heaven
The Great Tribulation

Four Creatures
- "Four living creatures" (Ezekiel 1:5)
- "And four great beasts" (Daniel 7:3)
- "One of the four beasts" (Revelation 6:1)

Seven-Sealed Book (Seven Trumpets/Seven Thunders)
- A book ... "therein lamentations...woe" (Ezekiel 2:10)
- "A book that is sealed" (Isaiah 29:11)
- "And He came and took the book." (Revelation 5:7)
- "The Lamb opened one of the seals." (Revelation 6:1)

The Latter Rain
- "The sun shall be turned into darkness" (Joel 2:31)
- "Whosoever shall call ... shall be saved." (Acts 2:21)
- "Came out of great tribulation, and have washed their robes" (Revelation 7:14)

Joel's Army (Spirits Out of Hell) Tormenting Men
- "... the appearance of horses" (Joel 2:4)
- "Like unto horses ... hair of women" (Revelation 9:7-8)

While chapters four and five are the transcending moments of the celebration of the church, victorious and glorified, chapter six starts the eviction of Satan and his spirits and the forthcoming judgment of sin on this earth. Everything contrary to God and His absolute righteousness has to be fully judged and cleansed from this universe. Chapter six begins that process. While Jesus was seen in glorified splendor in chapters one, two, and three, He is now seen as a slain Lamb performing the judicial acts for the perfect redemption of the created universe. It will be returned to the likeness of the Garden of Eden without one thorn infested bush or cloud in the sky.

The view in chapters six to eleven covers the whole of the seven years of the Great Tribulation from a heavenly view. The saints were raptured in the beginning of chapters four and are viewing and participating in this scene from a heavenly vantage point. First and Second Testament writers prophesied of many great truths that are seen in these chapters. Their chronological order is clearly set forth in the progression we view on the pages of the Holy Scripture in this book.

Revelation Twelve to Sixteen: Same Seven Years Seen From Earth
The Unholy Trinity
Satan
- "Thou shalt be brought down to hell." (Isaiah 14:15)
- "I beheld Satan as lightning fall from heaven." (Luke 10:18)
- "And the great dragon was cast out." (Revelation 12:9)

Antichrist
- "A ... beast, dreadful and terrible" (Daniel 7:7)
- "... A beast rise up out of the sea" (Revelation 13:1)

Anti-Spirit (False Anointing)
- "Arise false Christs, and false prophets." (Matthew 24:24)
- "... beheld another beast" (Revelation 13:11)

Seven Plaques (Seven Vials)
- "When thy judgments are in the earth" (Isaiah 26:9)
- "… in His hand a sharp sickle" (Revelation 14:14)

All Israel Shall Be Saved
- "… a time of trouble, such as never was" (Daniel 12:1)
- "I will pour upon (Israel) … grace" (Zechariah 12:10)
- "I will bring the third part through the fire." (Zechariah 13:9)
- "And so all Israel shall be saved." (Romans 11:26)

This covers the same seven years as chapters six through eleven but from an earthly view. Now, the scene moves to cover the casting out of the devil from the second heaven and the revealing of his false trinity: Satan himself as god, the first beast as Antichrist, and the second beast as the false prophet. It's important to see chapter twelve as a repeat of chapter four and following the same period but with an earthly picture of evil incarnate on the earth. The saints, are seen caught up in the first picture—chapter four—while the Jewish converts are seen in heaven with God in the second picture—chapter fourteen—of the same seven years.

Also, in the first picture of the seven years of Tribulation we see the two prophets that could not be killed, but were finally allowed by God to be killed and then raptured up to heaven before the watching eyes of the world. In the second picture, we see a remnant of Jews different from the 144,000, that had been sealed, also in heaven with God (Revelation 15:2-4).

Revelation Seventeen
Mystery Babylon, One World Religion
- "Neither shall he regard the God of his fathers." (Daniel 11:37)
- … multitude "corrupt by flatteries." (Daniel 11:32)

- A worldwide multitude that has lost all Biblical discernment and cannot be saved after the Rapture.
- "God shall send them strong delusion." (II Thessalonians 2:11)
- "The Great Whore that sitteth" (Revelation 17:1)

The events of this chapter and the next two all occur during the same seven years of Tribulation, but they must be viewed separately to fully understand them. This is the picture of the One World Religion that will reign during the seven years. Led by the second beast or the false prophet, or we may call him "the false anointed one," it will be an apostate religion with a "Christian" imitation and totally false. We see this religion of unity developing in our world today. Doctrine is out, but politically correct unity is in. Religion, in preparation for this coming seven years, must be a smorgasbord of ideas and theologies all equally held and tolerated. This liberal mindset is flooding the church world.

The one idea that will be excluded is Biblical infallibility. The final authority of Scripture is too narrow, the rejection of pagan ideas is too restrictive, the idea of an eternal Lake of Fire is too unmerciful, and any strong standard of God's commandments is plainly unacceptable. While this broad religion will give great support to the Antichrist and his One World Government, he and the false prophet will become competitors. The first Beast will declare Babylon the eternal city, while the second beast will declare and defend Rome as the eternal city. The Antichrist will burn the city of Rome and the ecclesiastical system of the One World Religion. When the Antichrist has full worldwide control, he will not need the religious system any longer.

Revelation Eighteen
Babylon Rebuilt
- "Babylon hath been a golden cup." (Jeremiah 51:7)

18

- "Babylon is fallen, is fallen." (Isaiah 21:9)
- "Babylon is fallen, is fallen." (Revelation 14:8)
- Antichrist slain in the entrance of Nimrod. (Micah 5:6)
- "Babylon, that mighty city ..." (Revelation 18:10)

The city of Babylon will have finally returned to its past glory, but will have an even greater glory than in the past. The palace built by Saddam Hussein overlooking the city of Babylon will soon be the palace of the Antichrist or the first beast. He will rule the world from his Babylon location. As an Assyrian, he will come to power by flatteries but rule by the same vicious cruelty as the ancient Assyrians. Babylon has been the center of Satan's activities since a short time after the creation. The great prophets of the First Testament, especially Isaiah and Jeremiah, prophesied of this revival of Babylon's mysticism and religious debauchery.

Since Babylon moved its dark religion to Rome as a deceptive action and faded off the radar, Satan has longed to recapture its original glory. The devil moved Saddam to start the process. The last tour and singing album by the Rolling Stones was entitled, "Back to Babylon." Who better than a demon-possessed singing group to call for a return to Ancient Babylon? The defeat of Saddam Hussein and the present struggle to establish a democracy in Iraq shows the perfect timing of Biblical prophecy. The entire region of Babylon will be totally obliterated and become a desolate wasteland during the future Millennium of Jesus Christ, and as will be documented, could even be the future location of the Lake of Fire.

Revelation Nineteen
The Marriage Supper
- "... out of the Ivory Palaces" (Psalm 45:8)
- "Come ... enter thou into thy chambers." (Isaiah 26:20)

- Abraham "looked for a city which hath foundations." (Hebrews 11:10)
- "... present it to Himself a glorious church" (Eph 5:27)
- "We shall reign on the earth." (Revelation 5:10)
- "Blessed ... called unto the Marriage Supper" (Rev. 19:9)

This chapter covers more than one subject, but the central theme is the "Marriage Supper." The greatest event in heaven during the seven years of the Great Tribulation is this wedding. The Son of God will be the Bridegroom and the raptured saints will be His Bride.

The banquet hall is in the city foursquare that John saw in chapters twenty-one and twenty-two. That city will not descend to the earth until after the Millennium—the one thousand year reign of Jesus Christ—has concluded. Yet, the Bride at the marriage will meet her Bridegroom in the city and will be given her rewards and mansion at some point before she descend to earth with Christ as His army to defeat Satan, his two beasts, and his army of the wicked, marked with the *Mark of the Beast* (Revelation 19:20), at the end of the seven-year Tribulation.

The saints that return with Christ in glorified bodies will be fully capable to ascend and descend between the city and the earth. We will reign with Him over all the earth from both our heavenly mansion and our earthly dwelling. Jesus Christ has been called the "Lamb" or the "Lamb of God" from Revelation four and five to the point where He descends with His saints to defeat the Antichrist and establish His kingdom on earth. This is another great proof of the Pre-Tribulation Rapture. The Lord of the church is wonderfully present in Revelation one, two, and three and immediately becomes the Lamb of God revealed as a judicially victorious judge in chapter four to chapter nineteen.

Revelation Twenty

The White Throne

Jesus Christ is your only escape!

- "Judgment cometh from the Lord." (Proverbs 29:26)
- "Judgment also will I lay to the line." (Isaiah 28:17)
- "Reserved unto fire ... judgment" (II Peter 3:7)
- "And I saw a great white throne." (Revelation 20:11)
- "Not ... in the book ... cast into the lake of fire." (Rev 20:15)

This great chapter covers the judgment of the devil and his being cast down into the bottomless pit. He will be out of commission for one thousand years, which is the great time of Christ's Millennium on earth. That is a wonderful period where the faithful saints are given their geographical dominion over the earth. We will reign with Him over this universe and enjoy a glorious Millennium of purity, peace, and prosperity. But the focus event of this chapter will be the Great White Throne Judgment that follows the One Thousand Year Reign of Jesus Christ.

The wicked dead will know nothing of the Great Marriage Supper, our eldership with Christ during the Tribulation Period, or our reign with Him as kings and priests on earth. Their resurrection is a resurrection of damnation that occurs right before the new heaven and new earth is revealed to the saints. Bodies of damnation suggest that every evil, rebellion, or wickedness known in life will be manifest in their resurrection. These are bodies that will live forever in the Lake of Fire and are continually filled with every appetite of the flesh and of evil spirits which they have followed. They will see the saints ready to enter into Heaven's eternal joys, but they will be barred at the door. As they are judged, the Book of Life with all its promises will be there; but the search for their name will be filled with great consternation. Trembling and great emotional sobs will fill the air, but mercy will be absent. The two kingdoms—darkness and light—will have finished their campaigns of conversions, each seeking to win the world for their master. The die is cast, and the eternal future for all souls is settled. It's the New Jerusalem and the new heaven and the new earth, or it's the Lake of Fire—an insane asylum for eternity.

Revelation Twenty-One and Twenty-Two
New Jerusalem
- "Behold, I create new heavens and a new earth." (Isaiah 65:17)
- Jesus said, "I go to prepare a place..." (John 14:2)
- "And I saw a new heaven and a new earth." (Revelation 21:1)
- "... prepared as a bride for her husband" (Revelation 21:2)
- "... saved shall walk in the light of it." (Revelation 21:24)
- "They shall reign for ever." (Revelation 22:5)

It's over! Eternity has finally begun. Sin is history and the devil is in the Lake of Fire, never to worry or bother another angel or soul again. His last hoorah was a failure. Everything he labored to accomplish, along with his false Christ and false prophet, is utterly destroyed. His kingdom of darkness is no more. The devil will have the darkest hole in the Lake of Fire for all eternity.

But, the saints have just begun to live. The new heaven and the new earth are a worldwide Garden. The entire universe is in perfect peace, and there is no one to mar the bliss. Sickness and disease are forever removed, death is a forgotten dark dream, and all tears are washed away. The Father and His Son are the Light of the world, and they are present to enjoy and be enjoyed.

To crown this new heaven and new earth is a golden city fifteen hundred miles square and fifteen hundred miles high. It descends from God out of heaven. Twelve foundations and twelve levels give us living space of 27,000,000 square miles just in the city. There will be no vast oceans on the new earth, and the great new heaven will give us an enlarged world to enjoy. There will be space to spare as we live in an unspotted world full of saints and angels all enjoying the Father and His Son.

Conclusion

What a revelation fills the pages of this "Masterpiece." Its organization is unparalleled, and its message is the hope of the ages. Some people read this book and only view the thorns of evil and judgment. But every thorn has a rose beside it, and every judgment has redemption in its finish. Sin must be forever vanquished, and to do so cannot be all beauty. This book answers the question of the doubters and fills the bosom of the believers with unspoiled assurance. After we view the progression of the titles given to His saints and the progression of the names assigned to our Lord, we will take each chapter verse-by-verse to watch a new heaven and a new earth unfold in the end. What a story this masterpiece presents.

Jesus Christ In The Book Of Revelation

> The Son of God is given many titles in the Book of Revelation. His central name proves that the Book of Revelation is primarily a book of redemption -- that title is "Lamb of God."

	Lord of the Church	The Lamb of God	Faithful and True	The King of Kings	The Bridegroom
Heavenly Picture	• There are forty-one titles given to Christ in Chapter One (Rev. 1:5-18). • Jesus Christ is seated at the Father's Right Hand in Heaven. • He directs the spiritual kingdom of His church (Rev. 2:2).	• Christ is with His Bride in Heavenly Jerusalem (Rev. 5:6). • He takes the Book from the Father's hand and opens it (Rev. 5:7-8). • He opens the seals and directs the judgments with His elders (Rev. 6:1).	• He is the mighty warrior leading His army against the Antichrist army (Rev. 19:11). • All the saints in Heaven mount white horses and descend as His army (Rev. 19:14).	• Christ takes His position on the Throne of David to reign as King. • Every kingdom on earth brings their glory to Jerusalem.	• New Jerusalem descends from Heaven and the Father reigns with Jesus Christ (Rev. 21:3). • The Father and Jesus Christ are the Light of the world (Rev. 21:23).
	Timeline		**Timeline**		
	Chapters 1,2,3	4:1 - 19:10	19:11-21	20:1 - 20:15	21:1 - 22:21
	The Lord Raptures His Church to Heaven				
Earthly Results	• Christ is walking in the midst of His overcoming saints on earth (Rev. 3:7). • He commands and charges His church to be pure in doctrine. • He is preparing His saints to be His Bride and is never seen as the Lord of the church after the seven letters to His churches.	• The believers on earth are called Tribulation Saints (Rev. 7). • Christ seals 144,000 Jewish believers to protect them from the Antichrist. • His wrath is poured out on the wicked world. • Satan and the Antichrist are allowed their last evil design.	• The Antichrist is slain by Christ in the Gate of Babylon (Micah 5:6). • The Jewish world is fully ready for Christ and are converted. • After Christ defeats the Antichrist, He quickly goes to Jerusalem and enters the Eastern Gate.	• The elders are now Christ's kings and priests. They reign over the entire earth except for Israel (Rev. 20:6). • The Jews inherit the total land mass promised to Abraham	• The River of Life and the Tree of Life become the divine source of Jesus Christ's eternal life flowing from the throne (Rev. 22:1-3). • The City of New Jerusalem is the capital of the world (Rev. 21:24).
Length of Time	The Total Age of the Church On Earth	Seven Years of the Great Tribulation	A Short Time Establishing His Kingdom On Earth	1,000 Year Millennium Reign	Eternity New Heaven & New Earth

THE LORD REVEALED IN HIS REVELATION

Introduction Two

The Book of Revelation is the revelation of Jesus Christ at the highest level. He, in all of His redemptive person, is the mountain peak of the book. While He and His Father are equal in all matters of the Godhead, He is the revelation of redemption for the entire universe. In the end, the Father will be all in all because Christ will deliver the kingdom to Him. There are many created beings that have a place in this book with the Son, His Father, and the Holy Spirit,—but second to the glory of our God is the glory of His saints. The four beasts are certainly glorious as His Cherubim that are always present when the Father is directing judgment and special activities on His earth. They will be called living creatures or Cherubim as the story progresses. There are other angels that participate and literally multitudes that ring the entire proceedings with their presence, but His saints are the reason for the book.

"Christ unveiled" has often been the first description of the Book of Revelation. It is indeed "a taking off of the cover" of the glories of the Son of God, but it is more. It is the removing of the veil from Him and from His stupendous plans and prophecies of His works of redemption and judgments and the glory to follow. His total plan for His saints is almost as glorious as He is, because it is His glory that He shares with His Bride. The first chapter reveals His personal glory as the foundation to reveal all the glories of His coming revelation. Never in any one chapter of the entire Word of God has any one person been described with so many adjectives and titles.

A Name That is Above All Names

The Father has given His victorious Son a "Name above every Name" (Philippians 2:9) and this chapter of God's masterpiece begins with a divine description. Forty-one adjectives and nouns are used to present Him to His chosen saints and His church. Every one of those descriptions was meant for His revelation to us. All the majesty that fills this book must have a divine foundation, and He is that foundation. In these titles and descriptions, He builds a superstructure of a holy house of literature in order that the words that create that house might carry us to the New Jerusalem of perfect existence and fulfillment. There is nothing about this house of words that is not divine and literal. It is all intended to be His story. Truth must flow out of Him because He is the Word of God. Chapter one is a foundational chapter, and represents the greatest display of His character, His triumph, and His glories ever revealed to humankind. It is breathtaking!

Let's read them without comment. *"... from Jesus Christ ... Who is the faithful witness ... the first begotten of the dead ... the prince of the kings of the earth ... that loved us ... washed us from our sins ... in His own blood ... He cometh with clouds ... every eye shall see Him ... they also which pierced Him ... all kindreds of the earth shall wail because of Him ... I am ... Alpha... Omega ... the beginning... the ending ... saith the Lord, ... which is ... which was ... which is to come ... the Almighty ... Alpha ... Omega ... the first ... the last ... the Son of man ... clothed with a garment down to the foot ... girt about the paps with a golden girdle ... His head and His hairs were white like wool ... His eyes were as a flame of fire ... His feet like unto fine brass, as if they burned in a furnace*

... His voice as the sound of many waters ... in His right hand seven stars ... out of His mouth went a sharp two-edged sword ... His countenance was as the sun shineth in His strength ... the first ... the last ... I am He that liveth, and was dead ... behold, I am alive for evermore ... Amen ... and have the keys of hell and of death" (Revelation 1:5-18). *"Write the things which thou hast seen, and the things which are, and the things which shall be hereafter"* (Revelation 1:19) and send them to the churches.

No such comprehensive description of Christ is found elsewhere in the Bible. He intended that we take this Book as our battle cry and fill our world with the hope of both Him and the pattern of our future. To even consider the church, filled with joy and the Holy Ghost without Christ and His plans for our future is mindless. These are the two things this great work of literary beauty is all about. The first verse sets the purpose in stone. *"The Revelation [unveiling} of Jesus Christ, which God [Father] gave unto him, to shew unto his servants [church] things [events] which must shortly come to pass; and he sent and signified it by his angel unto his servant John"* (Revelation 1:1). Let's follow the different titles of Jesus Christ as they change in this great story.

The Lord In The Midst Of His Church

While chapter one lifts our Lord Jesus Christ to the pinnacle of His glory, chapters two and three establish that His heart is His church and that He is constantly in their midst. He is seated at the Father's right hand, but by His Spirit, who is the omnipresent person of He and His Father, He walks in the midst of His church. He beholds us. He intercedes for us. He defends us against every enemy. He hears our prayers with the Father. He directs His Spirit and all His gifts. He calls and sends, and then goes before us in all matters of His church and His saints.

He begins the first letter to His churches by stating clearly His

Lord of the Church

- There are forty-one titles given to Christ in Chapter One (Rev. 1:5-18).
- Jesus Christ is seated at the Father's Right Hand in Heaven.
- He directs the spiritual kingdom of His church (Rev. 2:2).

TIMELINE
Chapters 1, 2, 3

- Christ is walking in the midst of His overcoming saints on earth (Rev. 3:7).
- He commands and charges His church to be pure in doctrine.
- He is preparing His saints to be His Bride and is never seen as the Lord of the church after the seven letters to His churches.

The Total Age of the Church On Earth

awesome presence. *"Unto the angel of the church of Ephesus write; These things saith he that holdeth the seven stars in his right hand, who walketh in the midst of the seven golden candlesticks"* (Revelation 2:1). It is only to Ephesus that He clarifies the unity of the seven churches and made the seven letters a united message. He takes His introduction unto Ephesus and then closes all seven letters with an equally uniting phrase, *"Behold, I stand at the door, and knock: if any man hear my voice, and open the door, I will come in to him, and will sup with him, and he with me"* (Revelation 3:20). These seven letters are made a united whole in Revelation chapters two and three.

The chart at the beginning of the chapter is a timeline designed to help you see the progression of Christ's titles that set forth the order of the book. Everything about the Book of Revelation is chronological, and can only be understood if the chronology is not broken. The chart sets the overall pattern and the progression of all end-times events from the church age to His Golden City and helps to keep the pattern strong and clear. The center of the book is the Master Himself and then His revelations.

The Lord As The Lamb of God

The Rapture occurs in Revelation 4:1 when God calls to John, who is exiled on the Isle of Patmos and says, *"Come up hither!"* From this time on, the Son of God is with the saints and together they are redeeming and cleansing this earth for the glory to come. From Revelation 4:1 the Lord Jesus Christ is pictured as the Lamb of God and is called *"Lamb"* or *"Lamb of God"* twenty-one times between this point and Revelation 19:9. Because The Lord Jesus Christ is the Lamb, He is qualified to take possession of the earth as its Great Judicial Kinsman Redeemer. The Kinsman Redeemer had to be next in kin to the rightful owner. Jesus Christ was next in kin to His Father and earned the right to redeem this universe. That right of ownership was won by His sacrifice on the cross and His broken body. The description of the exalting of this Lamb before the raptured multitude and the heavenly host that will participate in the great seven years of righteous judgment on the earth is as a *"Lamb as it had been slain"* (Revelation 5:6).

In describing the events taking place in the throne room of God, John writes, *"And I beheld, and, lo, in the midst of the throne and of the four beasts, and in the midst of the elders, stood a Lamb as it had been slain, having seven horns and seven eyes, which are the seven Spirits of God sent forth into all the earth"* (Revelation 5:6). Every time you see the term "Lamb" from chapter five to chapter nineteen, verse nine, the presence of the Lamb includes the presence of the Holy Spirit as having seven horns and seven eyes. Every act of the Lamb is possessed by the omnipotent power (seven horns) and the omniscient wisdom (seven eyes) manifest by the Holy Spirit.

This is an awesome picture and the story of the Son of God. It is impossible not to conclude that the entire scene has changed His role and title as "Lord of the Church" to the "Lamb of Judicial Redemption." Nothing is said of Him nor is anything rendered of Him by title or action from this point on in this masterpiece to show

The Lamb of God
- Christ is with His Bride in Heavenly Jerusalem (Rev. 5:6).
- He takes the Book from the Father's hand and opens it (Rev. 5:7-8).
- He opens the seals and directs the judgments with His elders (Rev. 6:1).

TIMELINE
Chapters 4:1 - 19:10

- The believers on earth are called Tribulation Saints (Rev. 7).
- Christ seals 144,000 Jewish believers to protect them from the Antichrist.
- His wrath is poured out on the wicked world.
- Satan and the Antichrist are allowed their last evil design.

Seven Years of the Great Tribulation

The Lord Raptures His Church to Heaven

29

Him present in His body, the church. While presently He walks in the midst of the seven candlesticks, which continues until the end of Revelation chapter three, the total expression of our Lord is now to prepare for His saints' future.

The word *church* is never used after the seven churches were addressed in seven letters in Revelation chapters two and three. The word *churches* is later used one time as the Lord refers to the churches concerning the total content of this great book. *"I Jesus have sent mine angel to testify unto you these things in the churches. I am the root and the offspring of David, and the bright and morning star"* (Revelation 22:16). It is clear that this is the Lord's complete endorsement of the total revelation and a command to take the Book of Revelation seriously, even as infallible truth.

The Lord As The Mighty Warrior

The Lamb of God becomes the mighty warrior just as soon as the seven years of cleansing and the redemption of the earth are complete. The earth cannot be the eternal kingdom of God until sin is perfectly judged and every vestige of Satan and his false trinity is vanquished. The devil's Antichrist and his false prophet must be taken by a great and mighty warrior and cast into the Lake of Fire. The Lamb of God has shown that His perfect sacrifice was a finished work, but now He must act as the victorious king. The Son of God quickly changes His role and title. We have not seen any of this great description of Him since the church was caught up at the beginning of chapter four, until now that He and His church are returning to this earth to establish His kingdom.

Jesus was called *"Alpha and Omega"* in Revelation chapter one and He is called *"Alpha and Omega"* again in Revelation 21:6. He was called the *"First and the Last"* to the church at Smyrna (Revelation 2:8), but not called that again until Revelation 22:13. The Son of

God was called *"Faithful"* in Revelation 3:14 to the church of Laodicea and again called *"Faithful"* in Revelation 19:11. Of course He was the fulfillment all those great titles and descriptions throughout the seven years of Tribulation from Revelation chapter six to Revelation chapter nineteen, but these titles were roles of His priesthood over His body, the church, and not applicable to His administration of the judgments of the earth. All of these great titles, and the way they are used, help us see the beautiful chronology of God's masterpiece of Revelation. This house of literature is perfect in every detail.

Christ mounts His white stallion, and calls His elders to join Him as they too are provided with white horses, because the time to settle earth's final conflict had come. The victorious Redeemer, along with his elders would now face the mighty task at hand. *"And I saw heaven opened, and behold a white horse; and he that sat upon him was called Faithful and True, and in righteousness he doth judge and make war. His eyes were as a flame of fire, and on his head were many crowns; and he had a name written, that no man knew, but he himself. And he was clothed with a vesture dipped in blood: and his name is called The Word of God. And the armies which were in heaven followed him upon white horses, clothed in fine linen, white and clean. And out of his mouth goeth a sharp sword, that with it he should smite the nations: and he shall rule them with a rod of iron: and he treadeth the winepress of the fierceness and wrath of Almighty God. And he hath on his vesture and on his thigh a name written, KING OF KINGS, AND LORD OF LORDS"* (Revelation 19:11-16). In these short verses, He is addressed by fifteen titles and descriptions altogether. Each of them is applicable to the

Faithful and True
- He is the mighty warrior leading His army against the Antichrist army (Rev. 19:11).
- All the saints in Heaven mount white horses and descend as His army (Rev. 19:14).

TIMELINE
Chapters 19:11-21

- The Antichrist is slain by Christ in the Gate of Babylon (Micah 5:6).
- The Jewish world is fully ready for Christ and are converted.
- After Christ defeats the Antichrist, He quickly goes to Jerusalem and enters the Eastern Gate.

A Short Time Establishing His Kingdom On Earth

role He will now fulfill as the earth's inhabitants are subdued, and His kingdom of righteousness is established on this earth. Every possible conflict against a righteous kingdom must be firmly adjudicated so that there will be no doubt of His kingdom success over the entire universe.

The King of Kings and The Lord of Lords

For one thousand years, the Son of God, along with His chosen Jewish family and the blood-washed saints, will rule the earth. *"... but they shall be priests of God and of Christ, and shall reign with him a thousand years"* (Revelation 20:6b). The disciples were absolutely convinced that Jesus Christ was going to set up the kingdom of God on earth when He was training them to be His apostles. They still held to the hope of freedom from Rome even after the resurrection. *"When they therefore were come together, they asked of him, saying, Lord, wilt thou at this time restore again the kingdom to Israel? And he said unto them, It is not for you to know the times or the seasons, which the Father hath put in his own power"* (Acts 1:6-7). But the time of the earthly kingdom was future, and the business of Jesus Christ was to birth His church and then set the promise of the kingdom at the appointed time.

Daniel prophesied of this great future kingdom after the judgments were complete. *"And in the days of these kings shall the God of heaven set up a kingdom, which shall never be destroyed: and the kingdom shall not be left to other people, but it shall break in pieces and consume all these kingdoms, and it shall stand for ever"* (Daniel 2:44). He added to this promise in another interpretation: *"Until the Ancient of days came, and judgment was given to the saints of the most*

The King of Kings

- Christ takes His position on the Throne of David to reign as King.
- Every kingdom on earth brings their glory to Jerusalem.

TIMELINE
Chapters 20:1 -20:15

- The elders are now Christ's kings and priests. They reign over the entire earth except for Israel (Rev. 20:6).
- The Jews inherit the total land mass promised to Abraham

1,000 Year Millennium Reign

High; and the time came that the saints possessed the kingdom"..."And the kingdom and dominion, and the greatness of the kingdom under the whole heaven, shall be given to the people of the saints of the most High, whose kingdom is an everlasting kingdom, and all dominions shall serve and obey him" (Daniel 7:22,27). The Son of God, who is Faithful and True, with eyes as a flame of fire, clothed with a vesture dipped in blood, speaking the Word of God, out of His mouth coming a two-edged sword, who alone is King of kings and Lord of lords, along with His saints, is going to rule the world in righteousness.

The Lord As Bridegroom

The eternal roles and titles of the Lord Jesus Christ will be everything He has ever represented, and he will be the Bridegroom of His chosen jewels, His bride. No name given to Him can be excluded because He is the name that is above every name. Studying the Book of Revelation shows clearly that this unveiling of Him unites every title He has worn beginning in Genesis, where He was the Word of God in creation, to the Book of Revelation, where He is the eternal Bridegroom. The city of New Jerusalem was His creation of ultimate value and beauty. Nothing in the past, of created value, can compare to this prize prepared for His bride. The present world knows no value with which to compare it. It is the final home for the highest honored of all saints. Men and women who have served faithfully, some even sacrificing their lives for Jesus Christ and carried their cross to His glory will dwell with Him in this city for eternity. This is the highest

> ### The Bridegroom
> - New Jerusalem descends from Heaven and the Father reigns with Jesus Christ (Rev. 21:3).
> - The Father and Jesus Christ are the Light of the world (Rev. 21:23).
>
> **TIMELINE**
> Chapters 21:1 - 22:21
>
> - The River of Life and the Tree of Life become the divine source of Jesus Christ's eternal life flowing from the throne (Rev. 22:1-3).
> - The City of New Jerusalem is the capital of the world (Rev. 21:24).
>
> ### Eternity
>
> ### New Heaven & New Earth

reward to be offered at the Marriage Supper.

The last two chapters of this book are the crowning glory of the Holy Scripture. There is no reasonable way for the Bible to end except as it actually ends. Our God never does one thing without perfection, and this is a perfect conclusion. This city will

The Book of Revelation is a house of words that finishes the Holy Bible in absolute completion.

adorn the earth like a jewel set in a golden display. The Father and the Son will become the Light of this city, and the beauty of it all will illuminate the entire universe so that there is no need of a sun. The city will be a temple of worship. The angels, Cherubim, Seraphim, and all the saints will find eternal joys together. heaven and earth will be a united universe, and His creation will find perfect pleasure in righteousness forever.

The Book of Revelation is surely a perfect house of words that finishes the Holy Bible in absolute completion. *"In the Beginning was the Word,"* (John 1:1) and words have always been God's choice way to describe His Son. This last book of the Bible is a house of literature, a masterpiece of revelation, and the chronological finality of Holy Scripture. Jesus is the Word, and this is His last word to His church and His saints.

The Church In The Book Of Revelation

The Saints of God are described by five different titles in the Book of Revelation. "Never called the church after Revelation 4:1."

	The Church	The Elders	His Army	Kings & Priests	His Bride
Heavenly Events	• Jesus Christ in His Glory (Rev 1:13-16). • Jesus Christ at the Father's right hand as our mediator (Hebrews 12:24). • Seven letters to commend and reprimand His church.	• Saints at the Bema • Saints Celebrate and prepare to reign (Rev 5:9-10). • Saints part of directing Tribulation on Earth (Rev 7:13).	• Jesus Christ and His army (saints) return to the earth (Rev 19:14).	God the Father will continue to reign in the Heavens with the Holy Angels. The White Throne Judgment	• New Jerusalem descends to the Earth (Rev 21:1-3).
Timeline	Chapters 1,2,3	4 - 19:4	19:14	20:6	21:2
	The Rapture Of The Church				
Earthly Events	• The church is the authority of Jesus Christ on Earth (Matt 16:18-19; 18:18-19). • Jesus is the Head (Eph 1:22-23). • The church full of the Holy Ghost. The church is never seen after Rev 4:1.	• The Unholy Trinity becomes the god of this earth (Rev 12-13). • Tribulation Saints wash their robes in the blood (Rev 7:9-17). • Seven Years of Great Tribulation. • People are saved all throughout this seven year period (Rev 7:9,14; 12:11). Demons invade the world (Rev 9:1-21).	• Saints are back to judge the nations (Rev 19:20; I Cor 6:2). • We will also judge the angels that rebelled with Satan (I Cor 6:3). • The saints will help to secure the kingdom of the Earth for our Lord.	• Jesus Christ is the King of Kings and Lord of Lords over the earth. • His saints will be kings, governors, and totally rule the nations of the world (Rev 19:11-21). • Holiness will fill the earth.	• New Jerusalem situated over earthly Jerusalem. • God the Father and the Son and God the Holy Spirit to reign together (Rev 21:22-23). • Jesus reminds us that this book is written to the church (Rev 22:16).
Length of Time	The Total Church Dispensation	Seven Years of the Great Tribulation H E L L On Earth	Short Time of Securing the Nations	1,000 Year Millennium Reign	For Eternity New Heaven & New Earth

I

THE TRIUMPHANT SAINTS IN THE BOOK OF REVELATION

Introduction Three

The Book of The Revelation of Jesus Christ was written out of Christ's love for His future bride. It is a love story composed of many breathtaking revelations and actions that have one primary conclusion: New Jerusalem, full of His beloved, surrounded by a multitude of angels and saints. All of this beauty will be enjoyed forever on a new earth situated within a new heaven, where God the Father and God the Son are the light and center of it all. The Father that gave His Son in redemption will enjoy this family for eternity, and we will worship and enjoy Him.

Following the presence of the saints of God in the Book of Revelation provides a great story of this masterpiece of literature. The redeemed are not obscure or unnecessary to this book; it was revealed and written for them. We are the purpose of the book. One of the unique truths about the entire Bible and all of God's revelations and miracles is that they always have a deep meaning for our lives. Our God does nothing as a show. Every revelation has meaning and purpose for His creation. Satan and his false religions will dazzle you with their display without any meaning or benefit except to capture your attention. The most important truth in discernment can be discovered in the presence or absence of genuine benefit and meaning. Our Father and His Son have revealed themselves and their revelations to inspire and fill your life with beauty, purpose, and purity.

The saints of God are given five different titles or positions of authority in the Book of Revelation. These titles reveal the progression of the story that the Lord is revealing to us. You can determine when the Rapture occurs by the change in the title and position held by the saints of God. When we cease to be called the church, we know that the church has moved up higher and must fulfill a different role in God's revelation. Later, we become His army to fight and defeat the Antichrist and his horde of the Beast's tattooed army, that is determined to destroy everything contrary to him. These different titles are themselves a masterful tool to communicate the end-time message and order of events. His saints are central to His plan for the redemption of His universe.

This book begins with a blessing promised to the saints if they read, hear, and keep the great truths that are contained in this revelation. *"Blessed is he that readeth, and they that hear the words of this prophecy, and keep those things which are written therein: for the time is at hand"* (Revelation 1:3). Then it ends with an even more wonderful and supernatural setting. *"And I heard a great voice out of heaven saying, Behold, the tabernacle of God is with men, and he will dwell with them, and they shall be his people, and God himself shall be with them, and be their God"* (Revelation 21:3). From the beginning of this Book to its ending, we are His love and passion. Every promise, every action of judgment, and every revelation of coming glory was all planned, ordained, and will be fulfilled so that His saints can enjoy Him for all eternity. What a day that will be!

Let me begin with a chart that clearly shows the progression of our titles and positions as the book unfolds. Please view the chart carefully. The Bible calls us "saints" throughout the sixty-five books, from Genesis to Jude. But the titles change in Revelation because this book reflects the activities assigned to us as we serve Him in fulfilling prophecy. The Kingdom of God is never void of His saints. *"For we are labourers together with God"* (I Corinthians 3:9). He has given to us the words of redemption. *"To wit, that God was in Christ, reconciling the world unto himself, not imputing their trespasses unto them; and hath committed unto us the word of reconciliation"* (II Corinthians 5:19). It is His promise that we are going to judge the world and angels. *"Do ye not know that the saints shall judge the world? and if the world shall be judged by you, are ye unworthy to judge the smallest matters? Know ye not that we shall judge angels? how much more things that pertain to this life?"* (I Corinthians 6:2-3). Our position in the coming redemption of all things is spectacular. We are at the center of this great Book of Revelation given to us by Jesus Christ Himself. He received it from the Father, and dictated it by angels and John, and commanded it to be written down and given to the church. How plain must He be to get our attention?

The Church
• Jesus Christ in His Glory (Rev 1:13-16).
• Jesus Christ at the Father's right hand as our mediator (Hebrews 12:24).
• Seven letters to commend and reprimand His church.

Timeline
Chapters 1, 2, 3
• The church is the authority of Jesus Christ on Earth (Matt 16:18-19; 18:18-19).
• Jesus is the Head (Eph 1:22-23).
• The church full of the Holy Ghost.
The church is never seen after Rev 4:1.

The Total Church Dispensation

The Saints Called "The Church"

The first title given to the saints is located in the first three chapters. The very title "church" constitutes a called-out assembly, set in authority to conduct His redemptive business in the world. His very language to His church in those three chapters denotes responsibility and a calling to service. The church is not a hiding place, but a serving place. The church is not where you go to be blessed, but where you go to bless others. For a group of people to claim to be His church is to accept the responsibility to obey His every command

39

and challenge. The seven letters to the sevenfold church are absolute instructions and directions to model the church life. Any church that does not model its doctrines and lifestyle after these letters is not His church, but their own club.

The church is is to be active in kingdom business. Our duty is to model the Gospel after Christ and literally seek to win the world. We must win them and then make disciples out of them so that they take up the business of the kingdom themselves. It is not just our duty to preach the Gospel and win the lost; it is also our duty to cast out devils, heal the sick, and set the captive free. We are never told to just pray for the sick. We are told to pray for them and to heal them by His authority, but never in our own authority. The church must be the church acting in total surrender and doing His business on earth in the exact model of His ministry. A Bible church is a "Book of Acts" and a "Book of Revelation" church.

The Elders Seated On Thrones

The saints are no longer called the church after John is caught up before the Throne of God. Immediately he saw the saints seated on lesser thrones before the Great Throne of the Father. The number of these elders is twenty-four, the perfect combination of First Testament saints represented by the twelve tribes of Israel and Second Testament saints represented by the disciples. They are glorified because they sit in His presence without being smitten to their faces. As they celebrate their glorious victory, there can be no doubt of the Rapture that has removed these saints from the earth to the city of heavenly Jerusalem. The number twenty-four is a symbolic number because the same group is a multitude in chapter five. *"And I beheld, and I heard the voice of many angels round about the throne and the beasts and the elders: and the number of them was ten thousand times ten thousand, and thousands of thousands"* (Revelation 5:11).

40

The Biblical description guarantees their transformation from the church to the reigning elders joining the Father and the Lamb as they direct in the judicial processes of redemption and judgment of the universe. *"And round about the throne were four and twenty seats: and upon the seats I saw four and twenty elders sitting, clothed in white raiment; and they had on their heads crowns of gold"* (Revelation 4:4). They are in authority, seated on thrones, clothed in white raiment, glorified, wearing crowns of gold, and rewarded. The great hope of the church is the Rapture, and this scene gives absolute certainty that the Rapture has occurred at this point in this great story.

From chapter four all the way to chapter nineteen, verse fourteen, the saints are called elders. This covers the entire seven years of the Great Tribulation. At the end of these seven years of judgment and redemption, Jesus Christ prepares to return to the earth to set up the Millennial Kingdom. Upon returning, He must first defeat the devil, the antichrist, and the false prophet, as well as the devil's army gathered from the nations of the world. They have gathered in Megiddo for this great battle that has been prophesied for millenniums. The elders have shared the seven years of judicial activities with Christ, while also celebrating the Marriage Supper. They are ready to take on another role as His army descending with Him back to earth.

The Elders
- **Saints at the Bema**
  - **Saints Celebrate and prepare to reign (Rev 5:9-10).**
  - **Saints part of directing Tribulation on Earth (Rev 7:13).**

Timeline
Chapters 4 - 19:4

- **The Unholy Trinity becomes the god of this earth (Rev 12-13).**
- **Tribulation Saints wash their robes in the blood (Rev 7:9-17).**
- **Seven Years of Great Tribulation.**
- **People are saved all throughout this seven year period (Rev 7:9,14; 12:11). Demons invade the world (Rev 9:1-21).**

Seven Years of the Great Tribulation

H E L L On Earth

His Army Riding White Horses
The saints were His church, and they became His elders at the

Rapture. Now it's time for His Second Coming, and they become His army. *"And I saw heaven opened, and behold a white horse; and he that sat upon him was called Faithful and True, and in righteousness he doth judge and make war. And the armies which were in heaven followed him upon white horses, clothed in fine linen, white and clean"* (Revelation 19:11,14). The saints are going to constitute an invincible army with the King of kings riding as the triumphant Word of God. This is the long awaited Second Coming of the Lord Jesus Christ to end the reign of terror by Satan and all evil. Jesus described this day perfectly. *"Immediately after the tribulation of those days shall the sun be darkened, and the moon shall not give her light, and the stars shall fall from heaven, and the powers of the heavens shall be shaken: And then shall appear the sign of the Son of man in heaven: and then shall all the tribes of the earth mourn, and they shall see the Son of man coming in the clouds of heaven with power and great glory. And he shall send his angels with a great sound of a trumpet, and they shall gather together his elect from the four winds, from one end of heaven to the other"* (Matthew 24:29-31).

Malachi prophesied that the saints of God would be removed to a safe place during the coming darkness that Jesus called the Great Tribulation. He concluded his promise with a beautiful addition that these saints would come back to earth with Him. *"Then they that feared the LORD spake often one to another: and the LORD hearkened, and heard it, and a book of remembrance was written before him for them that feared the LORD, and that thought upon his name. And they shall be mine, saith the LORD of hosts, in that day when I make up my jewels; and I will spare them, as a man spareth his own son that serveth him. Then shall ye return, and discern between the righteous and the wicked, between him that serveth God and him that serveth him not"* (Malachi 3:18). *"Then shall ye return"* clearly ties the First Testament saints with the Second Testament saints to fulfill the twenty-four elders in chapter four and also shows these saints are returning together as His army to conquer and take control of the earth. The saints of all the ages will be one company, first as His elders, but now His army to capture and rule a world that has been out of control.

His Kings and Priests

Mostly wicked men and women have ruled the world, but by prophecy the saints have always known that the day would come when righteousness and righteous people would rule the earth. The one thousand years, called the Millennium, is not just a time for Jesus Christ to rule, but also for His saints to rule with Him. In the first chapter of this book, He promised that such a day would fulfill this prophecy. His very purpose for this revelation was to set our hearts on the future. Hope is to live in this joyous expectation. *"And from Jesus Christ, who is the faithful witness, and the first begotten of the dead, and the prince of the kings of the earth. Unto him that loved us, and washed us from our sins in his own blood, And hath made us kings and priests unto God and his Father; to him be glory and dominion for ever and ever. Amen. Behold, he cometh with clouds; and every eye shall see him, and they also which pierced him: and all kindreds of the earth shall wail because of him. Even so, Amen"* (Revelation 1:5-7). His great purpose in His church is to prepare a people to be his "kings and priests on earth" and to rule with Him.

Now, this great prophetic revelation sets the time and date for this to be fulfilled. His army has conquered the earth. The evil army of Lucifer and his fallen host are vanquished and judged, and His saints are ready. *"Blessed and holy is he that hath part in the first resurrection: on such the second death hath no power, but they shall be priests of God*

Kings & Priests

God the Father will continue to reign in the Heavens with the Holy Angels.

The White Throne Judgment

Timeline
Chapter 20:6

• Jesus Christ is the King of Kings and Lord of Lords over the earth.
• His saints will be kings, governors, and totally rule the nations of the world (Rev 19:11-21).
• Holiness will fill the earth.

1,000 Year Millennium Reign

and of Christ, and shall reign with him a thousand years" (Revelation 20:6). The doctrine being promoted today called *Kingdom Dominion* is a lie of Lucifer. This doctrine arises from *Replacement Theology*, which takes Israel's promises and superimposes them on the church. The Millennial promises are beautifully represented in the First Testament and this Revelation's chronology puts their fulfillment in its exact place. The church and Israel will enjoy the Millennium together. Israel will rule the complete geographical area promised to Abraham, and it will be the garden center of the earth. The church will rule the Gentile world, and it also will become a garden. The Jews and the Gentiles will equally enjoy the promises of prosperity all together as the family and followers of our Christ and Lord.

Isaiah spoke vividly of this Millennium Day for the First Testament saints. *"Arise, shine; for thy light is come, and the glory of the LORD is risen upon thee. For, behold, the darkness shall cover the earth, and gross darkness the people: but the LORD shall arise upon thee, and his glory shall be seen upon thee. And the Gentiles shall come to thy light, and kings to the brightness of thy rising. Then thou shalt see, and flow together, and thine heart shall fear, and be enlarged; because the abundance of the sea shall be converted unto thee, the forces of the Gentiles shall come unto thee. Whereas thou hast been forsaken and hated, so that no man went through thee, I will make thee an eternal excellency, a joy of many generations. Thy people also shall be all righteous: they shall inherit the land for ever, the branch of my planting, the work of my hands, that I may be glorified"* (Isaiah 60:1-3,5,15,21). All of creation groans for this future day when the glory with God, along with the redeemed saints will reign as kings and priests with Jesus Christ as Lord of all. The one thousand years of righteousness will allow the earth's population to expand and set the minds of the natural world toward the hope of eternity. After a short period of temptation from Satan and the utter desolation of his ill-conceived efforts to attack the saints, the world will be ready to forever turn only to the Creator's glorious kingdom. It is time for time to be no more.

The Bride of Christ and His New World Order

Everything is going to be recreated in holiness. The marvelous city of New Jerusalem will descend out of God's heavenly city, and the earth and heavens will be utterly renewed in perfection without the tiniest flaw. The title of His chosen saints will forever be "The Bride of Jesus Christ."

His Bride
- New Jerusalem descends to the Earth (Rev 21:1-3).

The White Throne Judgment

Timeline
Chapter 21:2

New Jerusalem situated over earthly Jerusalem.
- God the Father and the Son and God the Holy Spirit to reign together (Rev 21:22-23).
- Jesus reminds us that this book is written to the church (Rev 22:16).

For Eternity

New Heaven & New Earth

We carried the burden during our natural life as His church, waiting each hour for Him to come as He promised. We served as His elders during the dark tribulation years. We mounted our white horses and rode like warriors to vanquish the armies of Lucifer. And we ruled honorably over His Millennial kingdom. Now it's time to enter into our greatest glory, take our residence in the city of His Bride, and serve as pillars in the temple of our God. His mark (or character) will be written on our brow, and we will enjoy a spotless eternity.

The city of New Jerusalem is beyond description. Yet its glory will not be comparable to our Beloved Father and His Beloved Son. The light and glory of eternity will be our Sovereign God and all that represents His eternal person. Everything about God, from His holiness

45

to His love for all creation, will be fully enjoyed and manifested. The city is a literal city with mansions beyond description, flowers of matchless beauty that never fade, and every possible creation of God without the curse of sin. It's all the best of life without the least amount of anything caused by the curse. Life will be as the Creator intended it to be before the fall of Lucifer and the fall of Adam.

The saints are truly the delight of the Creator. This masterpiece of literature has revealed the real life drama of His jewels in the end-time. Each revelation of their titles reflects the chronological progression of both this book and its fulfillment. You cannot alter one event, change its timeframe, or eliminate the results. In divine wisdom, the Son of God has given to us the blueprint and it's up to us to preach and teach this truth exactly as the Master has revealed it. The story is ours to tell.

THE "GLORY OF CHRIST" REVEALED

The greatest manifestation of the post-resurrected Christ is found in this first chapter of Revelation. How could students of the Bible not be enthralled as they read and search the words of this great introduction? It puts the Lord Jesus Christ exactly where He belongs, at the very peak of His glory and right in the midst of His saints. He is not an absentee landlord but the very present Lord and truly the head of His church.

This book is His most intimate communication to His beloved jewels. Every word He said as the Son of Man came directly from God. Now He is the First Begotten from the dead and has been rewarded by the Father. The Father has given Him a name that is above every name, and He manifests the glory of all those names in this Revelation. This book is the mountain peak, and this chapter is the first summit. The last summit will be seen in the last two chapters when He takes His abode in the city of New Jerusalem with His Bride.

This first chapter does four things that are very important to the understanding of the entire book. First, it gives us the clear source of the book; whom it is from, how it is communicated, and who is the saintly man that Christ entrusted with the content. Second, it provides us a very simple outline of the book. Third, it clearly communicates the purpose and the company to whom the book is written. Fourth and last, we see the sublime glory of the Lord Himself.

Everything in this book—all twenty-two chapters—must be read, studied, and grasped within sight of the towering presence of the Lord Jesus Christ. He is never far from any part of His story. He is the source of every truth and the keeper of every future promise and transaction. Nothing can fail, because He is the Master of every action. The source of this book leaves no one the right to ignore, treat lightly, or explain away this great Revelation. Touching this book negatively is dangerous to your soul. The Father Himself gave this great revelation to His only begotten Son. His Son then gave it to His servant John. An angel was chosen, no doubt one of the great Cherubim, to act between the Lord Himself and John. That settles the infallibility of this great book.

The word Revelation is an awesome word. We can define it as "taking the cover off" or "removing all of the veil" so that no one is hid from the content, and the content is not hid from anyone.

Second, an outline is provided to separate the three parts of the book. There will be a vision of the present position of our Lord, and the glory that will be revealed in His existing priesthood established in the Father's Son. Then His church dispensation is communicated in seven letters to seven churches. A picture of the prophetic future, after the church has finished her role in the world, is given over to the greater part of this Revelation.

This great Book of Revelation has only one goal. That goal is to give to the church an outline of her position with Jesus, along with her duties and charges in that position, and to clearly outline the prophetic future so the church can tell the world what that future holds for humankind. His Jewish family had the duty of bearing all prophecy of His plans and programs under the First Testament. Now He is making it clear that His church is duty-bound to carry His message of the Second Testament to the whole earth. The Jewish nation was never cast away. They were only set aside for a designated period called the dispensation of the church, and then they will be brought back into the picture. This book was written for the church, for every church, for every church period, and for every church member. All of us will answer to this duty of telling the world the content of this Revelation.

Third and last, the Lord is established as the Head of His church and is positioned at the Mount Everest of all mysterys and revelation. Christianity, without the triumphant King, becomes an immediate failure. He does not need a co-redeemer, and to suggest one serves only to lower the majesty of His position. No one book could incorporate every great title or name ascribed to Him, but this book comes close. It is an unveiling of His greatness and truly removes all questions that cast doubt upon Him. Revelation 1:8 tells us that He is *"Alpha and Omega, the beginning and the ending,"* Revelation 3:14 tells us He is the great *"Amen."*

Now we will take the introduction of this chapter and look at it verse by verse.

> *The Revelation of Jesus Christ, which God gave unto him, to shew unto his servants things which must shortly come to pass; and he sent and signified it by his angel unto his servant John. Who bare record of the word of God, and of the testimony of Jesus Christ, and of all things that he saw. Blessed is he that readeth, and they that hear the words of this prophecy, and keep those things which are written therein: for the time is at hand* (Revelation 1:1-3).

The word *Revelation* is an awesome word. We can define it as "taking the cover off" or "removing all of the veil" so that no one is hid from the content, and the content is not hid from anyone. We must quit saying, "This book is difficult," or "I cannot understand this book."

That flies in the face of the very name of the book. The Lord Himself called it His Revelation. Did He fail or have we failed? The answer is obvious. The statement *"the Revelation of Jesus Christ,"* means two things. It is about Him, and it was from Him. Like all mysteries of truth, they cannot be known except by allowing the Spirit of Truth to be our teacher. This book is the ultimate mystery and will be revealed to the ultimate seeker. Instead of saying, "I cannot understand the book," simply say, "I have not taken the time to discover the great secrets of the book."

John speaks of himself in verse two. What an honor this servant of Jesus Christ experienced. He watched, listened, and heard every portion of this great story and became an eyewitness for all of us. His words clearly testify that he missed nothing. He saw it all, he told it all, and we are expected to listen to it all. He identifies it as the *"testimony of Jesus Christ."* The eternal *"Word of God"* is showing John another portion of truth. John is to write it down and send it to the churches. Once John has made the source of the book very clear, he speaks to the church.

"Blessed" are those that *"read, hear, and keep"* the things written. Prophecy is history written in advance. God's people are the only people in the world that have the keys to the future in their hands. Most of the world grieves over what they cannot know about tomorrow, the next day, the next year, or the next decade. We have all of that and the next one hundred years and the next one thousand years and the next ten thousand years; yet we ignore it. We are *"blessed"* because we have nothing to worry about. The future is just as sure as was the past. So, John got the truth from the Maker of truth and has it all written in stone. He gives us a mandate to read it, hear it, obey it, and be happy.

John to the seven churches which are in Asia: Grace be unto you, and peace, from him which is, and which was, and which is to come; and from the seven Spirits which are before his throne; And from Jesus Christ, who is the faithful witness, and the first begotten of the dead, and the prince of the kings of the earth. Unto him that loved us, and washed us from our sins in his own blood, And hath made us kings and priests unto God and his Father; to him be glory and dominion for ever and ever. Amen. Behold, he cometh with clouds; and every eye shall see him, and they also which pierced him: and all kindreds of the earth shall wail because of him. Even so, Amen. I am Alpha and Omega, the beginning and the ending, saith the Lord, which is, and which was, and which is to come, the Almighty (Revelation 1:4-8).

John leaves no question about the people to whom this book is written. This book is the property of the church. Not only is it their property, it is their future and their responsibility. No treasure of great value is ever given to the saints to sit on, to hoard up, or to be put on the library shelf. This treasure is given to enrich the saints and to fill them with a hope that fills every day with expectation.

The seven churches represent the church universal which make up this church dispensation. No saint or church can ignore this special message. It is *"from Him, which is, and which was, and which is to come."* It is also the work of His Spirit—the Keeper of truth—so there can be no hint of failure. The presence of the seven-fold Spirit or the *"seven spirits which are before His throne"* places the omnipotence, omniscience, and omnipresence of His Holy Spirit squarely in the midst of this revelation to preserve, guarantee, and promote all that is being revealed.

The greatest revelations of God always come to the saints that suffer the most for Him.

The words, *"and from Jesus Christ,"* tie the presence of the Father in verse four to the presence of Jesus Christ in verse five and right on through this entire chapter. All of this is is given to help us grasp the picture of the greatness of Jesus Christ overshadowing this great book of Revelation. Here are the titles, actions, and descriptions of our Lord Jesus Christ listed in verses five through eight:

- **Jesus Christ** - Messiah, Son of man, Son of God
- **The Faithful Witness** - Truth Incarnate
- **The Faithful Martyr** – Unto death
- **First Begotten of the Dead** - First resurrected eternal body
- **Prince of the Kings of the Earth** - Every king shall bow
- **That loved us** - Took upon Himself the form of a servant
- **Washed us from our sins** - His blood has made us holy
- **His own blood** - Divine blood that is eternal
- **He cometh with clouds** - His promise is never forgotten
- **Every eye shall see Him** - Soon He will be known by all
- **They also which pierced Him** - His beloved kin are not forgotten
- **All kindred shall wail** - Judgment will touch every living thing
- **Amen** - He is the finality of life
- **I Am** – The first title God gave of Himself
- **Alpha** – The first word of all words ever spoken
- **Omega** – The last word to ever be spoken
- **The Beginning** - Time starts with Him
- **The End** – He is finality, the end of everything
- **The Lord** - His words are final - He is over all
- **Which is** - Self-existing and without beginning
- **Which was** - Came out of eternity to be known by all
- **Which is to come** - Will come again to finish all things
- **The Almighty** - Without Him was not anything made

These are twenty-three majestic word pictures of the Son of God. In our limited state of mind, words are still the most powerful means of communication. All the words above describing the altogether indescribable One are still only part of Him in this introduction. We will see eighteen more names or descriptions of Him. Identifying these titles helps us see the depth, height and breadth of this revelation. He wants our attention so that we never forget what He says. It all flows out of the Eternal Word and each word picture, though infinite in itself, is part of the whole being and makeup of our God and Savior, Jesus Christ.

> *I John, who also am your brother, and companion in tribulation, and in the kingdom and patience of Jesus Christ, was in the isle that is called Patmos, for the word of God and for the testimony of Jesus Christ. I was in the Spirit on the Lord's day, and heard behind me a great voice, as of a trumpet, Saying, I am Alpha and Omega, the first and the last: and, What thou seest, write in a book, and send it unto the seven churches which are in Asia; unto Ephesus, and unto Smyrna, and unto Pergamos, and unto Thyatira, and unto Sardis, and unto Philadelphia, and unto Laodicea* (Revelation 1:9-11).

The greatest revelations of God always come to the saints that suffer the most for Him. When the Lord is ready to do something great, He takes one of His servants and puts him in the fire to prove his mettle and to prepare the way for His glory. John is careful to tell his story without one moment of regret. He says, *"I am your brother."* He also reminds us that his fellowship with the saints was in tribulation and was born of patience that issued from Jesus Christ.

John's presence on the lonely isle of Patmos was as a prisoner doing hard labor; but it was for the right cause, and the right cause makes the worst of situations acceptable. John was exiled to this island for the crime of preaching the Word of God and bearing testimony to the person of Jesus Christ, and the preaching of the resurrection of Jesus Christ. It was because of the utter faithfulness and trustworthiness of John that Jesus Christ had chosen him for this awesome revelation and the writing of this masterpiece of divine literature.

In this trying place of deprivation, John was in the spirit of anointed worship and praise. The presence of a worshipping saint with the presence of the faithful Lord of the church can turn a windswept island into a sanctuary of the highest order. It was the Lord's Day, the day they always celebrated the resurrection, and John was having church.

John said, *"I was in the Spirit"* and heard *"a great voice as of a trumpet."* The Lord begins to speak, and this time John tells what he saw rather than what he knew. The eighteen descriptions and titles in verses five to eight are John's own acquaintance with the Lord. Now, John sees Him in His glory and hears the Lord's own declaration of Himself. The Lord now commands John to write a book and send it to His churches and names seven churches that fit the model of the church universal.

And I turned to see the voice that spake with me. And being turned, I saw seven golden candlesticks; And in the midst of the seven candlesticks one like unto the Son of man, clothed with a garment down to the foot, and girt about the paps with a golden girdle. His head and his hairs were white like wool, as white as snow; and his eyes were as a flame of fire; And his feet like unto fine brass, as if they burned in a furnace; and his voice as the sound of many waters. And he had in his right hand seven stars: and out of his mouth went a sharp two-edged sword: and his countenance was as the sun shineth in his strength. And when I saw him, I fell at his feet as dead. And he laid his right hand upon me, saying unto me, Fear not; I am the first and the last: I am he that liveth, and was dead; and behold, I am alive for evermore, Amen; and have the keys of hell and of death (Revelation 1:12-18).

John knew the first great description of Christ through his apostleship with Him. Now, John sees Him in His High Priest honors and His Lordship over the church. The church had never heard this great description. To see Christ seated at the Father's right hand, while also being told that He walks in the midst of the churches, was revolutionary to them.

John explains his vision of the Son of God and leaves us with no doubt that this is the exalted and glorified Christ. Many had seen Him ascend out of their sight and into heaven, and all had heard this great story many times, but now John is face to face with the risen Lord and gives us a vivid word description of His personage. another eighteen names, titles, and statements are added to the nineteen previously given:

- **I am Alpha and Omega** - The A to Z
- **One like unto the Son of Man** - The Christ we loved
- **Clothed with a garment down to the foot** – Readers will remember the Priestly robes
- **Girt about the paps with a golden girdle** - This attire can only describe the High Priest
- **His head and hair were white like wool** - Eternal
- **His eyes were as a flame of fire** - Awesome Holiness
- **His feet like unto fine brass** - Omnipotence
- **His voice as the sound of many waters** – Omnipresence
- **In His right hand were seven stars** - Angel charged to defend holiness in His churches
- **Out of His mouth a sharp, two-edged sword** - The Word of God incorruptible and unfailing

- **His countenance was as the sun shineth in his strength** - The glory of His Father
- **I am the first and the last** - And everything in between
- **And the last** – The end of all things
- **I am He that liveth** - This is life evermore
- **And was dead** - He was the Master of His own death
- **Behold, I am alive forevermore** - Death is defeated
- **Amen** - The work of God is finished - It's time to settle the last war
- **I have the keys of hell and of death** - The valley of the shadow of death is now a sun-kissed highway to Glory

This is a picture of Divinity that walked the pathways of human flesh until He would willingly die, enduring the pain of every human sin ever committed. As He lived in our midst, He robbed our enemy of his weapons. Now, this Victor has stepped back into the Father's presence and taken His rightful seat at the Altar of Grace wearing the robe of the High Priest and possessing all the rights of our Redeemer. He has all the possessions and appearance of final victory. He is the *"Amen"* of a new world soon to come.

Write the things which thou hast seen, and the things which are, and the things which shall be hereafter; The mystery of the seven stars which thou sawest in my right hand, and the seven golden candlesticks. The seven stars are the angels of the seven churches: and the seven candlesticks which thou sawest are the seven churches (Revelation 1:19-20).

Twelve times John is told by Christ to write this book or parts of it. He is clearly told to send it to the churches. This book cannot be ignored or treated lightly. The total church is to be saturated with its truths, commands, and all His promises.

Conclusion

Today's church would be turned on their heels if the glory of this revelation were heralded until it smote the darkness within the walls of our holy places. The fulfillment of every truth in these twenty-two chapters is as sure as the promises of His first coming were fulfilled to the letter. The fact that many First Testament followers did not believe the prophecies in their books did not change one thing. This will shortly be true again. The story starts with the eternal Son of God.

2

WALKING IN THE MIDST OF HIS CHURCH

The omnipresent Son of God is in the very midst of His church. The church cannot be His church until He is in its presence. The guarantee of any group of people being truly a church is only when He is there. His presence is tangible; it is as real as life. When He draws near, all that are present will know it. Nothing has made the church world more helpless and problematic than the denial of the literal dimension of Christ's Spirit. Every soul has a spiritual capacity, and that is the story of Christianity. Until the theology of the Bible leaves our head and arrives in our heart, we are nothing but religious. The bread of communion, representing His broken body, is death to the flesh, but the drinking of the cup, representing His shed blood, is life and resurrection.

Jesus Christ declared emphatically that His Words were Spirit. Everything about the devil's kingdom is paranormal, and all of it is but an imitation of the real. People that involve themselves with séances, fortune telling, and any degree of witchcraft will prove to you that it is tangible and can be manifested; yet, it is all a counterfeit shadow of the true God. Common sense will tell you that no imitation is as wonderful and life changing as the original. It is foolish to accept the world of evil and its reality and deny the even greater reality of the church of Jesus Christ and His supernatural revelation.

The church is either a spiritual dynamo or it is a failure. Either Jesus Christ is present or it is all empty religion.

The seven letters to the seven churches and all their beautiful content leaves no question of the reality of His church. There is a supernatural dimension to each church and all kinds of supernatu-

Until the theology of the Bible leaves our head and arrives at our heart, we are nothing but religious.

ral promises that these churches received from the Lord. The truths and doctrines of the Bible were carefully made a prime treasure for which these churches were to be held accountable.

They were highly commended for holding these truths against all attacks and they judged if doctrines of error were allowed to triumph. To Ephesus, the Lord said, *"And how thou canst not bear them which are evil: and thou hast tried them which say they are apostles, and are not, and hast found them liars"* (Revelation 2:2b). To Thyatira, He said *"Notwithstanding I have a few things against thee, because thou sufferest that woman Jezebel, which calleth herself a prophetess, to teach and to seduce my servants to commit fornication, and to eat things sacrificed unto idols"* (Revelation 2:20). The Bible holds all truth as the one greatest challenge for which His church will be accountable to God.

Placing these seven letters between the post-resurrection revelation of Jesus Christ, as seen in Revelation one, and the future prophecies to begin in Revelation four, is extremely important. The greatest mystical number in this masterpiece of literature is the number seven. This number is present in this one book of the Bible forty-four times. It is found in Scripture three hundred and ninety-five times. The Holy Spirit chose this number in His holy revelation to convey or reveal subjects in a whole or complete form. Anything seen with this mystical number is important in every part but great and vast in its totality. It's always associated as the number of completion, whether large or small, when used in a typological form.

Remember that each of the churches was an individual church that had a real local congregation. They also represented churches of this same characteristic in each period of church history. Each church also represented a period of extended years in the whole of the church age. The Ephesus church period began at Pentecost and continued for about seventy years (approximately AD 30 to AD 100). This was a special period, the greatest of all periods, but they were beginning to leave their first love. While studying church history, one finds that no church movement has ever maintained its vigor and vitality longer than one hundred years. The greatest hindrance in the church is always the loss of its first love. Let's look at the letter to the Church of Ephesus.

> *Unto the angel of the church of Ephesus write; These things saith he that holdeth the seven stars in his right hand, who walketh in the midst of the seven golden candlesticks* (Revelation 2:1).

Every church has a cherubim assigned to the congregation, beginning with the oversight of the under-shepherd and is dedicated to ministering to the whole flock of that local body. Anybody who negatively attacks, criticizes, or messes with that church will be in trouble. The devil, his evil spirits, the unconverted world, and even professing believers will soon discover that the Son of God, the Lord our Christ, defends His church, if that church is totally dependent on its Head. Satan can defeats a church, not because that victory was within his grasp, but because ministers and members defeated themselves. These seven letters show no victories for Satan, only failures in obedience and faithfulness in the church. We must not miss this point. Nowhere in Scripture, especially in these seven letters to His churches, is one victory ever credited to the devil. He cannot win because he is already totally defeated. The professing believers who simply do not apply Biblical principles to the struggle lose every battle—or what could have been a victory. These letters, including this first letter to Ephesus, show nothing but the absolute possibility of His church rising above every circumstance and fulfilling all that He has ordained for His saints. He holds the stars or Cherubim in His perfect grasp, and they are fully equipped for their task. Then, to assure victory, He walks in the midst of His church. *"For where two or three are gathered together in my name, there am I in the midst of them"* (Matthew 18:20).

> *I know thy works, and thy labour, and thy patience, and how thou canst not bear them which are evil: and thou hast tried them which say they are apostles, and are not, and hast found them liars: And hast borne, and hast patience, and for my name's sake hast laboured, and hast not fainted* (Revelation 2:2-3).

Nothing of our conduct or labor is missing from His omniscience, *"For we are laborers together with God"* (1 Corinthians 3:9), and He is fully prepared to use every pure action we provide with the promise of victory. The Son of God has made it plain that there is no design in His kingdom for defeat, *"And I will give unto thee the keys of the kingdom of heaven: and whatsoever thou shalt bind on earth shall be bound in heaven: and whatsoever thou shalt loose on earth shall be loosed in heaven"* (Matthew 16:19).

The Lord has already said that very plainly, *"And I say also unto thee, That thou art Peter, and upon this rock I will build my church; and the gates of hell shall not prevail against it"* (Matthew 16:18). The emphasis must be drawn between "His" church and "our" churches. Every time the church is defeated, it is never won by the devil, but it's lost by the church. The Head of the church has total awareness of all our labors in full surrender to His will. He never blesses our plans, except when those plans are His will and leading. Our own plans will accomplish nothing for the kingdom of Christ. *"The flesh profiteth nothing"* (John 6:63). This church at Ephesus was busy for His kingdom. He knew their works, their labor, and their patience; and He commended them.

He spoke only ten words of commendation before He began to emphasize His first agenda. Their faithfulness to defend truth against false apostles was high on His list. Every labor of the church must flow out of purity of doctrine. Today's church exalts works of compassion above the labor of truth. The Bible has always been perfectly clear that defending the infallible Word of God is the foundational responsibility of the body of Christ. Doctrines never issue from good works, but good works always issue from good doctrines. Destroy the foundation and all is in vain.

The Son of God has made it plain that there is no design in His kingdom for defeat.

> *Nevertheless I have somewhat against thee, because thou hast left thy first love. Remember therefore from whence thou art fallen, and repent, and do the first works; or else I will come unto thee quickly, and will remove thy candlestick out of his place, except thou repent* (Revelation 2:4-5).

This pure church that loved truth and had labored through the dark night had also left the first results of receiving truth. They had left their first love. The radical fire of love had been forsaken for the greater love of being diligent against error and dedication in labors. This has certainly occurred in every experience of His church, and it is the scourge of our day. It is impossible for a fervent believer to lose his or her first love. They must turn from it. The saints leave that radical fire of holy love for Christ because other things—often good things—crowd out the devotion of love. No Christian or church can ever be defeated until or unless they leave their first love. He pleaded with them to repent because the only path back to first love is repentance. They were told to do their first works: start at the bottom and return to Him and to the fire of abandonment to His love. This is the sweet joy of Christian living in a radical relationship of love.

No one abides long in the joy of discipleship without this fire. The person that has left his first love will usually deny it and claim to still possess that love in spite of all evidences. He is probably going to be angry when you suggest his loss. It is a loss that multitudes never recover. Most believers that have left their first love have an imitation love of religion and church that has replaced their Christ-centered love and are blind to their condition. Jesus says, *"Repent or else I will remove your candlestick."* Remember that it is among the candlesticks that He walks. The joy of His presence is one of the primary losses of leaving one's first love.

> But this thou hast, that thou hatest the deeds of the Nicolaitans, which I also hate. He that hath an ear, let him hear what the Spirit saith unto the churches; To him that overcometh will I give to eat of the tree of life, which is in the midst of the paradise of God (Revelation 2:6-7).

They still hated error and were full of fire against the doctrine of the Nicolaitans. This doctrine was the effort of some in the church structure to create systems of hierarchy so that a few could control the massive multitudes. Certain men wanted power and position because they had lost the sense of a Holy Ghost-led church. The whole idea was a moving away from the Lordship of Christ and the Spirit-led church life to a system of religion full of flesh and human control. It has been the failure of almost every great fellowship of believers at some point in the growth of their movement.

Every letter is concluded with a similar ending. Always the church is reminded that the sovereign Spirit of Christ is speaking. Deaf ears are not to be tolerated because this language is from the Spirit of God. Every believer must be an *overcomer*, because no promise is ever left for anyone but overcomers. Just like John introduced the Lord with one of the divine titles to each church and in each letter, He also closes each letter with an element of great triumph of victory to the victors. In this letter, He promises that the *overcomers* will eat of the tree of life in the midst of the paradise of God.

> *And unto the angel of the church in Smyrna write; These things saith the first and the last, which was dead, and is alive; I know thy works, and tribulation, and poverty, (but thou art rich) and I know the blasphemy of them which say they are Jews, and are not, but are the synagogue of Satan. Fear none of those things which thou shalt suffer: behold, the devil shall cast some of you into prison, that ye may be tried; and ye shall have tribulation ten days: be thou faithful unto death, and I will give thee a crown of life. He that hath an ear, let him hear what the Spirit saith unto the churches; He that overcometh shall not be hurt of the second death* (Revelation 2:8-11).

To Ephesus, He identifies the source of the letter as, *"He that holdest seven stars, and he that walks in the midst of the seven candlesticks."* To Smyrna, He says, *"These things saith the first and the last, which was dead and is alive."* There will be this beautiful progression of revelation concerning Him as the One Who writes to His church. The style of this masterful approach is so intriguing that we must be careful not to elevate the style over the messenger. Only God, incarnate in the flesh, and resurrected in glory, could possibly use such language. He is transcending, but He is also present to be loved and worshipped.

This church is without any words of correction. The presence of the Smyrna churches has graced every generation, and suffered untold tribulation; but they have won the day, if not in number, certainly in His court of acceptance. Almost every great awakening where multitudes of souls were converted, was birthed by Smyrna churches. I have never found one historical event of revival that did not begin by a local church or group of local churches. The Lord said, *"I know thy works and tribulation and poverty and also the blasphemy of those say that they are Jews and are not."* They claim to be the real thing as they attack the Smyrna crowd. It is extremely easy to see that every great move of God had the big religious crowd fighting against it. They always declare that they are the real church and that the Smyrna separatists are the problem. The book *The Pilgrim Church* by E.H. Broadbent proves this truth a multitude of times with historical facts.

The Smyrna churches have been the persecuted churches on many continents and in every period of church history. To read the *Foxe's Book of Martyrs* and witness the inhumane suffering of saints is life-changing. It tells of imprisonment, death, separation from families, children removed from their parents never to see them again, and horrible torture in an attempt to force great saints to recant; that is followed by being burned at the stake, torn asunder by wild beasts, or drowned. The Lord promises this church tribulation, but He also promises them a crown of life. While they would suffer much for Him, they were reminded that although they might be put to death in the flesh, they would not suffer the second death of eternal separation. The main time period of the Smyrna church was from AD 100 to AD 313, but this church has had a representation in every period as have all the others.

And to the angel of the church in Pergamos write; These things saith he which hath the sharp sword with two edges; I know thy works, and where thou dwellest, even where Satan's seat is: and thou holdest fast my name, and hast not denied my faith, even in those days wherein Antipas was my faithful martyr, who was slain among you, where Satan dwelleth (Revelation 2:12-13).

The Pergamos church was introduced by a very stern title, which described the Lord, *"These things saith he which hath the sharp sword with two edges."* The Word of God, as represented in this title and warning, is intended to be very strong. The marriage of Christ's church to the world was the darkest day in church history. Satan engineered this moving of Babylon to the head of the church, and the dark ages were not long in coming. We would think such a clear warning to His church would never be forgotten. It is never wrong for the church to set up its quarters right in the heart of evil, but it is always wrong when that happens by mixture instead of by conquest. The true church can literally pull down the gates of hell and those gates will have no defense. This appears to have happened in the beginning of the church age, but was quickly lost by the conquest of false doctrines and evil among themselves.

> *But I have a few things against thee, because thou hast there them that hold the doctrine of Balaam, who taught Balac to cast a stumbling-block before the children of Israel, to eat things sacrificed unto idols, and to commit fornication. So hast thou also them that hold the doctrine of the Nicolaitans, which thing I hate. Repent; or else I will come unto thee quickly, and will fight against them with the sword of my mouth* (Revelation 2:14-16).

The doctrine of Balaam was the great cause of defeat in this church. Instead of separation from evil and the conquest over evil, sin-loving preachers or leaders sought to bring the world in for evangelism, and the world beguiled them. Instead of storming evil by the power of God, they would try to win by influence and compromise. This has been the greatest defeat of every move of God. It's Balaam's doctrine—fornicate with the world, and they will want what we have. It is a lie from hell. The true church bars the world at

The watchword given to every church and every church age is "hold fast till I come."

the altar and pulls down the gates of hell. Remember, Jesus commended the church at Ephesus because they hated the deeds of the Nicolaitans. In this church, they have welcomed those that *"hold the doctrines of the Nicolaitans."* Now it's *"Repent or I will fight against you with the sword of my mouth"* or to say it plainly "with this Word of God." His only defense is His Word and our only offense is His Word.

> *He that hath an ear, let him hear what the Spirit saith unto the churches; To him that overcometh will I give to eat of the hidden manna, and will give him a white stone, and in the stone a new name written, which no man knoweth saving he that receiveth it* (Revelation 2:17).

Every ending is so worded that all seven endings are a perfect finish for the entire list of letters. Every church is plainly warned that the only victory is a full victory for those He calls overcomers. The new language of eternity requires a new name for our Lord Himself and a new name for the Bride of Christ. This church reflects the time period of AD 313 to AD 590.

> *And unto the angel of the church in Thyatira write; These things saith the Son of God, who hath his eyes like unto a flame of fire, and his feet are like fine brass; I know thy works, and charity, and service, and*

faith, and thy patience, and thy works; and the last to be more than the first. Notwithstanding I have a few things against thee, because thou sufferest that woman Jezebel, which calleth herself a prophetess, to teach and to seduce my servants to commit fornication, and to eat things sacrificed unto idols. And I gave her space to repent of her fornication; and she repented not. Behold, I will cast her into a bed, and them that commit adultery with her into great tribulation, except they repent of their deeds. And I will kill her children with death; and all the churches shall know that I am he which searcheth the reins and hearts: and I will give unto every one of you according to your works (Revelation 2:18-23).

The spiritual darkness that reigned in this church demanded a consuming title of the Lord to reflect His judgment and fury at compromise and sin. He plainly stated that their works had far bypassed their faith. Then, He revealed the death and destruction that the woman Jezebel had accomplished through the seduction of His church into utter failure. She would not repent, and He promised to cast her into great Tribulation. That system of Jezebel has survived until the present because she must be available in the end and be judged as He promised. Many opportunities to repent have been offered. History tells the story of great saints that pleaded with the false religious empires to change their ways but to no avail. This false system encompasses more than one organization and embraces almost every religious entity. There has never been a religious organization that has kept its evangelistic zeal for more than one hundred years. However, when that zeal was lost they proceeded to persecute the new move of God just like they were persecuted in their beginning.

The Lord sees His church as two-fold. The massive organizations are clearly tied to the woman Jezebel, but her boundaries are hidden in the closets of prayer and grace of the genuine saints that serve the Lord alone. He says, *"As many as have not known the depth of Satan, I will put upon you none other burden."* The pure church is seen as a type of a virgin or a bride. The false church is seen as a type of an impure woman or a Jezebel.

> *But unto you I say, and unto the rest in Thyatira, as many as have not this doctrine, and which have not known the depths of Satan, as they speak; I will put upon you none other burden. But that which ye have already hold fast till I come. And he that overcometh, and keepeth my works unto the end, to him will I give power over the nations: And he shall rule them with a rod of iron; as the vessels of a potter shall they be broken to shivers: even as I received of my Father. And I will give him the morning star. He that hath an ear, let him hear what the Spirit saith unto the churches* (Revelation 2:24-29).

The watchword given to every church and every church age is *"hold fast till I come."* There is an increasing emphasis given to this fourth church about the Rapture and the reward of being Rapture-ready. *"Hold fast till I come"* was a New Testament theme Jesus Christ taught in person that was carried throughout the world by the early church, even prior to the Book of Revelation. Here, He clarifies the promise of the reigning church during the millennium of Christ and His returning saints. *"To the overcomer, I will give power over the nations."* The Spirit has spoken and every saint is commanded to listen. This church age was from approximately AD 590 to AD 1517.

Conclusion

The second chapter of Revelation is the wonderful or sad story of four churches or church perils. The picture and promise for our future is bright with His irrevocable promises. The following three churches hear even more about the Rapture and the warning of coming tribulation. You cannot escape the fact that four themes govern these seven letters. It is faithfulness and devotion to His Infallible Word, separation from the world and all its systems, undying love for the Lord Himself, and a commitment to a Biblical lifestyle totally different from the world. He always calls His faithful followers *"overcomers."* The best words to describe the true church in the midst of the wicked world and ten thousand compromises is, *"These are my overcomers."*

I WILL KEEP THE OVERCOMER

There is an unprecedented level of love that Jesus Christ, in His exalted glory, clearly reveals for His Body, the church. These seven letters show that great love, His complete knowledge of His church, His correction, and above all His great plans for the church's future. He corrects because He will judge and reward nothing but faithfulness. There is a consciousness all through these letters of the impending tribulation and a desire to help His saints escape that dark hour and be found ready for the Rapture of His espoused bride. In every letter, He ends with a promise for the overcomers. The very word overcomer carries a dire warning of troubles to face and a glorious victory for facing those troubles and challenges with triumph.

Every one of the seven churches has had a counterpart in every hour of the church dispensation. Often, the Smyrna churches were hidden away in mountains or meeting in secret in the cities. The Thyatira churches were loving the woman Jezebel and reveling in the careless living she championed. The faithful of the Lord Jesus Christ were, in many cases, serving Christ in spite of rejection and suffering the hatred of those that compromised the truth. There has always been a remnant, in spite of all hellish actions on the part of the enemy within and the enemy without. The Lord of the church walked among His pilgrim people, whether it was in a cave, a dungeon, or a cathedral. These letters represent the most current and absolute facts about His relationship to His church in the entire Word of God.

> *And unto the angel of the church in Sardis write; These things saith he that hath the seven Spirits of God, and the seven stars; I know thy works, that thou hast a name that thou livest, and art dead. Be watchful, and strengthen the things which remain, that are ready to die: for I have not found thy works perfect before God. Remember therefore how thou hast received and heard, and hold fast, and repent. If therefore thou shalt not watch, I will come on thee as a thief, and thou shalt not know what hour I will come upon thee* (Revelation 3:1-3).

Church historians believe that the Sardis church represents the church of the reformation. Of course, that would only reflect the major events of Martin Luther, John Calvin, and other reformation leaders. It was during this period that smaller groups, mostly rejected and persecuted, were the real Biblical churches walking in fundamental Christianity. We will see references to those groups in Revelation 3:4. The churches of the reformation

There is an unprecedented level of love that Jesus Christ, in His exalted glory, clearly reveals for His Body, the church.

never truly turned from many of the doctrines and questionable teachings of the dark ages. There was almost no prophetic preaching that included this Book of Revelation and this great hope of the Pre-Tribulation Rapture. Replacement theology that relegated Israel to the ashes was still believed and preached by many. Post-millennialism or A-millennialism was the major doctrine of the reformation churches. Justification was a major step forward, but New

Testament Evangelism and Spirit-filled churches were still left for future progress. This period covered the years 1517-1790.

The Lord said, *"Thou hast a name that thou livest and art dead."* This statement could not describe the above truth better. The Lord pleaded, *"Be watchful, and strengthen the things which remain."* He makes great references to the Rapture, *"thou shalt not know what hour I will come upon thee."* There have been Sardis churches all throughout the church age and there are a multitude of these churches at present. He will shortly come upon them as a thief in the night.

Thou hast a few names even in Sardis which have not defiled their garments; and they shall walk with me in white: for they are worthy. He that overcometh, the same shall be clothed in white raiment; and I will not blot out his name out of the book of life, but I will confess his name before my Father, and before his angels. He that hath an ear, let him hear what the Spirit saith unto the churches (Revelation 3:4-6).

Here are those remnant saints that refused to be bound by the doctrines of men. These are saints of God, which have not defiled their garments. These are the Rapture-ready saints *"and they shall walk with me in white: for they are worthy."* If you will take a look at the elders in chapter four after the rapture, you will see the faithful company. These seven letters show that the great Lord of the church maintains perfect control. He knows our thoughts afar off, and His judgment is perfect. History reflects a pilgrim church far out of the mainstream but faithful to the Word of God.

Two books that every Christian should read are *Foxe's Book of Martyrs* and *The Pilgrim Church*. There are powerful records of that pilgrim church where literally millions of saints have been killed for their faith. The Anabaptist Christians existed over hundreds of years and covered several different periods of these churches. The

Waldensians and Albigenses were some of God's choice saints. There were thousands of lesser groups that filled communities with revival and then filled the same communities with their blood of martyrdom. There were a host of such saints whose names will not be honored until that marvelous day of reckoning. Every overcomer will be greatly rewarded and will be the hero of our future.

Do not miss the great promise to the church of Sardis. Remember that the seven letters contained many promises. All of these promises are really for all of His church. He said to those faithful to Him and that were overcomers of the flesh, the world, and the devil, *"But I will confess His name before my Father and before His angels."* That has to be the highest honor in the world.

> *And to the angel of the church in Philadelphia write; These things saith he that is holy, he that is true, he that hath the key of David, he that openeth, and no man shutteth; and shutteth, and no man openeth; I know thy works: behold, I have set before thee an open door, and no man can shut it: for thou hast a little strength, and hast kept my word, and hast not denied my name. Behold, I will make them of the synagogue of Satan, which say they are Jews, and are not, but do lie; behold, I will make them to come and worship before thy feet, and to know that I have loved thee (Revelation 3:7-9).*

The Philadelphia church is the perfect model and type of the church age existing from the end of the eighteenth century (approximately A.D. 1790) until the Rapture. The open door of evangelism, missions, and the general spiritual atmosphere has been phenomenal. The early church periods, typified in Ephesus and Smyrna, have been the only periods with which to compare. The dark ages snuffed out the light, and by God's grace the world witnessed a marvelous reoccurrence of revival. It is clear from Scripture and the history of this period that the move could have been more expansive and supernatural. He stated, *"For thou hast a little strength."* Both periods that include the Ephesus and Smyrna churches as well as the Philadelphia churches have faced many difficult periods of false religious, false prophets, and satanic attacks. Every one of the struggles has been duly recorded, and the false crowd will be required to worship before the feet of Jesus. Most of our church world has become so accepting of the false doctrines that they think a mixture is acceptable with God. The statement above is wonderful proof of our God's total commitment to pure truth.

I often hear Christians erroneously say, "I eat the meat and spit out the bone." These seven letters are positive truth that we should reject all Biblical error and have neither time nor space for heresy. The Philadelphia church period is extremely strong in denouncing the synagogues of Satan. A little error may not harm a few strong souls but always destroys a multitude in the end. Error progresses downhill and creates more and more damage as it worsens. The Lord promises great benefits and blessings to the defenders of His infallible Word. He will show the world His love for His revelations.

Because thou hast kept the word of my patience, I also will keep thee from the hour of temptation, which shall come upon all the world, to try them that dwell upon the earth. Behold, I come quickly: hold that fast which thou hast, that no man take thy crown. Him that overcometh will I make a pillar in the temple of my God, and he shall go no more out: and I will write upon him the name of my God, and the name of the city of my God, which is new Jerusalem, which cometh down out of heaven from my God: and I will write upon him my new name. He that hath an ear, let him hear what the Spirit saith unto the churches. (Revelation 3:10-13).

As I previously mentioned, the coming tribulation is evident all throughout these letters to the church. It has been made plain in the Second Testament that His saints are not appointed to wrath: *"For God hath not appointed us to wrath, but to obtain salvation by our Lord Jesus Christ"* (I Thessalonians 5:9). The term *overcomers* was very appropriate as the constant reminder that something was pending, and being overcomers was a prerogative for His church. He told the church of Thyatira that those who loved the woman Jezebel and her deception were going to be cast into the Great Tribulation. There is only one Great Tribulation. He warned the church of Sardis that were overcomers, *"I will not blot out his name."* A similar warning was given to the church of Laodicea.

His promise of the Rapture before the Tribulation to the church of Philadelphia is one of the surest in the entire Second Testament. The words are plain that a great event is about to happen on this earth *"which shall come upon all the world to try them that dwell upon the earth."* The entire world and all of mankind is going to be put through the utter judgment to try their souls unto life or death. There is only one way of escape, and He made it clear that we are the company that has the privilege. Even within the church there is a

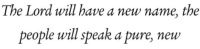

The Lord will have a new name, the people will speak a pure, new language; and His saints will be identified with His Son's new name written in eternal glorified bodies.

narrow margin. A very specific crowd will escape, and He describes them plainly. *"Because thou hast kept the word of my patience, I also will keep thee from the hour."* This can only be a reference to blood washed believers in Christ. No way to doubt or to swing a deal. The overcomers will be out of here before the terrible wrath of God is poured on this earth. It is a powerful promise from the Lord of the church and cannot be broken.

The Master adds a warning, *"Watch ye therefore, and pray always, that ye may be accounted worthy to escape all these things that shall come to pass, and to stand before the Son of man. And in the daytime he was teaching in the temple; and at night he went out, and abode in the mount that is called the Mount of Olives. And all the people came early in the morning to Him in the temple, for to hear him"* (Luke 21:36-38). The Bible affirms to us that the entire judgment period begins with His church. He states, *"For the time is come that judgment must begin at the house of God"* (I Peter 4:17a). The promises that end each letter grow in beauty and purpose to excite His saints. We were never meant to live gloomy lives. The word *hope* in Scripture means "joyous anticipation." Hope is the certainty of the promises that cannot fail to fill the hearts of the faithful. The Lord will have a new name, the people will speak a pure, new language; and His saints will be identified with His Son's new name written in eternal glorified bodies. Hear carefully what the Holy Spirit is saying to the churches.

> *And unto the angel of the church of the Laodiceans write; These things saith the Amen, the faithful and true witness, the beginning of the creation of God* (Revelation 3:14).

He uses one of His most magnificent names as He begins His final letter to the last of the church age. Not only is this the last of the church age, it is the most dire warning to the church world from then until now. He says this letter is from *"The Amen."* I'm always amazed at the doomsayers when they predict the world's ideas of how this earth will be destroyed. *"The Amen"* is going to take care of that, and He will have the last word. He is also named *"the faithful and true witness."* The names of our Lord used in each address to the churches serves to strengthen the commendations and condemnations. The truths He speaks can be rejected, but this rejection will result in absolute judgment. Every word will be fulfilled and every correction will be obeyed or serve as witness in the coming judgment. These great teachings are not suggestions.

I know thy works, that thou art neither cold nor hot: I would thou wert cold or hot. So then because thou art lukewarm, and neither cold nor hot, I will spue thee out of my mouth. Because thou sayest, I am rich, and increased with goods, and have need of nothing; and knowest not that thou art wretched, and miserable, and poor, and blind, and naked: I counsel thee to buy of me gold tried in the fire, that thou mayest be rich; and white raiment, that thou mayest be clothed, and that the shame of thy nakedness do not appear; and anoint thine eyes with eyesalve, that thou mayest see (Revelation 3:15-18).

This church is in dark trouble. The meaning of her name is an expression of her character. The *"church of man rule"* is a period in which every man is a law unto himself and where the Holy Scripture has been reduced to a cafeteria diet. This "pick and choose" treatment of the Word

> *His love was not a distant love but a love of one standing at the door.*

of God is death to the soul in every case. This church period marks the last of the church age and shows that the prophetic words of Jesus Christ, as recorded in Matthew, has indeed occurred; *"And because iniquity shall abound, the love of many shall wax cold"* (Matthew 24:12). The fire of the Holy Ghost is gone, and the church world, for the most part, is spiritually dead, although it has been estimated that there are close to 80 million so called evangelicals in the United States today.

His judgment of this condition is severe. Our present church life is a confused dichotomy. We have the experimental element where doctrine is unimportant and the opposite systems of theology where experience is rejected. Both extremes are contrary to Scripture. A lukewarm church life can be attributed to both extremes. While one extreme is death without experiencing the life of the Holy Spirit, the opposite extreme is experiencing religion without the guideline of great truths. Both of these mindsets lead to separation from God in Hell, and have plagued the church in every period of church history, but have certainly reached a zenith in this last church age. He condemns the coldness of such church life and rejects it from the body life of His own Rapture-ready Bride. He said, *"I will spue them out of my mouth."*

Such churches are normally the richest and largest in the world. All worldly church members normally want a church free of strong guidelines, where self can reign unchecked. It does not matter much in what extreme direction a church may go as long as there are no restraints on self. Any system of religion will grow, prosper, and become great if the cross life is absent. The one area that unconverted or unsanctified flesh cannot handle is the separated life of Bible righteousness. This Laodicean church has made the cross life the worst enemy and has championed unsanctified living. The Lord's words make that very plain, *"I counsel thee to buy of me gold tried in the fire, that thou mayest be rich; and white raiment, that thou mayest be clothed, and that the shame of thy nakedness do not appear."* Spiritual death has robbed this church of life because the spiritual is only present in death to self.

> *As many as I love, I rebuke and chasten: be zealous therefore, and repent. Behold, I stand at the door, and knock: if any man hear my voice, and open the door, I will come in to him, and will sup with him, and he with me. To him that overcometh will I grant to sit with me in my throne, even as*

I also overcame, and am set down with my Father in his throne. He that hath an ear, let him hear what the Spirit saith unto the churches (Revelation 3:19-22).

His love is the love of a Father to His children, and it is because of this great love that He says, *"As many as I love, I rebuke and chasten."* Who could ever want a love that allows the one loved to destroy themselves? Still, His love was not a distant love but a love likened to a Father standing at the door. The Lord is ready to so consume with love that His rebuke is nothing less than joy. His love walks in the midst of His church offering His great promises.

This closing statement to the church shows the perfect unity of the seven letters. All of His overcomers will be judged individually and rewarded individually, but there is still a unity in His promises. This last inclusiveness is to all overcomers. *"To him that overcometh will I grant to sit with me in my throne, even as I also overcame, and am set down with my Father in his throne."*

Conclusion

Every identification of the Lord to His church recalls a portion of His revelation in chapter one and every promise is part of the sum total given to all seven of His churches. Also, in each ending to all seven churches, He states, *"what the Spirit saith unto the churches."* Notice, He says *"churches"* in the plural. They are separate and different but all part of one church. It's important that no correction is rejected. Each letter is a final warning and promise. The Rapture is at hand, and there will be no additional warning before He appears.

COME UP HITHER

4

Any view of this chapter that does not allow for the triumphant Rapture of the saints is woefully inadequate and an embarrassment to the truth. It is the grandest picture of the true church and the overcoming saints who were brought up from the Lion's mouth into the King's throne. The blood-washed saints that were hated by the world had faced their persecutors for the last time. Giving up the world, they had gained the grandest seats around the throne of the Father. This chapter is the beginning of the glory that has been promised to the saints since the opening of the Holy Bible. From seats around the throne to the city of the throne, the saints will never suffer shame again. They are His saints; they will take up positions as His elders until they march forth as His army, reign as Kings, and possess the city of the Bride.

Revelation chapter four moves us past the Church Age, where His saints are pilgrims and strangers on this earth. After the opening of chapter four, everything revealed in this book is future prophecy. The pilgrim saints become serving elders that sit on lesser thrones and participate with the Father and the Son in the redemption of this earth. Redemption in the Bible is always a judicial business incorporating cleansing, judgment, and the renewing and perfecting of that which sin has corrupted. The authorized elders, Cherubim, and angels will serve the Lamb of God during this process. This chapter is the opening volley, and ultimately the universe will be perfectly redeemed. From the rebellion in heaven, where Satan and his angels were cast to the earth, until Satan presents his false Christ and false spirit, every act of evil must be presented and judged at the bar of justice. It will be seven years of perfect redemption until the earth is fit for the King of Kings to rule and reign.

The great Jehovah God is seated on His throne in the celestial heavens and is fully prepared for the heavenly court. Over six thousand years have passed since a serpent possessed by Lucifer walked into the garden and deceived God's perfect couple, Adam and Eve. From the venom of lies in the garden, sin has touched every offspring of Adam. The upheaval of the earth by the Noahic flood left its scars on a sin-cursed earth. There is not one element of the created world unspoiled by the flood of evil, and it's now time for redemption. The celestial city of Jerusalem, now in heaven, and its inhabitants are the only untouched geography in the cosmos, and the court will be held in its temple. David must have had a slight view of this seven-year session. *"Great is the LORD, and greatly to be praised in the city of our God, in the mountain of his holiness. Beautiful for situation, the joy of the whole earth is mount Zion, on the sides of the north, the city of the great King. God is known in her palaces for a refuge"* (Psalms 48:1-3).

The court proceeding that must go forth out of this city demands a Pre-Tribulation Rapture to transfer the saints from their graves or from their living on earth to fulfill their appointed place in the judgments. This earth is the Lord's and He has appointed it to His saints to posses for eternity. It has been clearly stated that we shall judge this earth, and our removal to this grand event is unquestionably guaranteed. The fight against the Rapture is a last-ditch battle from the devil to prevent us from our heavenly task. The proceeding cannot begin until we arrive at our appointed seats before the throne.

After this I looked, and, behold, a door was opened in heaven: and the first voice which I heard was as it were of a trumpet talking with me; which said, Come up hither, and I will shew thee things which must be hereafter (Revelation 4:1).

There is no event on God's calendar that demands a door opened into heaven from the earth's advantage except the Rapture. This great vision by John incorporates all the fine details that Scripture associates with the saints being caught up to meet the Lord in the air. *"For the Lord himself shall descend from heaven with a shout, with the voice of the archangel, and with the trump of God: and the dead in Christ shall rise first: Then we which are alive and remain shall be caught up together with them in the clouds, to meet the Lord in the air: and so shall we ever be with the Lord"* (I Thessalonians 4:16-17).

Before John sees the throne in heaven, he hears the voice of Jesus Christ *"as it were of a trumpet"* saying, *"Come up hither."* The trumpet voice gave details to John to make sure the church would understand this further information as *"hereafter"* or following the letters to the seven churches. Nothing from this

The great Jehovah God is seated on His throne in the celestial heavens and is fully prepared for the heavenly court.

point in Revelation can be a historical event. This was clearly stated in the introduction of chapter one. *"Write the things which thou hast seen, and the things which are, and the things which shall be hereafter"* (Revelation 1:19). All through chapter one, two, and three the whole vision and scene is the High Priestly appearance of Jesus Christ and His letters to His churches.

John is clearly caught up into the heavens to view further proceedings that demand his presence. He is going to witness the glorified saints seated in positions of honor and dressed in attire that would be impossible on earth. Everything he sees and writes from this verse has no connection to the Church Age and its kingdom business, which the Scripture identifies as the spiritual kingdom *"that cometh not with observation. And when he was demanded of the Pharisees, when the kingdom of God should come, he answered them and said, The kingdom of God cometh not with observation: Neither shall they say, Lo here! or, lo there! for, behold, the kingdom of God is within you"* (Luke 17:20-21).

> *And immediately I was in the spirit: and, behold, a throne was set in heaven, and one sat on the throne. And he that sat was to look upon like a jasper and a sardine stone: and there was a rainbow round about the throne, in sight like unto an emerald* (Revelation 4:2-3).

What John was about to witness demanded that a spiritual dimension temporarily overshadow him. This again proves that his vision was beyond the physically observable age of the church and was a prophetic view of future events. No one can stand before God's throne or even view God's throne until our bodies are glorified. *"For in this we groan, earnestly desiring to be clothed upon with our house which is from heaven"* (2 Corinthians 5:2). This vision given to John was for our future hope and demands the Rapture to fulfill its glory.

In the Spirit, John looks on the majestic throne of Almighty Jehovah, where our Heavenly Father is seated in His glory. The description given to us is limited by human language inadequate to reach to such heights of splendor. The glory was such that the writer could only compare it with the grandeur of rare jewels. There was a gleam of glory and overwhelming splendor making Him incomparable to earthly beauty. The dazzling colors of a rainbow were seen overshadowing the throne and its occupant. The throne itself was in sight like unto an emerald. No earthly wonder has ever been so described.

How can we question that something is about to transpire that the ages of human pain has longed to behold? Ten thousand gods have imitated God the Father and have tried to possess His kingdom. They all have faded into defeat. The last of those gods are soon to disappear. His presence settles the God-questions of the rebellious multitudes. The proceedings that will issue from His throne will not leave any questions or doubts. His glorious

There is no event on God's calendar that demands a door opened into heaven from the earth's advantage except the Rapture.

presence became the backdrop of the rest of this great masterpiece of literature. Every scene from this point forward must be understood as the acts and transactions of Him, His Son, His Holy Spirit, and His appointed elders and angels. He is sovereign God, and all glory and honor must flow from His throne.

> *And round about the throne were four and twenty seats: and upon the seats I saw four and twenty elders sitting, clothed in white raiment; and they had on their heads crowns of gold. And out of the throne proceeded lightnings and thunderings and voices: and there were seven lamps of fire burning before the throne, which are the seven Spirits of God. And before the throne there was a sea of glass like unto crystal: and in the midst of the throne, and round about the throne, were four beasts full of eyes before and behind* (Revelation 4:4-6).

All three of these verses begin with references to the throne of God and He that is seated in His majesty, *"And round about the throne...And out of the throne... And before the throne."* That is breathtaking language. First, *"round about the throne"* are the saints of God that have been promoted to elders. No more pilgrims and strangers traveling through a weary land, but exalted, glorified, and seated *"round about the throne."* The judgment seat of Christ has occurred, and His saints have been promoted to their lofty positions. They are seated after a lifetime of

pilgrimage and sorrows. They are clothed in sparkling-white raiment, which is the righteousness of the glorified elders. They are
crowned with crowns of gold, and this is just the first day of eternity for all of them.

"And out of the throne" and *"before the throne"* describes both the
activity and the person of His Holy Spirit. The Holy Spirit is a divine
member of the Godhead and He is described as both proceeding *"out
of the throne"* and *"before the throne."* Our divine God is indescribable
and this reflection of His Spirit reveals the intimacy that the Father,
the Son, and the Holy Spirit represent. The Spirit is here revealed in
the totality of His office, and
great spiritual activities are
manifest. The Holy Spirit is
grace in redemption, but He will
be fire in judgment. *"Seven lamps
of fire"* are the evidence of the

*In the Spirit, John looks on the
majestic throne of Almighty Jehovah,
where our Heavenly Father is
seated in His glory.*

coming refining of this earth until *"righteousness covers the earth as the
waters cover the sea."*

The great Cherubim of God, called the four beasts, are truly a
multitude that are the keepers of righteousness in the earth. They
always move in the wake of the Holy Spirit and defend everything
and everyone that is pure in God's kingdom. Because the saints have
become elders around the throne and because the Holy Spirit has
moved His epicenter back to the throne, the Cherubim are present in
heaven for the beginning of earth's redemption. Four is the earthly
number, and this host will be deeply involved in the process to refine
and redeem this universe. They will shortly be dispatched back to
this earth for the coming redemption.

*And the first beast was like a lion, and the second beast like a calf,
and the third beast had a face as a man, and the fourth beast was like*

a flying eagle. And the four beasts had each of them six wings about him; and they were full of eyes within: and they rest not day and night, saying, Holy, holy, holy, Lord God Almighty, which was, and is, and is to come (Revelation 4:7-8).

These two verses unite the four living creatures (a multitude) of the Book of Revelation with the same four living creatures of Ezekiel. Their appearance in Ezekiel is described similar to the so-called unidentified objects that you hear and read about in today's paranormal world. This earth is soon to be conscious of incredible heavenly activities and these

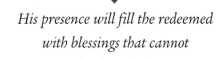

His presence will fill the redeemed with blessings that cannot be described.

living creatures, Cherubim, will defend holiness on a scale unknown in the church dispensation. Their appearance as a lion, a calf, a man, and a flying eagle reflects the united intelligence with the strength and mobility that will define these activities. This earth will understand this activity as God-appointed action and judgment.

They have great speed—as light—great ability to discern right and wrong as *"eyes within,"* and they rest not day or night. Their constant action and declarations will be for the glory of God. Their glory throughout the earth will be to declare God's glory and will powerfully make the earth aware of the Heavenly Father on His throne directing the proceedings on the earth. Of course, to begin with, this will start in heaven and then proceed to the earth as the seals are opened in chapter six and forward to chapter nineteen. The entire chapters of four and five are a prelude of celebration before the beginning of the sorrows that the inhabitants of this earth will be subject to endure.

And when those beasts give glory and honour and thanks to him that sat on the throne, who liveth for ever and ever, The four and twenty elders

*fall down before him that sat on the throne, and worship him that liveth
for ever and ever, and cast their crowns before the throne, saying, Thou
art worthy, O Lord, to receive glory and honour and power: for thou
hast created all things, and for thy pleasure they are and were created*
(Revelation 4:9-11).

A great time of worship and adoration of the Heavenly Father
must precede the events that are developing. Nothing in God's universe and no action on the part of our Creator ever proceeds until
worship has reached its crescendo. There is no truth in the Bible that
is greater in reach than to learn that no one can ever become a great
prayer warrior until first they are great in worship. These heavenly
events of which the Book of Revelation is a grand part is literally
flooded with worship to our great sovereign God. The Cherubim
have rocked the heavens with *"Holy, Holy, Holy"* adding, *"Lord God
Almighty which liveth forever."* Now the multitudes, represented as
twenty-four elders, join the heavenly worship. This is the first time
in human history that glorified saints, and elders, have been privileged to sing together with angels.

There are songs they sing without us and songs we will soon sing
together with them. There are also songs we sing without them, but
in this case we are joined together. As the redeemed elders, worship
becomes so majestic that these glorified elders begin to cast their
crowns at His feet before the throne. This is ultimate praise when all
our rewards shall seem as nothing before the face of Him who sits on
His throne.

Our frailty of flesh forbids that we understand the beauty of this
coming time of heavenly worship. The state of our new bodies and the
breath of our minds and emotional being will allow us to worship as
it was intended when God created man. There will be no glory in
heaven that exceeds this beauty of heavenly worship. His presence

will fill the redeemed with blessings that cannot be described.

Conclusion

In chapter five, we will see the forfeited deed of this earth that Adam allowed the devil to steal. Chapter four is the prelude to the viewing of this great title deed of His earth that will soon be free of all offense. The twenty-four elders are a multitude from both the First and Second Testament saints. This is the first time in the Holy Bible that the twelve tribes are united with the twelve apostles in a prophetic number to represent the espoused Bride. When we view the Bride's city, New Jerusalem, we will see the twenty-four elders again. The twelve gates of this city are named after the twelve tribes and the twelve foundations are named after the twelve apostles. *"And had a wall great and high, and had twelve gates, and at the gates twelve angels, and names written thereon, which are the names of the twelve tribes of the children of Israel: On the east three gates; on the north three gates; on the south three gates; and on the west three gates. And the wall of the city had twelve foundations, and in them the names of the twelve apostles of the Lamb"* (Revelation 21:12-14). *"Come up hither"* is the call of the Rapture and this call could ring out at any moment. Be prepared with your wedding garment at any hour!

THE TITLE DEED OF THE EARTH, SEVEN-SEALED BOOK

If there is one chapter in God's Holy Word that stands out as the mountain peak for our future, this must be it. This earth has become a cesspool; filth, garbage, human debauchery, and demonic activities are riding like a victorious army across the entire world, spreading its moral sewer as they go. But as you read this story, you will see that darkness is ripe for judgment and that our Holy God will have the last word. The devil's business for six thousand years has been to turn the beautiful into the ugly, the well-watered plains into a wilderness, and to spread sorrow and destruction on this earth.

Satan walked proudly into the Garden of Eden for the very purpose of supplanting God's wonderful design in that luxurious place. When he had lied, deceived, and stolen his way into the hearts of Adam and Eve, he had to crawl his way out of that formerly harmonious place. Although he had stolen the title deed of this earth, he certainly had no glory for his success. From that day he has been the god of this earth. Every false religion is his design, and every god other than the true God is nothing but the devil disguised in a religious coat. Any person that is willing to follow the present design of praying without naming the name of Jesus as their right of entrance is actually praying to one of those false gods. The false god of this world is riding his way to hell on the back of the false one-world religion, and a multitude is riding with him.

This fifth chapter of Revelation is the Father and Son's revelation of the coming redemption of this earth. This entire cosmos that we live in and the earth that we live on is ripe for redemption. The darker it gets and the more evil we see triumphing, the closer we are getting to the earth's cleansing. The cup of wrath must be filled to the brim.

The devil's business for six thousand years has been to turn the beautiful into the ugly, the well-watered plains into a wilderness, and to spread sorrow and destruction on this earth.

God acts only in full judicial perfection. Satan must be allowed, along with his false trinity, to complete their claim on this earth. The Father intends for this world's population to see the devil for what he really represents. Satan has never had any powers but those which were conceded to him by God's created family. Satan is an interloper and masquerader. He lies and cheats his way to every evil victory. Right now, the world scene reveals his closing actions. The culture of the coming personified Antichrist is spreading into worldwide acceptance. Satan is preparing for his last hellish endeavor.

The next critical event must be the Rapture, which will be followed by the opening of the book containing the title deed of this earth. The saints must be in heaven to assist the Father and the Son in this triumphant takeover of the earth. We are the ones to whom He has promised the right to rule this earth for Him. He never meant for Adam and Eve to give up the right of authority over the earth. They were told to take dominion, to rule and direct a holy government for the Creator, and to enjoy this planet. It was an absolutely perfect world of exquisite beauty. The devil deceived his way into the heart of man, and mankind became his servants. The Rapture has removed the elect chosen saints to His presence (Revelation chapter four) and the great God will now act to begin the process of eviction. The multitudes of Satan's followers will be allowed a fling of passing authority as we—the raptured saints—unite with the heavenly leadership and God's angelic host to judge and then cast out the offending powers of evil. Let's look at Revelation chapter five, verse by verse.

And I saw in the right hand of him that sat on the throne a book written within and on the backside, sealed with seven seals. And I saw a strong angel proclaiming with a loud voice, Who is worthy to open the book, and to loose the seals thereof? (Revelation 5:1-2).

In the previous chapter, we witnessed the throne of God with the First and Second Testament saints worshipping in the Father's presence, unashamed and glorified. For the first time in human history since the fall in the garden, saints could worship before their God without falling on their faces. No doubts can be raised that these saints had been raptured. They are not the spirits of the saintly dead, but are glorified with bodies. They are seated before the exalted Creator on lesser thrones and are fully prepared to sit with Him in authority and to participate with Him in the redemptive process. The scene He is directing before these saints would be impossible without the resurrection of the dead and their removal to His throne room.

Now God appears before this host of the redeemed with this magnificent book in His right hand. This book not only contains content within, but it is sealed with seven seals and written on the backside. The inside script contains the process that will follow after the book is opened, but the outside contains the rights to open the book. This great heavenly angel, no doubt a Brigadier General of heaven's highest order, proclaims with a loud voice a question: *"Who is worthy to open the book, and to loose the seals therof?"* The heavenly Godhead of the Father, the Son, the Holy Ghost, and the great leadership of angels knew that no ordinary member of the mighty angelic host could accomplish this redemptive act. Glorious created beings were certainly of great honor, and yet they were incapable of this divine act to redeem the earth.

> *And no man in heaven, nor in earth, neither under the earth, was able to open the book, neither to look thereon. And I wept much, because no man was found worthy to open and to read the book, neither to look thereon* (Revelation 5:3-4).

Please remember that John, who was answering this question, was the physical John on the Isle of Patmos, not the glorified John that would soon be among the glorified multitude. So, this answer was from the fleshly mind of the earthly John before his death, as he was beholding this vision. When he heard this great question—*"Who is worthy to open the book?"*—, all he could do was weep. From his Jewish background, he understood the process of redeeming property that had been sold or taken as debt or even stolen by an interloper. The redeeming member of the family that had sold or had been evicted from the property had to be the next of kin. He surely did not understand all of the connecting dots, or there would have been shouting instead of weeping.

The Son of God then stepped forward to His Father's grand presence with the seven-sealed book in His hand.

John was seeing this entire picture, and the verses show us that a survey of all creation quickly occurred before his face. Cherubim, Seraphim, and all the created angelic hosts were surveyed, but they stood incapable of opening this book. The earth's populace was considered, but it was hopeless. They even surveyed all the dead since Adam and no one was found worthy.

John wept much because he knew the hell that this earth had experienced, and he knew the hope of tomorrow when this earth would become the kingdom of God again. Did he doubt for a moment that no one would be found? I cannot answer that, although I doubt it. I can tell you that he knew the future was bleak until a "Kinsman Redeemer" could be found to set this earth straight. I can imagine that this veritable giant of the faith could say with certainty that God his Father and Christ His Lord had a plan, but somehow he could not grasp it and his weeping stirred his heart with concern. But then voices rang out with the answer.

> *And one of the elders saith unto me, Weep not: behold, the Lion of the tribe of Juda, the Root of David, hath prevailed to open the book, and to loose the seven seals thereof. And I beheld, and, lo, in the midst of the throne and of the four beasts, and in the midst of the elders, stood a Lamb as it had been slain, having seven horns and seven eyes, which are the seven Spirits of God sent forth into all the earth. And he came and took the book out of the right hand of him that sat upon the throne* (Revelation 5:5-7).

No heavenly scene can transcend this event. Since the fall of man in the Garden of Eden, the Great God and His Son have anticipated this day. Heaven gave its Crown Prince to step from its presence into a virgin's womb to be born a fleshly man and die a horrible death. Angels ascended and descended about Him as He fulfilled His redemptive role in His Father's great plan. His whole life was a series of multiple choices to never deviate from the plan. He knew death on the cross was His lot in life, but each step to that cross was more than robot activity. He felt each moment of rejection, each word of blasphemy, and, finally, each pain of crucifixion. In order to be the Kinsman Redeemer, He had to be one of us and yet rise above us so that no act of sin would ever mar the sacrifice. To do what had to be done, to put this earth back on track again, required a spotless Lamb hanging on a cruel tree until each drop of divine blood could shake a godless earth back to the Father's design.

The church now steps into her future role in this vision of tomorrow. An elder and glorified saint answers John's mournful response. The answer is a wonderful description of our Lord's heritage as well as His victory. He had to be a Kinsman. It was not enough that He was the "Son of God," but He had to be the *"Lion of the tribe of Judah"* and the *"Root of David."* He had to fulfill every prophecy and be of Jewish genealogy. Anyone that seeks to attack the nation of Israel or to deny their relationship to Christ or the prophetic future of the Jews is clearly speaking for the devil himself. Jesus said it well when He said, *"Salvation is of the Jews"* (John 4:22). The Son of God's death was the final act of sacrifice and was followed immediately by His descent into the realm of the First Testament abode of the righteous dead. After He had finished that victory for His own mostly Jewish forbearers, He arose as the first fruits of our coming resurrection.

There is surely an angel standing somewhere near the portals of glory awaiting the word to make the trumpet blast.

John saw Him standing triumphantly in the midst of the Father's throne, surrounded by His Cherubim. All of this in the midst of the raptured saints, encircling and clearly endearing to the seven Spirits or the person of the Holy Spirit. "Awesome" is the only word to describe such a sight. The Father is triumphant, the Son is triumphant, the Holy Spirit is triumphant, and the Cherubim are triumphant. But, do not forget the saints of God, because all of this triumph is ordained and offered as the glorious triumph of His Bride, the church.

The Son of God then stepped forward into His Father's grand presence with the seven-sealed book in His hand. There is no hesitation, because the Father, in preparation for this moment, has exalted the Son of God. Thirty three years of pilgrimage, followed by a willing sacrifice on a cross and a glorious resurrection; and then He was seated at the Father's right hand so that all the process was finished except to take the book and to let the final redemption of this earth begin. And begin it will, just as soon as the Bridegroom calls for His Bride. He would never take back the earth unless He had His Bride ready to possess her inheritance.

> *And when he had taken the book, the four beasts and four and twenty elders fell down before the Lamb, having every one of them harps, and golden vials full of odours, which are the prayers of saints. And they sung a new song, saying, Thou art worthy to take the book, and to open the seals thereof: for thou wast slain, and hast redeemed us to God by thy blood out of every kindred, and tongue, and people, and nation; And hast made us unto our God kings and priests: and we shall reign on the earth* (Revelation 5:8-10).

Let the shouting begin! If the church could get a little picture, just a simple view of what awaits the victorious saints when the process of redeeming this earth begins, we would start the shouting now. This hour of glory is just as certain as the sun rose this morning. O, yes, this is a future prophecy; and it cannot be relegated to church history; and it cannot begin until the saints are transported, via the Rapture, into the very throne room of heaven, where Christ, even now, sits at the right hand of His Father. There is surely an angel standing somewhere near the portals of glory awaiting the word to make the trumpet blast. As soon as the Lamb had taken the book from the Father, the Cherubim and elders fell down before

Him and began the heavenly worship of the coming victories.

The elders were all possessors of harps and vials of triumphant prayers, and the mixing of the music and the great odors of prayers made heaven become a place of glory and praise. The saints and elders began to sing a song that answered the great weeping of John and the question of the great angel that asked, *"Who is worthy?"* The elders will sing, *"Thou art worthy."* It's very apparent that the opening of this seven-sealed book is a misunderstood truth of today's church world. In reality we are these elders and we have the privilege of their understanding this future event. They had endured exactly

As much as Satan has sought to destroy this earth and to make it uninhabitable, it is still the Lord's earth.

what we are now enduring, an earth where sin reigns and a world of people that are easily offended and are ready to devour. But, they had passed into the hope that is waiting every unfailing saint. They were where we are soon to be. They were experiencing what we are soon to experience. They were ready to unite with the Lamb to cleanse and purify the corrupted earth.

Listen to the second stanza of their song. First, they glorified Him, but then they sang of their present and future. They sang it as those already possessing it because, just like our redemption from sin in our life, so is this future redemption. The death of Jesus Christ has already paid the price. It's already done! The elders now continue to sing the second stanza.

And I beheld, and I heard the voice of many angels round about the throne and the beasts and the elders: and the number of them was ten thousand times ten thousand, and thousands of thousands; Saying with a loud voice, Worthy is the Lamb that was slain to receive power, and riches, and wisdom, and strength, and honour, and glory, and blessing.

And every creature which is in heaven, and on the earth, and under the earth, and such as are in the sea, and all that are in them, heard I saying, Blessing, and honour, and glory, and power, be unto him that sitteth upon the throne, and unto the Lamb for ever and ever. And the four beasts said, Amen. And the four and twenty elders fell down and worshipped him that liveth for ever and ever (Revelation 5:11-14).

Wherever Satan has authority and dark evil deeds have been allowed, the entire culture slowly turns into a cesspool.

Now, we move beyond the symbolic number of twenty-four—twelve representing the Old Testament saints and twelve representing the New Testament saints—and we see the multitudes they truly represent. The term "ten thousand times ten thousand" in the original Greek means "myriads times myriads," which means an "exceeding multitude times an exceeding multitude." If you can multiply an innumerable number times an innumerable number, you will have a little idea of this great host.

This worship event is impossible to describe or understand. These saints are glorified with their new bodies, totally uninhibited by the limitation of flesh, and worship in heaven will be our natural culture. We are already spirit-beings or, in other words, we have a spirit within. When we are glorified with our resurrected bodies that are made in Christ's likeness, our spirit will be holy in nature and will possess a new body that is holy in nature. *"Beloved, now are we the sons of God, and it doth not yet appear what we shall be: but we know that, when he shall appear, we shall be like him; for we shall see him as he is"* (I John 3:2).

Conclusion

This earth is soon to be the possession of His saints. As much as Satan has sought to destroy this earth and to make it uninhabitable, it is still the Lord's earth. *"For the earth is the Lord's, and the fulness thereof"* (I Corinthians 10:26). Every molecule of this present cosmos, except the Lake of Fire, will be purified and made spotless. We will breathe in an atmosphere that is perfectly pure. We will enjoy the fruit of the earth delivered of its curse and live forever without the aging process. The animals will be a joy and every man will be a friend. The presence of God will fill His universe until there is no place for sorrow or sadness. The legal book in my Father's right hand has been completed and finished on the cross, and the drama or story is ready to unfold.

SATAN'S EVICTION NOTICE

The saints of God are soon going to inherit this earth and rule it with a rod of iron. *"The earth is the Lord's, and the fulness thereof"* (I Corinthians 10:26). Remember, the second stanza of their song in chapter five *"And hast made us unto our God kings and priests: and we shall reign - rule - be in total authority - on the earth"* (Revelation 5:10). Satan has been the god of this world for six thousand years and has consistently turned the fruitful valleys into deserts and wildernesses. Wherever Satan has authority and dark evil deeds have been allowed, the entire culture slowly turns into a cesspool. *"The wicked shall be turned into hell, and all the nations that forget God"* (Psalm 9:17). We see it occurring right now all across our nation and in most of the world. Homosexuality and lesbianism is being championed by the media and the entertainment industry. Much of the church world is like *"dumb dogs, they cannot bark"* (Isaiah 56:10). But, it is almost over for the devil and his crowd.

Revelation chapter six is the prophetic story of the beginning of the end for the evil reign of Satan and his horde of spirits and evil mankind. It's incredibly sad that most of the world had rather serve the world's god than the Creator God. The whole world system is quickly becoming evil to the core and set against everything that centers in Jesus Christ. The term *"god"* is becoming a world phenomenon, while the name *"Jesus"* is utterly rejected and squashed. Most of the church world is adopting the new theology of the One-World Church, which is being called by many names, such as *"sinner-sensitive"* or *"the emerging church"* and other names. They believe that if you commit not to unsettle the sinner, then they will be delighted to become Christians. It's the new easy way to hell; and it's exactly what Jesus said would reign in the last days before He returns to evict the devil from his stolen post as the *"god of this world."*

It's almost impossible to believe that the church world could be so theologically dumb and ignorant of truth. The Book of Revelation has been rejected as to its prophetic values and its chronological picture of the end. You cannot read this book literally and take it literally as our Lord Jesus Christ intended without being overwhelmed with its perfect beauty of what is either occurring or about to occur. Every evil act and every lifestyle contrary to the Holy Bible is about to be judged by the exact standard of holy truth. Every religious person that refuses to live a godly, set-apart life according to the whole Word of God will be brokenhearted at the revelation of the coming judgment of the church. The Scripture declares that *"judgment must begin at the house of God: and if it first begin at us, what shall the end be of them that obey not the gospel of God?"* (I Peter 4:17). The compromise of Bible Holiness is the greatest tragedy ever to occur in the House of God. It will damn an overwhelming multitude of church souls.

Satan's Eviction

The devil is truly on his last rampage. Once the great celebration of Revelation chapter five is finished, it will be time to begin the opening of the seven-sealed book. This book contains the title deed of this earth and the process of its redemption out of the hands of the interloper named Lucifer. Satan's six-thousand-year reign of terror is about to end, and he will be evicted from his falsely acquired kingdom. The process of this eviction is extremely thorough and nothing of his evil designs and deceptions will remain. As Daniel prophesied, *"And in the days of these kings shall the God of heaven set up a kingdom, which shall never be destroyed: and the kingdom shall not be left to other people, but it shall break in pieces and consume all these kingdoms, and it shall stand for ever"* (Daniel 2:44). The Son of God, seen as a Lamb slain, has earned the perfect judicial right to direct the process, and His elders, the glorified raptured saints, will share the glory of His victory.

> *And I saw when the Lamb opened one of the seals, and I heard, as it were the noise of thunder, one of the four beasts saying, Come and see. And I saw, and behold a white horse: and he that sat on him had a bow; and a crown was given unto him: and he went forth conquering, and to conquer* (Revelation 6:1-2).

The champion of this grand finale is the Lamb of God. His death was more than a sacrifice to cleanse our personal sins; it was the complete sacrifice to redeem this universe and to evict the devil out of God's total kingdom. It was the end of the devil. Satan has been out on bail since that very moment, and His saints have been gathering evidence to put him away forever. Now, the process begins. Jesus opens the first seal and we hear a *"noise of thunder"* as one of the Cherubim/beasts says, *"Come and see."* These four Cherubim, called beasts in our King James Bible, have been evident in Scripture all the way back to Genesis chapter three. They are God's keepers of holiness in the earth, so any activity of God's righteousness relating to this earth must include their activity. These Cherubim will be manifest on this earth during the entire process of evicting Lucifer and cleansing this earth.

Immediately a *"white horse"* appears and begins his ride through the earth. Throughout Scripture, "four horses" have been the conveyors of judgment in this earth. They ride together when the

Creator God is sending forth His powers to recompense evil and bring it to task. This horse has a *"bow and a crown"* and he goes forth *"conquering and to conquer."* Many see him as the Antichrist, but I see him as representing the going forth of righteousness to judge and to disquiet every work of evil. It certainly can include the releasing of Antichrist activities because the Lamb of God and His servants of Cherubim and saints or elders will orchestrate every detail of this seven-year period, and Satan can do nothing except by God's design and plan.

"Conquering and to conquer" suggests that Satan's reign of terror is coming to an end. God is doing the conquering, not the devil. The going forth of judgment is a judgment of wickedness and evil and the conquering of the dark forces that represent Satan's army of evil powers and spirits. These four horses are intimately connected, and nothing can be said of one without fitting the pattern of all four. They are intimately connected and related to each other as a whole. It's all part of the mighty right hand of the Great Judge bringing redemption from wickedness to this universe.

> *The compromise of Bible holiness is the greatest tragedy ever to occur in the House of God. It will damn an overwhelming multitude of church souls.*

And when he had opened the second seal, I heard the second beast say, Come and see. And there went out another horse that was red: and power was given to him that sat thereon to take peace from the earth, and that they should kill one another: and there was given unto him a great sword (Revelation 6:3-4).

Now, we hear the second Cherubim crying out as thunder, *"Come and see."* There is something stupendous about their cry, *"Come and see."* It certainly suggests a series of events in the earth that demand attention. This is not entertainment; this is judgment. The process shows that this period will escalate as it continues. Hour-by-hour the earth will grow darker and the judgment will increase as human pain and sorrow explodes. The whole period of seven years will be a full and total judgment of cleansing.

The second horse is the color of red, the color being a symbol of death and deep convulsions of excruciating pain. This horde has power to take peace from the earth and to stir men's hearts toward a dark desire to destroy. We see this destructive culture developing presently but only in its early stages. The mass murdering by world-wide terrorism is just a beginning. Their god is the source of direction for their terror. We have no better proof that false gods are demons that are already showing the coming terror of the future. The theme of this second seal appears as "a great sword" in the earth.

And when he had opened the third seal, I heard the third beast say, Come and see. And I beheld, and lo a black horse; and he that sat on him had a pair of balances in his hand. And I heard a voice in the midst of the four beasts say, a measure of wheat for a penny, and three measures of barley for a penny; and see thou hurt not the oil and the wine (Revelation 6:5-6).

The darkness, as revealed in this seal, is now reaching the pandemic stage. This third Cherubim cries, "Come and see," and what we see is sheer horror. The horse is black, showing the symbol of a hellish blackness descending on this earth. The rider of this horse has a scale or a pair of balances in his hand suggesting a famine on a total scale. Now, we see all four of the Cherubim together and one cries out with a mournful cry of coming drought, crop failure, starvation, and death. The insanity that follows the disaster of starvation and famine is impossible to describe. Never has there been such a worldwide famine at the same time. To even consider the kind of beastly human behavior during a worldwide loss of the food chain is terror.

> *And when he had opened the fourth seal, I heard the voice of the fourth beast say, Come and see. And I looked, and behold a pale horse: and his name that sat on him was Death, and Hell followed with him. And power was given unto them over the fourth part of the earth, to kill with sword, and with hunger, and with death, and with the beasts of the earth* (Revelation 6:7-8).

Now, the last of the four Cherubim issues his cry, *"Come and see,"* and the fourth horse, pale in color, rides. The horse is named *"Death and Hell"* because the increasing destruction guarantees death on an unimaginable scale. Literally hundreds of millions of souls are dying, being killed, slain by massacring beasts, and killed by each

The Rapture will remove such a small minority of church members that the existing church will hardly catch their breath.

other. We saw thousands being buried in mass graves after the December 26, 2004 tsunami in the Far East. At this stage of the seven years of hell on earth, millions will be quickly buried in massive graves. The psychological effects of this period of history will create an atmosphere of insanity on a worldwide scale.

As you read this commentary, you must remember that all of this is a panoramic view of the real Lucifer that is about to be evicted. Every expression of evil is nothing but Lucifer personified. He is more of a beast than man has yet to see but will in this fulfilling of prophecy be impossible to miss. This horse, named *"Death and Hell,"* is given power over the fourth part of the earth. It appears that one fourth of the earth's population will be killed by the effects of this horse and rider. At a population of six billion plus, that could represent over one and one-half billion deaths. They will be killed by every possible means, from a sword to starving wild beasts. By this time, the earth will be in a worldwide pandemic. The impossibility of burying the dead will unleash disease and malignity impossible to contain. All of this is guaranteed to escalate until the world will be ready to help evict the devil and his army of unclean spirits. The Father will insure that the world learns the true source of all sorrow.

And when he had opened the fifth seal, I saw under the altar the souls of them that were slain for the word of God, and for the testimony which they held: And they cried with a loud voice, saying, How long, O Lord, holy and true, dost thou not judge and avenge our blood on them that dwell on the earth? And white robes were given unto every one of them; and it was said unto them, that they should rest yet for a little season, until their fellowservants also and their brethren, that should be killed as they were, should be fulfilled (Revelation 6:9-11).

All hell has broken loose against the multitudes of the professing church that has missed the Rapture. The church world, as a whole, has rejected holiness of lifestyle and the godly standard of Biblical separation. You cannot tell the average professing Christian from the un-professing world. Self-will is the scourge of today's religious movements. Cross-bearing and total surrender of all selfish plans and lifestyles is the one and only standard for a Rapture-ready believer. The Rapture will remove such a small minority of church members that the existing church will hardly catch their breath. Multitudes will suddenly show up at churches looking for answers from unprepared preachers that must hurriedly study the Book of Revelation and other great Biblical books.

At this time, the only hope for the left behind is to prepare to be martyrs for Christ at the terrible cost this period will demand. The

One World Church will deny the Rapture as having any significance or will give it a twisted explanation. The multitude of decent people that failed to be prepared will know the truth and will certainly make every effort to repent and prepare for the dark days ahead. Many backsliders and apostates will discover that it is too late to repent and will be hardened by the deceitfulness of sin.

Those that do surrender totally to Christ will be hunted and killed by the gathering group of Christ-haters and Antichrist followers. These souls are heard to cry out for God to judge such a godless crowd that floods the world with their Christ-hating vengeance. The very words of these martyrs reveal the depth of slaughter that men will experience. They cry out from their grave, *"Dost thou not judge and avenge our blood on them that dwell on the earth?"* They will be given white robes as they await multitudes of other saints that will repent and be slain. The very wording of this truth suggests that the martyrdom of souls, as they repent, will continue unabridged throughout the seven years of this Great Tribulation.

And I beheld when he had opened the sixth seal, and, lo, there was a great earthquake; and the sun became black as sackcloth of hair, and the moon became as blood; And the stars of heaven fell unto the earth, even as a fig tree casteth her untimely figs, when she is shaken of a mighty wind. And the heaven departed as a scroll when it is rolled together; and every mountain and island were moved out of their places. And the kings of the earth, and the great men, and the rich men, and the chief captains, and the mighty men, and every bondman, and every free man, hid themselves in the dens and in the rocks of the mountains; And said to the mountains and rocks, Fall on us, and hide us from the face of him that sitteth on the throne, and from the wrath of the Lamb: For the great day of his wrath is come; and who shall be able to stand? (Revelation 6:12-17).

While varying events are described in this entire chapter, it is important to see all of them as ongoing revelations that will each continue for an indefinite time. This is the beginning of great and unprecedented sorrow. A sixth seal reveals an earth—the very structure of the earth and the heavens above the earth—all experiencing an upheaval that matches the time of Noah's great flood. God's universe is a united whole, and each expression of this universe affects all of its systems. This great earthquake certainly appears to be one of a kind that the earth had never experienced before. The sun becoming black as sackcloth of hair could suggest the kind of catastrophe that will send such earthly segments into the atmosphere that it darkens the entire sky. Earthquakes often unleash other elements in a domino effect as we saw in the recent

At this time, the only hope for the left behind is to prepare to be martyrs for Christ at the terrible cost this period will demand.

tsunami. The moon turning to blood shows the effect our planetary bodies have on each other. The falling of stars says the same thing.

Now, the universe begins to move in such an upheaval, that the flood of Noah comes to mind. All of this earthly consternation is actually a redemptive process. The acts of God and the earth's upheaval would suggest that it is repairing itself back to its original splendor. Mountains that were raised during Noah's flood will now be returned to a more garden-like landscape. When the seven years are completed, this world will once again to be resplendent and prosperous.

The mighty kings and all earthly authorities are going to see the sources of their power and wealth slipping into destruction. Earthly upheavals of unknown dimensions have filled the greatest of men with insane fear, and this will be on a level that our minds are incapable of understanding. It will be a total upheaval. Suicide will become a welcome escape for those that do not know God.

This truth shows men praying to the mountains to fall on them and to aid them in death. Finally, the world population admits that God judges sin as they proclaim, *"The great day of His wrath is come."*

Conclusion

This chapter and the story it contains is the beginning of Satan's total eviction from the earth. The world will know that his reign as "god" has proven to be the grand disaster of which the Father had warned. The church must see the Book of Revelation as redemptive and not destructive. Surely, dark and wicked deeds and all their results must be judged, destroyed, cleansed, and purified. It may look like calamity, but so does all the building materials of a mansion and the adjoining gardens when the raw materials are only collected and work is yet to begin. This seven-sealed book contains all the dark transactions, but it also is the blueprint for a new earth, wherein dwelleth righteousness.

SAVED OUT OF DOOM'S DAY

This chapter opens with the entire earth filled with the wrath of the Father and the Lamb against sin and wickedness. Satan, the enemy of all that is holy, has produced his greatest imitation of religion in human history. Blasphemy against the Creator and all that is holy has filled the earth. A war in the heavens has cast Satan to the earth, and his time is short. He and his unholy trinity will fight to the finish, and the world's armies will join his struggle. It's a Doom's Day scenario.

As we study the Book of Revelation, chapters six through eleven, we must remember that the time frame of this story is the exact same seven years as the time frame of chapters twelve to nineteen. Accordingly, chapters six and seven are approximately the same time as chapters twelve and thirteen. Satan has been cast out of heaven to earth and is on a rampage against all truth and all that believe and obey truth. The wrath of God and the anger of Satan, along with his false trinity, are everywhere. Men are dying like flies. It's doom's day to the fullest extent. The Father and the Lamb must judge everything of sin before they can redeem the earth. The evil trinity has been reduced to a very short time frame to mount their offense against the kingdom of God

Darkness is at its greatest level, yet there is a rainbow of brilliant color above the Father's throne, and mercy is extended. The throne of God is the backdrop of this entire seven years of tribulation. The rainbow over His throne must never fade from view as we behold the scene of redemption and judgment. The Father is sovereign, holy, and full of grace but perfect in judgment of sin. This book is as lit-

Satan has been cast out of heaven to earth and is on a rampage against all truth and all that believe and obey truth.

eral as every other book of the Bible, and every scene of mercy and grace must be defended. The view that states that this book and its story is all darkness and sorrow has done great injus-

tice to this masterpiece. The one word that rises above all others is the word *redemption*. This earth and all of God's universe is experiencing the final moments of purification, cleansing, and renewal that will end in a world fit for no one but the Holy God and His holy family, a world of kings and priests.

This seventh chapter of Revelation is clearly a brief moment where the great God and the Lamb stop everything that is occurring to reveal the extent of their mercy. Within this one chapter, the Jewish world and the Gentile world both witness the unfailing love of God. This chapter has the appearance of occurring in the middle of the seven years of the Great Tribulation. There is no finality to that, but it does fit the overall scheme of events. In the First Testament, the prophets of Israel call this period of seven years a time of Jacob's Trouble. At least two-thirds of all the Jewish race will die or be killed. *"And it shall come to pass, that in all the land, saith the LORD, two parts therein shall be cut off and die; but the third shall be left therein. And I will bring the third part through the fire, and will refine them as silver is refined, and will try them as gold is tried: they shall call on my name, and I will hear them: I will say, It is my people: and they shall say, The LORD is my God"* (Zechariah 13:8-9).

The book of Revelation was written for and to the church, but we see the Lord's kinsmen and all the promises to them surface several times. The twenty-four elders place the redeemed of Israel in their proper order. The twenty-four elders represent both First Testament saints and church age saints. This chapter makes it clear that Israel is not forgotten, and chapters fourteen and fifteen put a remnant of Israel in His presence that were saved out from the troubles of the Great Tribulation. The twelve Gates of Pearl in New Jerusalem—named for the twelve tribes—shows that God has a permanent place for them in His plan for mankind. They will possess the whole geography of God's promises to Abraham during the thousand years of His reign on earth, and the ancient city of Jerusalem will be the joy of the earth. This book, though written to the church, does not forget Israel.

We will see the multitude that has been saved, converted, and redeemed out of the Gentile world as the judgments of God fill the earth and the masquerade of Satan reveals his evil design. Never has the population of the earth been privileged to see the contrast of God's hatred for sin and Satan's true nature of sin so clearly. The greater multitude will refuse to repent, but those that do will not be forgotten. A great company will find repentance impossible and will serve Satan and his Antichrist, while they believe that he is their true god. To suggest that salvation will be easy in this dark period would be a disservice to truth and to the great multitude that will be desperate for direction. Salvation will depend upon a person's willingness to be a martyr and to be hated many times worse than the hatred experienced in this present day. The world will finally see that the Jehovah God of Holy Scripture is the only true God. The choices will be simple because God's judgments will be known by the whole world.

And after these things I saw four angels standing on the four corners of the earth, holding the four winds of the earth, that the wind should not blow on the earth, nor on the sea, nor on any tree. And I saw another angel ascending from the east, having the seal of the living God: and he cried with a loud voice to the four angels, to whom it was given to hurt the earth and the sea, Saying, Hurt not the earth, neither the sea, nor the trees, till we have sealed the servants of our God in their foreheads (Revelation 7:1-3).

This pause in the proceeding of judgments is remarkable. The world is under great wrath from the Father and the Lamb. They are also under an assault from Satan and his army at the same time. It's like everything comes to a standstill as the angels of God manifest their incredible powers. Even Satan's activities must be stayed. All the elements of nature will suddenly be calmed, and the earth's population will be filled with a sense of a divine encounter. His angels, probably Cherubim in this case, are awesome creatures. When they manifest powers as great as suggested in this text, a foreboding of their great strength will touch all creation. *"Holding the four winds of the earth"* will create a hush or calm that strikes incredible fear.

The Father is sovereign, holy, and full of grace but perfect in judgment of sin.

These angels were already on a mission to disrupt the processes of nature. Their activities were in motion so that the sudden calm was like the eye of a hurricane with a storm raging on both sides. It is apparent that this action to seal the servants of God from the nation of Israel suggests that the effort by the Antichrist to massacre the Jewish race is well underway and the Lord is acting to preserve the remnant. This also suggests that the abomination of desolation had been erected in the temple, and Israel had learned of their mistake when they made a covenant with the Antichrist. One third of Israel will be preserved and saved. This action by the Lamb guarantees their future in His plans. The sealed saints will be His witnesses among the remnant.

And I heard the number of them which were sealed: and there were sealed an hundred and forty and four thousand of all the tribes of the children of Israel. Of the tribe of Juda were sealed twelve thousand. Of the tribe of Reuben were sealed twelve thousand. Of the tribe of Gad were sealed twelve thousand. Of the tribe of Aser were sealed twelve thousand. Of the tribe of Nepthalim were sealed twelve thousand. Of the tribe of Manasses were sealed twelve thousand. Of the tribe of Simeon were sealed twelve thousand. Of the tribe of Levi were sealed twelve thousand. Of the tribe of Issachar were sealed twelve thousand. Of the tribe of Zabulon were sealed twelve thousand. Of the tribe of Joseph were sealed twelve thousand. Of the tribe of Benjamin were sealed twelve thousand (Revelation 7:4-8).

This great action by the Lamb to set aside a fixed number of His kin for witnesses to Himself is quite amazing. They have already been thoroughly converted after the Rapture. They are called "servants of our God" and were probably faithful orthodox Jews that were busy preparing for the Messiah before they learned of the Rapture and realized they had missed this grand event. No one can be saved apart from the Lamb's blood, and this seal confirms his or her faith in Christ. Please note that this seal is called *"the seal of the Living God"* to distinguish this mark from the seal of the Antichrist.

The tasks of these faithful believers from among the Jews, and their protection while they are His witnesses, would suggest several things. They will become powerful witnesses to Jesus Christ's messiahship to the entire Jewish world. They will certainly prepare all of Israel to be converted in one single day when the Son of Man arrives in Jerusalem after He wins the Battle of Armageddon. His one hundred and forty-four thousand will be heaven with the Lamb before the seven years of tribulation is over and will likely be guests at the wedding event and supper already underway in Heavenly Jerusalem.

They also may help prepare Israel for the coming kingdom of Israel during the Millennium. This large number of protected Jews will certainly have a wonderful part in Israel's future, both before they are caught up, and when they return with Christ to reign on earth.

> *After this I beheld, and, lo, a great multitude, which no man could number, of all nations, and kindreds, and people, and tongues, stood before the throne, and before the Lamb, clothed with white robes, and palms in their hands; And cried with a loud voice, saying, Salvation to our God which sitteth upon the throne, and unto the Lamb* (Revelation 7:9-10).

This multitude of Gentile believers are never called the church and never given a reference to suggest the church. The saints in chapter four are symbolically numbered twenty-four elders, which clearly connects them to the First and Second Testaments. That was the First Testament saints and the Second Testament church that was raptured up together to meet the Lord. There is little room for debate on that fact. This new multitude is unique and arrives while the church is celebrating her victory in heaven, and the Lord's elders are helping direct the proceedings of tribulation and redemption on earth. The saints that became elders were seated on thrones, but these victorious saints have only palm branches. They had certainly

The devil and his false trinity will direct their main offense against any reference or connection to the Bible and the beloved of the Lamb.

won a victory but not the same victory. Both companies are clothed in white robes, but the Pre-Tribulation saints had crowns on their head. That is a distinctive difference.

This company of Tribulation saints will never be a part of the Bride but could well be guests of the Bride at the Marriage Supper. Reference was made to the martyrdom of saints on earth in chapter six in the opening of the fifth seal. Already a great number had been killed but were told to wait while others suffered the same death. The devil and his false trinity will direct their main offense against any reference or connection to the Bible and the beloved of the Lamb. While Satan will offer great support to the one world church, he will stamp out any idea of the truth. One of the most dangerous locations after the Rapture will be a Bible-believer's meeting. The multitude that will be converted will be too large to hide, and their readiness for martyrdom will certainly give boldness to stand up for Christ. When death will be welcomed because of the great sorrows and suffering, the converted will no longer fear the consequence of the boldness of their faith.

When they arrive in the Heavenly Jerusalem, they will break forth in worship that will excite the elders, angels, and the Cherubim to a fresh time of praise. These Tribulation saints will immediately be welcomed to the throne of God and the presence of the Lamb. They will cry with loud voices, *"Salvation to our God which sitteth upon the throne and unto the Lamb."* Every fresh arrival into the City of New Jerusalem in heaven will proceed to the throne because the Father is the focus of the city. The Son of God will always be in the presence of the Father and will be equal in receiving the praise and adoration belonging to our Creator and Sovereign God.

> *And all the angels stood round about the throne, and about the elders and the four beasts, and fell before the throne on their faces, and worshipped God, Saying, Amen: Blessing, and glory, and wisdom, and thanksgiving, and honour, and power, and might, be unto our God for ever and ever. Amen* (Revelation 7:11-12).

The great hosts of elders, the great multitude of angels, and the living creatures or Cherubim break forth in another time of worship that has always been the culture of heaven. The pleasure of heaven will be the worship of our triune God which is now revealed to His victorious elders and Tribulation saints.

Everything is in the proximity of the throne. This vast multitude falls on their faces to be careful to give all honor to the Father and the Son. This is certainly victory worship because of the salvation of this multitude out of the Great Tribulation. This is not a light thing because these saints had paid the ultimate price. If angels rejoice over one sinner saved in our present world, can you imagine the glory of a great number being saved in spite of the devil's vengeance?

God the Father and the Lamb are receiving the great praise and many acclamations because redemption has been won by the sacrifices of the Lamb. Their praise and their word offering, *"Blessing and glory and wisdom and thanksgiving and honor and power and might,"* show that this is no ordinary event. Mercy has come at a terrible price. This world was on a fast track to total oblivion, but the Father and His Son have manifested all the glory that belongs to Divinity. They divested themselves of the privileges of their divine right as God the Eternal and God The Son, to redeem a fallen race and now to redeem a depraved world. This worship is going to be forever and ever.

> *And one of the elders answered, saying unto me, What are these which are arrayed in white robes? and whence came they? And I said unto him, Sir, thou knowest. And he said to me, These are they which came out of great tribulation, and have washed their robes, and made them white in the blood of the Lamb* (Revelation 7:13-14).

The question asked by this elder is the same we hear today in many theological circles. This great multitude has been a mystery to many because the world thinks of the Antichrist and his dark invasion without remembering Jesus Christ and His powers to save. The Bible declares, *"for when thy judgments are in the earth, the inhabitants of the world will learn righteousness"* (Isaiah 26:9b). This earth is going to face such a revelation of God's righteous judgment that great numbers of the earth's population will turn to the Heavenly Father and wash themselves in the Blood of the Lamb. The Book of Revelation must be understood as a book of redemption, not a book of annihilation. God is not going to destroy this earth, but He is going to destroy sin and all its ugliness. The salvation of this multitude is proof of the positiveness of this book.

There can be no doubt that these martyred converts came out of the Mid-Tribulation period. The same elder that asks the question answers the question. The question was asked of John, and John answered him, *"Thou knoweth."* This elder was part of God's team, so he knew what was occurring on earth. His answer is clear, *"These are they which came out of the Great Tribulation."* The Son of God identifies the Great Tribulation in His discourse on the mountain, which was called the Olivet Discourse. He called it the Great Tribulation and clearly tied it to Daniel's seventh weak. *"When ye therefore shall see the abomination of desolation, spoken of by Daniel the prophet, stand in the holy place, (whoso readeth, let him understand)"* (Matthew 24:15).

> *Therefore are they before the throne of God, and serve him day and night in his temple: and he that sitteth on the throne shall dwell among them. They shall hunger no more, neither thirst any more; neither shall the sun light on them, nor any heat. For the Lamb which is in the midst of the throne shall feed them, and shall lead them unto living fountains of waters: and God shall wipe away all tears from their eyes* (Revelation 7:15-17).

The promises to this multitude of redeemed Tribulation saints are great but clearly different from the elders that were raptured before the seven years began. When this beautiful truth is understood, it clearly solves the debate of the times of the Rapture. You cannot confuse this with the pre-tribulation Rapture of the saints that occurred in chapter four. These Tribulation saints are clearly a distinct group and separate from the Pre-tribulation raptured saints. They are never called elders as in chapter four and they never sit on lesser thrones. They do not receive crowns, but they enter into all other glories of the redeemed. They *"serve Him day and night"* and *"hunger no more, neither shall the sun light on them,"* because, now, He and the Lamb are the light of all the redeemed. The Lamb will be in the midst of them and will lead them into life everlasting. We can see that they have glorified bodies and are free forever of the tears and fears of this life.

Conclusion

This is a marvelous chapter. The chapter closes the way it opened for the Tribulation judgment to begin again. No chapter in this book reveals mercy and forgiveness more beautifully. The Great Tribulation is an event planned from the day that darkness fell in the Garden. The Father never doubted that He would redeem His world and that mercy would win for eternity. The presence of the one hundred and forty-four thousand converted and sealed out of the nation of Israel brings all the hope of the First Testament into the middle of this masterpiece. The fact that the world is not cut-off from salvation during His judgment shows us this forgiveness of sin that gave us His Son in the first place. Our God is holy, but love is His greatest emotion.

WHEN GOD AVENGES HIS SAINTS

The true saints of God will never suffer in vain. Every heart-rending prayer, every period of great intercession for the kingdom of God to come, and every person that endures tribulation, persecution, or temptation will be avenged and rewarded for their faithfulness. You cannot give a cup of water to a righteous person and not be guaranteed your reward, *"For whosoever shall give you a cup of water to drink in My name because ye belong to Christ, verily I say unto you, he shall not lose his reward"* (Mark 9:41). The Father and His Son never redeem a person in vain and will never fail to justify, sanctify, and multiply those overcoming saints that take up their cross and follow Him. When the books are opened and the time of the reconciliation of all things has come, the faithful believers will discover that the Father has planned the end perfectly. The Apostle Paul said it beautifully, *"But as it is written, Eye hath not seen, nor ear heard, neither have entered into the heart of man, the things which God hath prepared for them that love him"* (1 Corinthians 2:9).

This great chapter of the Book of Revelation is mainly about the avenging of His saints. Even the attention-getting first verse suggests great things to come. The Bible and secular history is replete with the injustice and persecution of the righteous people of the earth. It has always cost to be an all-out Bible-believer and to live the genuine life of a Bible-believing person. When the converted man or woman has stepped out of darkness into the light, the light will never fail to shine from that converted person, and darkness will be offended. *"These things I have spoken unto you, that in me ye might have peace. In the world ye shall have tribulation: but be of good cheer; I have overcome the world"* (John 16:33). The world may not hate us, but the enemy that rules their lives will hate the light that uncovers their deeds. It cannot fail unless the heart of the wicked is open for them to be converted!

Revelation chapter eight is the supernatural beginning of the avenging of His saints. Vengeance is evil in the hands of men but righteous in the hands of God. Then, it is called justice. This promise has been left to us, and we are to leave vengeance in His hands and wait for the right to prevail. It is impossible for right not to prevail if we will keep our hands free and our heart full of patience and faith.

The Father and His Son never redeem a person in vain and will never fail to justify, sanctify, and multiply those overcoming saints that take up their cross and follow Him.

"Dearly beloved, avenge not yourselves, but rather give place unto wrath: for it is written, Vengeance is mine; I will repay, saith the Lord" (Romans 12:19). Every act of wickedness against righteousness will be perfectly vindicated, and every unrepentant sinner will answer for his sins.

The entire Book of Revelation is about justice and redemption. It's impossible to have one without the other. There is no perfect redemption without justice and there is no true justice without redemption. Our Father has never condemned the righteous with the wicked. Justice is the principle reason that the Rapture must occur before the seven dark years of tribulation. When the Creator judged the earth with a flood, Noah had to be removed first. *"But Noah found grace in the eyes of the LORD"* (Genesis 6:8). When Sodom and Gomorrah went up in flames, Lot had to be removed first. The angel said, *"Haste thee, escape thither for I cannot do any thing till thou be come thither"* (Genesis 19:22). Any person that unfairly judges the righteous is laying a snare for themselves. When you are unfairly treated, put it in God's hand and go on in righteousness. Forgive and forget!

And when he had opened the seventh seal, there was silence in heaven about the space of half an hour (Revelation 8:1).

The Lamb, the Son of God, will open all seven seals. This is clearly His activity. Nothing makes this book so breathtaking as the proximity of everything and every event to the Lamb and to His Father on His throne. This seal and its opening startled heaven into silence. The entire populace of heavenly Jerusalem has anxiously waited for the day when Satan will be judged and evicted from the universe. The angels are well aware of the broken heart of God over man's first rebellion and even more conscious of the moments surrounding the

The entire Book of Revelation is about justice and redemption. It's impossible to have one without the other.

death of the Son of God to redeem. That redeemed host from the earth has joined the heavenly hosts. A holy awe envelopes this city and even the "Holy, Holy, Holies" of the Seraphim and Cherubim revere the call of silence as preparation is made to avenge the overcomers out of a sin-cursed world.

Recording angels have never missed an event on God's earth. Every injustice is recorded daily . Every sin that has not been removed by the Lamb's blood is written in a book and awaiting justice. The acts of wicked men to destroy the righteous are perfectly prepared for this hour. And as stupendous as it may seem, every saintly prayer and every weeping believer waiting on His God and crying out for mercy, both for themselves and others, is all recorded. The prayer of the saints will soon become fire in the earth and the books have it all on record.

And I saw the seven angels which stood before God; and to them were given seven trumpets. And another angel came and stood at the altar, having a golden censer; and there was given unto him much incense, that he should offer And the smoke of the incense, which came with the prayers of the saints, ascended up before God out of the angel's hand. And the angel took the censer, and filled it with fire of the altar, and cast it into the earth: and there were voices, and thunderings, and lightnings, and an earthquake (Revelation 8:2-5).

Seven angels with seven trumpets are coming straight from the Father's presence. This is the only opening of the seven seals that special angels are given special prominence, and that prominence has the favor of the Father. Of course, all of the activities flow from the unity of the Father and His Son, but to see a special mention suggests something very close to His heart. Nothing connected with this earth holds any favor more special than His redeemed and their discipleship and tribulation during their earthly pilgrimage. They must be vindicated, and the time has arrived.

An eighth angel appeared before the altar, and he had in his possession a golden censer. This was no doubt taken from the great Temple of heaven of which the Temple of Solomon was but a shadow. Bible students have given only scant attention to this temple. Melchizedek was the high priest of that temple and descended to offer a foreshadow of communion to Abraham. Connecting that golden censer to the temple and the prayers of the saints is especially important. The prayers of the saints would naturally be preserved in the temple for it is the very center of all redemption. The blood of Jesus Christ is on the altar in that same heavenly temple, the very center of the activities of the seven years of the Great Tribulation. The Apostle Paul notes every anointed prayer as special. Prayer has always been the lifeline of His church. *"And hath raised us up together, and made us sit together in heavenly places in Christ Jesus"* (Ephesians 2:6).

The power and authorities vested in these great volumes of prayer is quite overwhelming. The angel already held in his possession the prayers of the saints and now receives incense to add and finish this offering ready to be offered. Everything is on hold, silence is evident, and the angel is about to unleash the authority that will affect the universe and all heaven, but the effect will be on earth. It's important to note that this includes the prayers of all saints. This offering is made directly before the throne of the Father on the very central altar of heaven, called the golden altar. You can rest assured that this is the central most sacred spot of heavenly Jerusalem and has the attention of the entire heavenly host.

Once this offering is finished, the smoke and aroma ascends up before the Father as an acceptable act of worship. Every prayer in Christ's name offered by a believing saint is held in store for action. Sometimes the action is immediate according to the will of God, and sometimes it is preserved until the proper hour; but they are always heard. When I read of the saints of God from Pentecost to the present, and see the price in blood that the many martyrs have paid, I get just a little of the emotion that will be manifested on that day. Think of Polycarp, the Huguenots, Hussites, the millions that were slaughtered during the Dark Ages, and the thousands that were slaughtered by reformation leaders when their dictates were disobeyed. I long for this hour with all those saints that are awaiting vindication.

Now, the action will begin on earth. Every prayer delivered by a saint of God as they were led to the stakes to be burned alive or to the waters in which to be drowned or the many other deaths of martyrdom are all stored up for vengeance. I read of a sixteen-year-old young lady that would not recant her faith in Christ alone, who was carried by the inquisitors to a horse trough and held under water until she was dead. Then, her body was cast on the fire to be burned.

Those inquisitors, and all like them, will one day be made to bow before the throne of the Father in heaven and before the feet of the martyred saints. *"Behold, I will make them of the synagogue of Satan, which say they are Jews, and are not, but do lie; behold, I will make them to come and worship before thy feet, and to know that I have loved thee"* (Revelation 3:9). Every debt of every persecutor must be paid.

After the prayers touched the heart of God, this angel took his censer, filled it with fire from the altar, and cast it onto the earth. You can believe that this Tribulation Period now takes on a new level of judgment. Now, the Father and the Lamb are not just judging the earth, they are judging every act of evil against every saint of God for six thousand plus years. The effect is immediate as voices, thunderings, lightnings, and earthquakes begin to move across the earth from east to west and from north to south. Not one piece of real estate will escape this action. The vengeance of righteousness against wickedness, light against darkness, and purity against impurity will utterly fill the earth. God's saints will be vindicated. This action will continue until the end of the seven years is complete.

We should remember that in the final reckoning before our Father, it is not our music or our great sermons that truly matter, as important as they are, but the prayers we have prayed. The greatest work of His saints is found in their fellowship and communion with Him. Intercession for the lost, prayer for the multiplying of His words, weeping over the vileness that invades this earth, and wonderful communion with the Father and the Son is the pure order of righteousness. To allow our works to out-pace our prayer life is our shame. More than our labor, He wants our loving togetherness.

And the seven angels which had the seven trumpets prepared themselves to sound. The first angel sounded, and there followed hail and fire mingled with blood, and they were cast upon the earth: and the

third part of trees was burnt up, and all green grass was burnt up.
And the second angel sounded, and as it were a great mountain burn-
ing with fire was cast into the sea: and the third part of the sea became
blood; And the third part of the creatures which were in the sea, and
had life, died; and the third part of the ships were destroyed
(Revelation 8:6-9).

A properly blown trumpet is an awesome musical instrument. It
can sound incredibly startling when the sounds are meant to startle.
At this point in the Book of Revelation, the wicked population of
this earth is hell-bent to destroy and eliminate every vestige of
morality and any remembrance of the God of Holy Scripture. A new
god is being proclaimed and
loved, and the new freedom has

We should remember that in the final
reckoning before our Father, it is not
our music or our great sermons, as
important as they are when
Biblically offered, but the prayers we
have prayed.

unfettered the flesh of men to
the full satisfaction of their
wildest lusts. Its freedom, and
the new religion, are full of the
dreams of wealth and pleasure.
But even in the midst of their
pleasure, the trumpet begins to sound and the earth begins to shud-
der. The events on this earth are out of control, and the very sound
of that trumpet is like a wake-up call.

When the first angel sounded, the heavens turned black, and a
storm broke out like midnight on the world. Everyone had heard the
trumpet, and the storm was so instantaneous that the two could not
be separated. The hail was murderous and destructive, killing tens of
thousands and literally destroying everything in its wake. To add to its
fury, the hail became a mixture of fire, and blood. One third of the
earth's trees were destroyed before the storm had subsided, and there
was no grass left. It was a fire-parched world when it was all over.

Without warning and probably no more than a few days, maybe hours later, there is another great sound of a trumpet. The world shudders again and the world news outlet goes on alert. The earth is struggling to return to normal. Yet, everyone is expecting the worst. Finally, the news agencys get the story that a great mountain had fallen from out of nowhere burning with fire. It had fallen to the sea and the first release of waves began to paint the true picture. A third of the earth's large bodies of water have been turned to blood. In many places it has congealed and is already an unbearable stench. Pleasure, money, vacation! Nothing mattered except survival. The seas of the world are a disaster. At least one third of every creature in the world's bodies of water are dead. At least a third of the ships have gone down with all their crew on board. It is a second disaster on top of the first.

To allow our works to out-pace our prayer life is our shame. More than our labor, He wants our loving togetherness.

> *And the third angel sounded, and there fell a great star from heaven, burning as it were a lamp, and it fell upon the third part of the rivers, and upon the fountains of waters; And the name of the star is called Wormwood: and the third part of the waters became wormwood; and many men died of the waters, because they were made bitter* (Revelation 8:10-11).

Consternation, death, desperate efforts to bury the dead, looting, and scrambling for food are occurring on a worldwide basis. The world is in shock! Days, maybe weeks, pass and then suddenly a third trumpet sounds. The past months have been unbearable, and another shock creates utter insanity. As the world watches for the results of this trumpet, the sky turns threatening and a great star is hurling in a path toward the earth. The entire earth trembles and shakes on impact. It has fallen like a lamp full of fire and destruction. Its effect is upon the rivers and all the fountains of water. The sea is already undrinkable, and now the water supplies issuing out of the earth are utterly contaminated. Multitudes die as they drink, in desperate thirst, from the poisoned waters.

And the fourth angel sounded, and the third part of the sun was smitten, and the third part of the moon, and the third part of the stars; so as the third part of them was darkened, and the day shone not for a third part of it, and the night likewise. And I beheld, and heard an angel flying through the midst of heaven, saying with a loud voice, Woe, woe, woe, to the inhabiters of the earth by reason of the other voices of the trumpet of the three angels, which are yet to sound! (Revelation 8:12-13).

The trees and green grasses have mostly been parched, the seas and oceans are a disaster, and the water supplies of the world are poisoned. Now, heaven itself must speak of the judgment of a Holy but angry God. Millions of His servants have been slaughtered. Godly people have been hated and martyred simply for being Godly. The Father promised vengeance on a rebellious and unbending world, and its time has come. The fourth angel sounds and the heavens respond. A third of the sun goes black, then a third part of the moon, and then a third part of the stars so that the earth is engulfed in total darkness for at least five hours out of every daylight period. Nothing can be more awesome than blackness without a shade of light. Insanity is the only answer for the total universe except for those who know truth and have repented. They wait in confidence knowing that the time is short and Jesus will return to establish His kingdom.

Conclusion

Suddenly an angel appears in the sky and heralds a message that the world will hear in great sorrow and fear. It's not over, and the angel sounds the warning. Everyone will hear the angel's words. There are three woes to go. The angel will declare, *"Woe, woe, woe, to the inhabiters of the earth by reason of the other voices of the trumpet of the three angels, which are yet to sound!"* (Revelation 8:13).

The time schedule would suggest that the period of these seven angels is three and one-half years. There will be different events that happen simultaneously, and there will be no rest for the world or the wicked. They will surely find places and times to continue their sins and moral rebellion, but each event will only make this world more dangerous.

THE GATES OF HELL ARE OPENED

The great divide between the earth and its inhabitants and hell and its inhabitants has always remained a mystery. Upper Sheol in the First Testament was the abode of the righteous dead, and Lower Sheol and Hell fire was the abode of the wicked dead. Even between these two separate locations, there was an impossible gap. Abraham plainly told the rich man in hell that none could pass between the two abodes. *"And beside all this, between us and you there is a great gulf fixed: so that they which would pass from hence to you cannot; neither can they pass to us, that would come from thence"* (Luke 16:26). Jesus told this great story to teach the truth of man's eternal destiny. The gulf between the two abodes was very narrow compared to the gulf between the earth and hell. In fact, man is forbidden to ever consider communication with the dead across that gulf.

Scripture teaches us clearly that the abode of the wicked is in the heart of the earth. Upper Sheol no longer exists because Jesus Christ led the captives out of their captivity, and they ascended with Him to dwell in His presence. They are awaiting the resurrection of their body. The righteous dead in the Old Testament could not escape death and its bondage until Jesus Christ was crucified and arose from the dead. Now, the gulf is only between Lower Sheol and the earth. No one should attempt any contact with hell or the people that are damned to eternal fire. Those in hell are awaiting the White Throne Judgment, where they will appear to give account to the rejected Creator of this universe, whom they have rejected.

Hell is not just a place of wicked men and women but also a place where fallen angels are already being judged. Jude spoke of this when warning the church about wicked men. *"And the angels which kept not their first estate, but left their own habitation, he hath reserved in everlasting*

The righteous dead in the Old Testament could not escape death and its bondage until Jesus Christ was crucified and arose from the dead.

chains under darkness unto the judgment of the great day. Even as Sodom and Gomorrah, and the cities about them in like-manner, giving themselves over to fornication, and going after strange flesh, are set forth for an example, suffering the

vengeance of eternal fire" (Jude 1:6-7). The apostle Peter also reminded us of the judgments of angels that had already begun. *"For if God spared not the angels that sinned, but cast them down to hell, and delivered them into chains of darkness, to be reserved unto judgment"* (II Peter 2:4). When the Son of God met demon-possessed individuals, the demons would beg not to be dismissed into the deep, clearly referring to Hell or the bottomless pit.

Humans can become so wicked that they take on the same characteristics of fallen angels or demons. Jude gave reference to humans that had become beasts. *"Likewise also these filthy dreamers defile the flesh, despise dominion, and speak evil of dignities. But these speak evil of those things which they know not: but what they know naturally, as brute beasts, in those things they corrupt themselves. Woe unto them! For they have gone in the way of Cain, and ran greedily after the error of Balaam for reward, and perished in the gainsaying of Core"* (Jude 1:8,10, 11). Calling humans *"brute beast"* certainly suggests a dark state of character. Hell is inhabited with the darkest of all fallen angels and the godless and wicked throughout more than six thousand years of human history. They have festered in their vileness and grow increasingly wicked by the day. Our Father and the Lamb are going to unleash a multitude of this wicked crowd right onto the earth.

Joel, an Old Testament prophet gave a preview of this ninth chapter of Revelation:

> *Blow ye the trumpet in Zion, and sound an alarm in my holy mountain: let all the inhabitants of the land tremble: for the day of the LORD cometh, for it is nigh at hand; A day of darkness and of gloominess, a day of clouds and of thick darkness, as the morning spread upon the mountains: a great people and a strong; there hath not been ever the like, neither shall be any more after it, even to the years of many generations. A fire devoureth before them; and behind them a flame burneth: the land is as the garden of Eden before them, and behind them a desolate wilderness; yea, and nothing shall escape them. The appearance of them is as the appearance of horses; and as horsemen, so shall they run. Like the noise of chariots on the tops of mountains shall they leap, like the noise of a flame of fire that devoureth the stubble, as a strong people set in battle array. Before their face the people shall be much pained: all faces shall gather blackness. They shall run like mighty men; they shall climb the wall like men of war; and they shall march every one on his ways, and they shall not break their ranks: Neither shall one thrust another; they shall walk every one in his path: and when they fall upon the sword, they shall not be wounded* (Joel 2:1-8).

There is no possible interpretation of this passage but the truth before us. Joel's army is clearly paranormal, wicked, and they set out to not only destroy the earth, but to inflict great pain on its inhabitants. All future judgment and end-time prophecies find their perfect fulfillment in this masterpiece of literature.

The chasm between hell and the bottomless pit at the deepest extreme of hell is about to be bridged to the earth for the Great Tribulation. Satan and his followers will use every wicked resource

Hell is not just a place of wicked men and women but also a place where fallen angels are already being judged.

to work havoc, and the Father will use them to judge and destroy their own kind. The devil's history is full of the destruction of his own followers. The demon-possessed often speak of their own war with each demon-possessed individual who tried to climb the ladder of priesthood in their dark realm. There is no doubt that Satan's kingdom is in the realm of darkness, and every aspect of their character is darkness and destruction.

And the fifth angel sounded, and I saw a star fall from heaven unto the earth: and to him was given the key of the bottomless pit. And he opened the bottomless pit; and there arose a smoke out of the pit, as the smoke of a great furnace; and the sun and the air were darkened by reason of the smoke of the pit (Revelation 9:1-2).

The darkest place in God's universe is about to open onto the earth. Remember that Jesus Christ, the Lamb, opened the seventh seal, and out from that seal appeared seven angels with seven trumpets. This is the fifth of those angels sounding their trumpets. Another angel, one of the seven Cherubim assigned to His churches, descended quickly from heaven. Remember, an individual angel or cherubim was assigned to each church during the Church Dispensation. The seven stars were the angels of the seven churches, which are now established in heaven since the Rapture. They are the defenders of righteousness in the earth and that includes redemption and judgment. This great star or Cherubim has a key to the bottomless pit. No one, demon or human, that has ever been assigned to that pit has ever been released. The gate has never been unlocked on the exit side of this dark chasm. Everything and everyone inside the bottomless pit is as wicked as they could possibly be. They are corrupt with corrupting personalities and have longed for an opportunity to vent their fury. If this crowd had not been held in captivity, this earth would have descended into an even darker and deeper vileness. Their captivity has been part of God's restrictive plan until the fated hour should arrive.

When the great gate is opened, the smoke of this furnace quickly darkens the universe. The sun and moon is hid, and the atmosphere is darkened by the very spirit and darkness out of this frightful abyss. No doubt the smoke is but a conveyor of a stench and presence that darkens the mind of every soul it touches. There will be no pure light until this open door to hell is closed, and it will not be closed until this seal is finished.

> *And there came out of the smoke locusts upon the earth: and unto them was given power, as the scorpions of the earth have power. And it was commanded them that they should not hurt the grass of the earth, neither any green thing, neither any tree; but only those men which have not the seal of God in their foreheads. And to them it was given that they should not kill them, but that they should be tormented five months: and their torment was as the torment of a scorpion, when he striketh a man. And in those days shall men seek death, and shall not find it; and shall desire to die, and death shall flee from them* (Revelation 9:3-6).

These creatures are nothing less than demons with dark powers that Satan has trained and mobilized for his honor and for this time. Hell and the bottomless pit is indeed a place of fire and brimstone, but it cannot devour spirits or souls. It can only torment and create an atmosphere of misery. In this abyss, the spirits and souls will scheme, plan, and anticipate the day when they can spread their misery. That day has come in this text. Like hordes of locust, hungry to devour, they have power to sting like scorpions and inflict pain that will seem unbearable.

They will be commanded to hurt nothing of nature, but only the wicked that have rejected the God of Righteousness and do not have the seal of the Father and His Lamb in their forehead. They cannot kill these wicked souls but are commanded to torment them. The torment lasts for five months, with a pain that goes to the depth of human captivity. The wicked have killed and maimed the righteous and God-honoring; now, the tide has turned. This great multitude will seek to die and will make every effort to take their own life, but death will be beyond their reach.

Chapter eight started this period of God's revenge on the godless that mercy could not touch. They cannot blame the Father or the Lamb because mercy and forgiveness was held before this world for at least the first three and a half years. Even now, the door is open to repent, but this multitude wants no repentance. Now, the misery is too dark to see past.

> *And the shapes of the locusts were like unto horses prepared unto battle; and on their heads were as it were crowns like gold, and their faces were as the faces of men. And they had hair as the hair of women, and their teeth were as the teeth of lions. And they had breastplates, as it were breastplates of iron; and the sound of their wings was as the sound of chariots of many horses running to battle. And they had tails like unto scorpions, and there were stings in their tails: and their power was to hurt men five months* (Revelation 9:7-10).

The appearance given to these spirits and souls was planned to create the very atmosphere of the bottomless pit. Misery loves misery;

now, misery has invaded the world. Their appearance is like horses, crowned with gold and having faces like men. They have hair like women and teeth like lions. They wear breastplates of iron, and they have wings like many chariots racing to destroy. Their tails are quick to inflict pain and torment. It's a scene of hell on earth, for, indeed, hell has invaded the earth.

These amazing creatures are servants of Satan and they are venting Satan's fury on his own worshippers. Satanism has never made sense because it is the opposite of a sane mind. God the Father actually uses Satan to punish himself and his followers and to show that the very nature of evil is to destroy itself. Evil does not have the ability to do good. This seven years of Tribulation will reveal all that is evil for a final display of its nature.

And they had a king over them, which is the angel of the bottomless pit, whose name in the Hebrew tongue is Abaddon, but in the Greek tongue hath his name Apollyon. One woe is past; and, behold, there come two woes more hereafter (Revelation 9:11-12).

Satan's kingdom is organized. The Book of Ephesians shows four levels of the hierarchy of Lucifer. *"For we wrestle not against flesh and blood, but against principalities, against powers, against the rulers of darkness of this world, against spiritual wickedness in high places"* (Ephesians 6:12). The organization of evil is off the radar of human sight and understanding. We fail to see how sinister it is in our normal world. The Book of Revelation actually pulls the cover off and we can begin to catch a better picture. This king over the bottomless pit is a destroyer. He is one of hell's most powerful creatures.

Everything represented in the names given to Satan in Scripture shows that there is no capacity for good even to his own. This king has prepared his army well. They do their job under his leadership,

and their only reward is more of hell. One woe is over, but two more
are on the way.

> *And the sixth angel sounded, and I heard a voice from the four horns*
> *of the golden altar which is before God, Saying to the sixth angel which*
> *had the trumpet, Loose the four angels which are bound in the great*
> *river Euphrates* (Revelation 9:13-14).

A voice rings out from the very altar of God. The sixth angel has
blown his trumpet and the depth of judgment must be manifested.
Satan has always been on a leash. He can do only what he is allowed.
These four angels have been bound because of previous deceptions
and dark deeds. They are masterminds of evil, and have by necessity
been bound, awaiting judgment day. Their location of dwelling is in
the Babylonian vicinity because this is Satan's stronghold. They
must be loosed to finish the task that wickedness demands. It's fitting that during Satan's last rampages his powers will be concen-
trated out of his natural habitat. Babylon will be fully rebuilt and
occupied. His Antichrist will rule from this city. Evil will develop
right out of Babylon and will spread out over the whole earth.

> *And the four angels were loosed, which were prepared for an hour,*
> *and a day, and a month, and a year, for to slay the third part of men.*
> *And the number of the army of the horsemen were two hundred thou-*
> *sand thousand: and I heard the number of them. And thus I saw the*
> *horses in the vision, and them that sat on them, having breastplates of*
> *fire, and of jacinth, and brimstone: and the heads of the horses were as*
> *the heads of lions; and out of their mouths issued fire and smoke and*
> *brimstone. By these three was the third part of men killed, by the fire,*
> *and by the smoke, and by the brimstone, which issued out of their*
> *mouths. For their power is in their mouth, and in their tails: for their*

tails were like unto serpents, and had heads, and with them they do hurt (Revelation 9:15-19).

Hell's fury will certainly arise from the center of the Beast's kingdom. There is certainly some connection between the first half of this chapter and this second multitude of spirits. They both issue from the earth or beneath the earth. Their former dwelling place is Hell or the abyss. They all serve the devil and his principalities. Their period of destruction is one year, one month, one day, and one hour. They will make use of every minute, and one-third of earth's population will be slain.

The size of this great demonic army is threatening to consider. Two hundred million trained, equipped, and vicious demonic spirits will go out from one geographical area to invade the earth. Two hundred million suicide bombers all dressed in explosives could not do the damage this multitude will do. John saw the vision and describes them. He called them *"horseman"*—or half horse, half man—with *"breastplates of fire, jacinth and brimstone."* Their heads are like lions and they breath out smoke, fire, and brimstone. The very sight of this army is enough to cause the world to seek death before they even arrive.

Their power is both from their mouth and in the tail. They kill coming and going. This kind of creature is being portrayed in mythology and has been trivialized until Revelation seems a joke. When the national news shows this evil footage, the fun will disappear. Demons have previously taken on the appearance of holy angels or an angel of light, but that capacity is no longer available. When the angels of God cast Satan out of his second heavenly empire, he will be stripped of his powers to appear holy as angels. His only appearance must derive from his character, and this vision is the result. What you are really seeing in this vision is Satan and his demons exactly as they are in their culture. Finally, Satan will look like the devil and all of his horde of spirits will look the same.

And the rest of the men which were not killed by these plagues yet repented not of the works of their hands, that they should not worship devils, and idols of gold, and silver, and brass, and stone, and of wood: which neither can see, nor hear, nor walk: Neither repented they of their murders, nor of their sorceries, nor of their fornication, nor of their thefts (Revelation 9:20-21).

Conclusion

Unimaginably, there is still a multitude that will not repent. The call to repentance has not subsided. Angels are always flying through the heavens calling men to repent. We will see that in future passages. The flesh loves its gods of self, devils, idols, and wealth. The sin of Adam was caused by the desire for things, especially things that touch the emotions. God must have known that if man fell, it would be because He gave him that wonderful creative ability to be emotional, to feel things, and to have emotions of desire, success, and triumph. Man's most beautiful creativity is his emotions, but emotions are also his downfall when the heart is deceived.

At this point, the world's population is almost totally given to the lust of unbridled emotions. Nothing can help a man when his emotions are unchecked, and Satan will produce just that kind of world when God gives him free reign for the coming seven years of tribulation.

The Seven Years of Great Tribulation

Rapture of Saints Up To God's Throne	Two Pictures of the Rapture (Rev 4-11)	Rapture & Tribulation Seen From Heaven	Saints Around The Throne	Tribulation Begins	Tribulation Saints Suffer & Die
	"The door was open from heaven. John heard, "Come up hither…" (Rev 4:1-4)		"And round about the throne were four and twenty seats: and upon the seats I saw four and twenty elders sitting, clothed in white raiment; and they had on their heads crowns of gold." (Rev 4:4)	*The seven-sealed book is opened.* "And I saw, and behold a white horse: and he that sat on him had a bow; and a crown was given unto him: and he went forth conquering, and to conquer." (Rev 6:2)	"And when he opened the fifth seal, I saw under the altar the souls of them that were slain for the word of God…And they cried…How long, Lord, holy and true, dost thou not judge and avenge our blood on them that dwell on the earth?" (Rev 6:10)

Same Event	**First Picture (Rev 4-11) Deals more specific with first 3 1/2 years**				
				Timeline	
	"The woman (visible church) gives birth to the manchild (invisible church). The manchild is caught up to God's throne. (Rev 12:1-5)	Rapture & Tribulation Seen From Earth	"And she brought forth a man child, who was to rule all nations with a rod of iron: and her child was caught up unto God, and to his throne." (Rev 12:5)	"And the great dragon was cast out, that old serpent, called the Devil, and Satan, which deceiveth the whole world: he was cast out into the earth, and his angels were cast out with him." (Rev 12:9) Satan is cast down and leads his evil army.	"And they overcame him by the blood of the Lamb, and by the word of their testimony; and they loved not their lives unto the death." "And dragon … persecuted the woman which brought forth the man child." (Rev 12:11) Satan hates the remnant of believers that defy his "One World Religion"

Comments	Nothing in Revelation after 4:1 can be historic, but all future.	Two different pictures of the same event.		Earth becomes a place of evil invasion.	Multitudes will be saved and die as martyrs.

The Book of Revelation gives us two different pictures of the same Rapture and Seven Years of Tribulation.

144,000 Jews Are Sealed: Caught Up To The Throne	Seven Seals, Trumpets & Vials	Satan & Demons Loose On Earth	The Temple of God is Opened In Heaven. The Marriage of the Lamb is Come.	Tribulation Ends - Christ's Kingdom Begins.	The Millennium (1000 Years) Begins (Jesus Christ Reigns)
"And I heard the number of them which were sealed: and there were sealed an hundred and forty and four thousand of all the tribes of the children of Israel." (Rev 7:4)	"And the seven angels which had the seven trumpets prepared themselves to sound. The first angel sounded, and there followed hail and fire mingled with blood, and they were cast upon the earth ..." (Rev 8:6-7)	"And the fifth angel sounded, and I saw a star fall from heaven unto the earth: and to him was given the key of the bottomless pit . . . and there arose a smoke out of the pit, as the smoke of a great furnace; and the sun and the air were darkened ..." (Rev 9:1-2)	"And the temple of God was opened in heaven, and there was seen in his temple the ark of his testament: and there were lightnings, and voices, and thunderings . . . and great hail." (Rev 11:19)	Great voices saying, "The Kingdoms of this world are become the kingdoms of our Lord and of His Christ." (Rev 11:15)	

Timeline

Second Picture (Rev 12-19)
Deals more with second 3 1/2 years.

"And I looked, and, lo, a Lamb stood on the mount Sion, and with him an hundred forty and four thousand, having his Father's name written in their foreheads." "These were redeemed from among men ... to the Lamb." (Rev 14:1,4b)	"And I saw another sign in heaven, great and marvellous, seven angels having the seven last plagues; for in them is filled up the wrath of God." "And I heard a great voice out of the temple saying to the seven angels, Go your ways, and pour out the vials of the wrath of God upon the earth." (Rev 15:1;16:1)	"And they worshipped the dragon which gave power unto the beast: and they worshipped the beast . . . And it was given unto him to make war with the saints, and to overcome them: and power was given him over all . . . nations." (Rev 13:4,7)	"Let us be glad and rejoice, and give honour to him: for the marriage of the Lamb is come, and his wife hath made herself ready." "And he saith unto me, Write, Blessed are they which are called unto the marriage supper of the Lamb..." (Rev 19:7,9)	"And I saw heaven opened, and behold a white horse; and he that sat upon him was called Faithful and True, and in righteousness he doth judge and make war." (Rev 19:11)	
remnant of Jews are messengers to all Israel and protected.		This is Satan's last hurrah.		Jesus comes to finish the seven years and set up His kingdom.	

This is Jacob's trouble. All Israel will soon be saved.	Satan turns the earth into a wilderness.	Satan no longer has access to God's Throne. He is limited to the earth.	The seven years end with a great triumph of the Kingdom of Jesus Christ.	The earth has been redeemed.	Comments

THE LORD OF THE MILLENNIUM KINGDOM

The Book of Revelation is a masterpiece of end-time prophecies, revealing hidden truths and declaring marvelous mysteries—mysteries that excite the soul and inspire the appetite for that glorious day that is surely coming. This chapter is a transition helping to divide the twin pictures of the same period. The Rapture and the Tribulation period have been placed chronologically in this book of the Bible, which has not been so in the other books. Both the Rapture and the seven years of tribulation have been pictured twice, once from a heavenly view and once from an earthly view.

First, John sees this period and the two events, the Rapture and the seven years of Tribulation in chapter four to eleven while he is caught up to heaven. It has to be a heavenly view because John is right in the middle of both the Rapture and the Great Tribulation, seeing them from a scene above the earth. These two events, the glorious Rapture and then the horrible seven years of hellish activities, are seen as God's or the Lamb's direct action and, in some cases, actions allowed to Satan. John sees the saints out of the Gentile nations and he also sees the Jewish believers evident in each of the two stories.

Second, he sees these events from an earthly viewpoint. Satan is visibly trying to hinder and defeat the Rapture, but he fails. After this failure, Satan and archangel Michael, each with armies, engage in a heavenly battle in the atmospheric domain. This battle is seen in the twelfth chapter. John sees the man-child disappear and then watches Satan being cast down to the earth, where he prepares for his rally against the great Creator and the Lamb. John had seen all of this from his lofty place in the heavenly vision, but now the details take on a more physical and human understanding in the story of chapter twelve to nineteen. The dark effect on the earth can be readily described as John walks among the folly of human action.

This double view of the Rapture and the Tribulation years can be confusing until you understand the reasons why the Lamb of God

The Book of Revelation is a masterpiece of end-time prophecies, revealing hidden truths and declaring marvelous mysteries that is surely coming.

wanted us to view both perspectives. The heavenly view helps us understand the mercy and redemption that never ends during the entire period. The earthly view makes God's judgment of sin more real and forever removes any doubt that nothing of sin can survive what is about to occur. Let me bring a timeline into this picture so you can see each view in perspective. This book of God's revelation was meant to settle all future prophecy in the order in which it will occur.

When we start reading each verse of chapter ten and studying it in its order, we will see that John is on earth and no longer caught up to heaven. He now witnesses the Lord coming down to earth. He even speaks of his vision differently and in a more physical sense. The Lord is called a messenger, but John's description leaves no doubt as to who He is. This chapter presents an incredible prelude to the first picture of the ending of the Seven Years of Tribulation and the beginning of the Millennial Kingdom. John has seen the opening of the seven-sealed book and the seven seals themselves, and now he will view it totally opened and disclosed. Read these verses carefully.

And I saw another mighty angel come down from heaven, clothed with a cloud: and a rainbow was upon his head, and his face was as it were the sun, and his feet as pillars of fire: And he had in his hand a little book open: and he set his right foot upon the sea, and his left foot on the earth (Revelation 10:1-2).

This description of the Lord as an angel in this introduction is not an accident or a mistranslation. The Son of God was called the *"angel of the Lord"* often in the First Testament. Although Revelation is written to the church, the church is commanded never to forget Israel's great place in prophecy. The ending of the seven years of the Great Tribulation will be good news to the nation of Israel. The description of the Lord in these verses identifies Him with His glory as seen in the first chapter of this masterpiece. He is described as clothed with a cloud. *"Behold, He cometh with clouds"* (Revelation 1:7). This description continues, *"and his face was as it were the sun, and his feet as pillars of fire."* Again, the description collaborates

This book of God's revelation was meant to settle all future prophecy in the order in which it will occur.

with John's vision, *"And his feet like unto fine brass, as if they burned in a furnace...and his countenance was as the sun shineth in his strength"* (Revelation 1:14, 16). Identifying Him as the One who possesses the Little Book, settled any doubt of His right to the task at hand. The book was opened, and He was clearly described as the One that opened each of the seven seals. This business is relegated the Lamb. He alone has redeemed this great universe, and His action proves that the task is almost completed. The process has developed to the point of possessing the earth *"and he set his right foot upon the sea, and his left foot on the earth."*

And cried with a loud voice, as when a lion roareth: and when he had cried, seven thunders uttered their voices. And when the seven thunders had uttered their voices, I was about to write: and I heard a voice from heaven saying unto me, Seal up those things which the seven thunders uttered, and write them not (Revelation 10:3-4).

His voice and His word are synonymous. His voice commands because He is divine and speaks creatively. His great cry sets action in motion and great Cherubim or angels step forward to thunder. John is on the earth now; pen and parchment are in his hands. The results of those seven thunders must have awakened something magnificent or awesome in judgment.

For whatever reason, the Lord speaks and commands John not to write. Something so significant is about to happen, and yet God tells John not to write about it. The Book of Revelation was not given to impress us or to scare us. Very likely this is event is hid from us to eliminate such thoughts. The complete meaning of this book is redemption and the judgment of sin, and nothing must be revealed that clouds the vision of truth.

And the angel which I saw stand upon the sea and upon the earth lifted up his hand to heaven, And sware by him that liveth for ever and ever, who created heaven, and the things that therein are, and the earth, and the things that therein are, and the sea, and the things which are therein, that there should be time no longer (Revelation 10:5-6).

This declaration will be fulfilled at the end of both descriptions of the coming judgments. If we did not understand the division between the two distinct pictures of the seven years of tribulation, these verses would make no sense. This world has been a cesspool; evil had badgered every step of God's saints. Prophets have declared

His truth, and many of them were killed for their obedience. Living the Godly life has cost millions of His saints their lives. The God we love and serve is keeping a perfect record, and the entire universe is very close to a new day where the righteous will shine as the sun for ever and ever.

The Lord of Lords alone would possess the right to proclaim what we are witnessing from His lips. Standing upon land and sea, He utters words that only God the Creator or Christ the Lamb has the right to declare. Nothing can stop His word from triumphing. Only the Creator alone can make an oath because only He can alter the outcome. The Son is invoking the name of His Father. He has been given full right to so speak and to so act. He invokes all creation as well as the name and power of the Creator and declares that time—the measuring off of days and months from eternity—shall be no more. These words must be understood in context. The

The Book of Revelation was not given to impress us or to scare us. The complete meaning of this book is redemption and the judgment of sin, and nothing must be revealed that clouds the vision of truth.

whole of this great revelation and its entire context will change this world and usher in the eternal kingdom.

But in the days of the voice of the seventh angel, when he shall begin to sound, the mystery of God should be finished, as he hath declared to his servants the prophets. And the voice which I heard from heaven spake unto me again, and said, Go and take the little book which is open in the hand of the angel which standeth upon the sea and upon the earth. And I went unto the angel, and said unto him, Give me the little book. And he said unto me, Take it, and eat it up; and it shall make thy belly bitter, but it shall be in thy mouth sweet as honey. And I took the little book out of the angel's hand, and ate it up; and it was in my mouth sweet as honey: and as soon as I had eaten it, my belly was bitter (Revelation 10:7-10).

The entire revelation of this scene is carefully declared in the first verse. The seven years of tribulation is almost finished and the message is clear that it will be so when the seventh angel sounds his trumpet. This occurs in Revelation chapters eleven and fifteen. The kingdom of God will fill this earth with righteousness even as the waters fill the sea. The Lord invokes His prophets of old and confirms the purity of their prophecies. Revelation actually unites the First Testament with the complete revelations of the New Testament. This book is the capstone of all of God's truth.

Now, the great voice of God tells John to go and take the book that is in the hand of the Lord who has proclaimed the great triumph. John did so and was commanded to take and eat the book. The Lord promises it would be sweet to the taste but bitter in its digestion. This is the perfect picture of God's truth and of every prophet that has proclaimed His word. Every man of God has experienced the bitterness and sweetness of the truth. A man that forgets to weep over the bitter will lose the glorious sense of the sweet. God's word is like a hammer that breaks the rock in pieces.

The kingdom of God will fill this earth with righteousness even as the waters fill the sea.

The eating of this book by John points us to the next scene that we will view in chapters twelve through nineteen. While it covers the same period as the scene that begins with chapter six and ends with chapter eleven, the picture will be from the midst of those sorrows and it will not be pretty. That's the true beauty of the sweet and bitter results of John eating the little book. The Word of God is always sweet, every word, but that word must also judge and bring all men to accountability. And that is bitter to the soul.

And he said unto me, Thou must prophesy again before many peoples, and nations, and tongues, and kings (Revelation 10:11).

John is on the island of Patmos, but he will be released, and this is the Lord's beautiful way of declaring that promise. The suffering was great; but the joy of preaching, waiting, and prophesying to the multitude certainly makes all the pain worthwhile. Men today think of a prophet as having a beautiful and intriguing life. Nothing could be further from the truth. God needs servants that have counted the cost and are ready to pay the ultimate price.

Conclusion

This chapter fulfills a beautiful purpose. It's like an hour of sun in the middle of a stormy day. Throughout this book there are breathless moments of joy and excitement, promises and small picturesque views of our exciting future. Revelation was never meant to scare the saints but to show the glorious promises fulfilled. This chapter also has its scene of foreboding and sorrows. The next scene of the seven years is literally hell on earth. The devil will be given his dues and will then pay the price of his rebellion. All who follow his folly will reap with him the results of that folly. Chapter eleven will finish this scene and take us before the great temple opened in heaven.

THE TEMPLE IS OPEN IN HEAVEN

This great chapter begins with the temple in earthly Jerusalem and ends with the temple in heavenly Jerusalem. These two cities are destined to be the center of all God's universe for eternity. The present focus is a sense of the finality and the finishing of redemptive and judgmental activities. The Antichrist both loves and hates earthly Jerusalem because of the ageless battle between his capital—Babylon—and the Father's chosen capital—Jerusalem. Babylon and Jerusalem are the antitheses of each other, and the final struggle between them is gathering momentum. To be the god of this world, Satan must control Jerusalem as well as Babylon. His Antichrist has established his image in the outer court of the Jerusalem temple, and the majority of the Jewish population has fled the city and sought refuge wherever possible.

The Jewish leaders will be terribly deceived by the Antichrist—actually accepting him as their messiah—but the installation of the Antichrist image in the temple will convince them of their error. In His Olivet discourse, Jesus Christ warned them of the results of their deception. *"When ye therefore shall see the abomination of desolation, spoken of by Daniel the prophet, stand in the holy place, (whoso readeth, let him understand:) Then let them which be in Judaea flee into the mountains: Let him which is on the housetop not come down to take any thing out of his house: Neither let him which is in the field return back to take his clothes. And woe unto them that are with child, and to them that give suck in those days! But*

155

pray ye that your flight be not in the winter, neither on the sabbath day: For then shall be great tribulation, such as was not since the beginning of the world to this time, no, nor ever shall be. And except those days should be shortened, there should no flesh be saved: but for the elect's sake those days shall be shortened" (Matthew 24:15-22). The leaders of the Jewish temple have watched Daniel's prophecy fulfilled right before their eyes.

Daniel had prophesied of this coming judgment and gave clear details of the seven year period. In the middle of the seven years—one week of years—this beastly imitation would be manifested and placed in the Jewish temple. *"And he shall confirm the covenant with many for one week: and in the midst of the week he shall cause the sacrifice and the oblation to cease, and for the overspreading of abominations he shall make it desolate,*

The Antichrist both loves and hates earthly Jerusalem because of the ageless battle between his capital—Babylon—and the Father's chosen capital—Jerusalem.

even until the consummation, and that determined shall be poured upon the desolate" (Daniel 9:27). The fateful hours have arrived in this prophecy, and Jerusalem is in the center of a worldwide effort by the Antichrist to establish full power on a global basis. This beast of a man will hate the nation of Israel for their effort to deny his right to the temple, and the Jews will be slaughtered wherever they can be found.

The prophets called this period Jacob's Trouble:

"And at that time shall Michael stand up, the great prince which standeth for the children of thy people: and there shall be a time of trouble, such as never was since there was a nation even to that same time: and at that time thy people shall be delivered, every one that shall be found written in the book. And many of them that sleep in the dust of the earth shall awake, some to everlasting life, and some to

shame and everlasting contempt. And they that be wise shall shine as the brightness of the firmament; and they that turn many to righteousness as the stars for ever and ever. But thou, O Daniel, shut up the words, and seal the book, even to the time of the end: many shall run to and fro, and knowledge shall be increased. Then I Daniel looked, and, behold, there stood other two, the one on this side of the bank of the river, and the other on that side of the bank of the river. And one said to the man clothed in linen, which was upon the waters of the river, How long shall it be to the end of these wonders? And I heard the man clothed in linen, which was upon the waters of the river, when he held up his right hand and his left hand unto heaven, and sware by him that liveth for ever that it shall be for a time, times, and an half; and when he shall have accomplished to scatter the power of the holy people, all these things shall be finished. And I heard, but I understood not: then said I, O my Lord, what shall be the end of these things? And he said, Go thy way, Daniel: for the words are closed up and sealed till the time of the end. Many shall be purified, and made white, and tried; but the wicked shall do wickedly: and none of the wicked shall understand; but the wise shall understand. And from the time that the daily sacrifice shall be taken away, and the abomination that maketh desolate set up, there shall be a thousand two hundred and ninety days. Blessed is he that waiteth, and cometh to the thousand three hundred and five and thirty days. But go thou thy way till the end be: for thou shalt rest, and stand in thy lot at the end of the days" (Daniel 12:1-13).

Again, let's understand the two different word pictures of the Seven Years of Tribulation. The first view is seen in chapters six to eleven of the Book of Revelation. This is the final chapter of that picture. The first view focuses on the first three and one-half years and gives us only a bird's-eye view of the last three and one-half years. Chapter eleven is the short view of the last half of the seven years.

The next view of the seven years gives us a full view of the last three and one-half years and only a short view of the first half. These two views together present us with a masterful picture of these seven years of the Great Tribulation. The first view focuses primarily on the heavenly action and the second view primarily on the earthly action. Most of what is seen in the first full picture is the activities of the Father and the Lamb. Also, most of what occurs in the second view is the diabolical activities of the devil, his Antichrist, and his false prophet.

Chapter twelve will actually start at the same hour, or point in time as the fourth chapter. Remember that chapter eleven is the short view of the last half of the seven years. Chapter twelve will be the short view of the first half of the seven-year period, and chapter thirteen will start in the middle of this seven-year period. This simple information will help you to understand the progress of this actual period in the close of human history. This point in this masterpiece is the basis of most confusion in this picture of end-time prophesy. Revelation eleven must be seen as the end of the Tribulation years. Then we will begin back at the beginning but with the other side of the story. The Lamb of God has been the focus in chapter twelve; the Antichrist will be the focus in chapter thirteen.

> *And there was given me a reed like unto a rod: and the angel stood, saying, Rise, and measure the temple of God, and the altar, and them that worship therein. But the court which is without the temple leave out, and measure it not; for it is given unto the Gentiles: and the holy city shall they tread under foot forty and two months* (Revelation 11:1-2).

We are at the middle of the seven-year period. The abomination spoken of by Daniel is now erected in the Jewish temple's Holy Place. Remember that the temple has a Holy of Holies, which is the court where the Ark of the Covenant once stood. There is a possibility that it will be found and that it will be present at this prophetic moment when this Scripture is fulfilled. There are Jewish worshippers in that holy place at this moment in prophecy, and they apparently refuse to leave. When John was told to measure the temple, the altar, he was also told that there would be worshippers in the temple while he was measuring. This was a confirmation that Jewish worshippers would possess this temple. There will be Jewish believers in this area of the temple and the Antichrist does not force them out. For some unknown reason, they are not removed.

The court outside the Holy of Holies is not measured because it is in the possession of this beast of the Antichrist. The second verse confirms that the Gentiles, led by the Antichrist, will possess the rest of the temple and will control it for three and one-half years, or forty-two months.

The Book of Revelation is written to the church, but Israel must be seen in her part of this great struggle.

The Antichrist could possibly allow those worshippers that possess the Holy of Holies to remain either as a public relations ploy or because they are in possession of military ability that could destroy the entire temple complex if the Antichrist threatens to evict them. It will be a stand off that lays the groundwork for the Battle of Armageddon, when the Antichrist has an army ready to obliterate Jerusalem.

The two opening verses reveal an awesome period developing for the Jewish nation. Again, this Book of Revelation is written to the church, but Israel must be seen in her part of this great struggle.

And I will give power unto my two witnesses, and they shall prophesy a thousand two hundred and threescore days, clothed in sackcloth. These are the two olive trees, and the two candlesticks standing before the God of the earth. And if any man will hurt them, fire proceedeth out of their mouth, and devoureth their enemies: and if any man will hurt them, he must in this manner be killed (Revelation 11:3-5).

God now empowers two great Jewish prophets to begin a ministry that captures the attention of the whole world. These two men probably have a connection to those worshippers in the Holy of Holies, and the world will both hear and see their ministry and their struggle to awaken men to the righteousness of God. It's beautiful to see this contrast of the Antichrist and his image in the Jewish temple and these two prophets that begin to expose the Antichrist for who he is. That image will be able to speak and will be given some form of paranormal life. At the same time, these prophets will bellow out their rebuke and expose the devil's lies.

Their ministry will cover this same last half of the seven-year period so that the Antichrist will never get a free pass. God's two prophets will hound the Antichrist everywhere he goes. They will warn this entire globe of Satan's false trinity and his lies. These prophets will be clothed in sackcloth so no one will fail to recognize them. They possess a supernatural anointing, and God calls them His two *"olive trees"* or *"candlesticks."* They are invincible to their enemies, and no one can kill them. When it says, *"fire proceedeth out of their mouth,"* this could be speaking of their supernatural words that are instantly fulfilled when they speak. These men will be miracle workers from the Heavenly Father, and their miracles will be a stark contrast to the Antichrist and his false prophet and the false wonders.

These have power to shut heaven, that it rain not in the days of their prophecy: and have power over waters to turn them to blood, and to smite the earth with all plagues, as often as they will. And when they shall have finished their testimony, the beast that ascendeth out of the

*bottomless pit shall make war against them, and shall overcome them,
and kill them* (Revelation 11:6-7).

The world will see and hear the power of Holy Scripture from the
lips of these two Godly men. Wicked men will be instantly rebuked
with action. When men refuse to hear the Word of God, these
prophets will get their attention with miracles that control all natural activities. If the circumstances require it, they will turn water to
blood and call for plagues that reveal God's wrath at sin. Their
action will be the exact penalties of the transgressors. Holiness and
wickedness will be seen in perfect contrast.

When God is finished with them, the Beast will have power to kill
them, but not until God Himself is wonderfully exalted. Satan and his
emissaries are always on a leash. The battle between the Antichrist and
these two prophets is called a war. Apparently, it will be a protracted
struggle. Armies will be engaged, and these prophets will be chased
across continents and finally captured. The Father intends for their
death to show the hatred that the Antichrist has for the truth. When
they are dead, this world will be advised, and the news media will proclaim it as a victory for their champion, the Beast.

*And their dead bodies shall lie in the street of the great city, which spir-
itually is called Sodom and Egypt, where also our Lord was crucified.
And they of the people and kindreds and tongues and nations shall see
their dead bodies three days and an half, and shall not suffer their
dead bodies to be put in graves* (Revelation 11:8-10).

The world rejoices as the news is broadcast via radio, the internet
and television. The prophets are dead. They are made a laughing-
stock, and their dead bodies are allowed to decompose right in the
street of Jerusalem. Jerusalem will be under Antichrist control, and

the character of the city will be like that of Sodom and Egypt—that means that the city is a cesspool of moral degeneration. There will be rejoicing and shouting by the most depraved of human beings right around their decomposing bodies.

The world pleads for a view of these hated prophets in death. Their bodies will be on display and used in the vilest abominations. They have preached righteousness to an unrighteous world, and the treatment must be in full satisfaction of the rage against restraints. Nothing makes wicked men angrier than to be told of their wickedness. This picture has got to be the very last drops of the vile actions that finish *"God's cup of wrath."* The world calls for a party. To them it's like the devil has won, and the days of Godly men and women whose very lifestyle is a rebuke is finally over. But it is not over!

And after three days and an half the Spirit of life from God entered into them, and they stood upon their feet; and great fear fell upon them which saw them. And they heard a great voice from heaven saying unto them, Come up hither. And they ascended up to heaven in a cloud; and their enemies beheld them (Revelation 11:11-12).

In the midst of their party, while they view the rotten corpses that are being abused, something begins to happen that this world has never viewed. Those two dead prophets suddenly begin to change. Rotten flesh turns to life, their physical appearance turns fresh and new, and breath enters into their once dead bodies. In the presence of this world, while television cameras catch each detail, they stand alive upon their feet. There is no doubt that their first words will be the Gospel message and the price of sinful living. Giddy and foolish men and women will suddenly turn ghostly and riddled with fear. Fear will take hold of men like a thousand deaths. Their victory turns to defeat in their face. The world begins to mourn.

The Lamb of God thunders His trumpet as He calls out to the resurrected prophets, *"Come up hither."* They will be caught up before a watching world and will ascend to God in a cloud. Words fail to express this moment that will clearly be seen by the shocked partying multitudes. Victory is turned to defeat in one short period, minutes at the most. The Bible says, while *"their enemies beheld them."* No wonder God planned the war and allowed their death, so that He could reveal the triumph of His righteousness.

> *And the same hour was there a great earthquake, and the tenth part of the city fell, and in the earthquake were slain of men seven thousand: and the remnant were affrighted, and gave glory to the God of heaven* (Revelation11:13).

Probably no event of the seven years will capture the attention of this world more fully than this. Fear descends like a black and threatening cloud. The forty-two months of these two prophets, their death, their resurrection, and their ascension bring the seven years of the Great Tribulation to its last, short closing days. We see the rest of the events in the following chapters of Revelation: thirteen through eighteen. Much of it will happen simultaneously with these prophets preaching God's word. During the same hour of the prophets' resurrection, there is a great earthquake. *"Seven thousand men were destroyed,"* and the remnant *"were affrighted."* And the scripture says, they *"gave glory to God."* Did they repent? The Bible does not say.

❖

> *The Lamb of God thunders His trumpet as He calls out to the resurrected prophets, "Come up hither."*

The second woe is past; and, behold, the third woe cometh quickly.

And the seventh angel sounded; and there were great voices in heaven, saying, The kingdoms of this world are become the kingdoms of our Lord, and of his Christ; and he shall reign for ever and ever (Revelation 11:14-15).

The words above help us understand that while we are viewing different aspects of this hour, most of it occurs at the same time as other things we will view. The fact that two woes are past and the third is coming does not mean progression, but rather one sorrow on top of two sorrows. The third woe that this seventh angel sounds is like a warning of what is to come, as this seven year period continues to unfold. While we will return to view many events in the second full story of these same years, now we pause to see the end of it all.

The angels of the Lord and the elders in heaven are heard proclaiming *"the kingdoms of this world are become the kingdoms of our Lord and of His Christ, and He shall reign for ever and ever."* Everything that occurs in this entire Book of Revelation is preparation for His kingdom. Nothing shall be lost, but the lost themselves. All this misery is misery of sin and rebellion. All the sorrows are the sorrows of unbelief and disobedience. Nothing in this book spells anything but glory for His saints.

And the four and twenty elders, which sat before God on their seats, fell upon their faces, and worshipped God, Saying, We give thee thanks, O Lord God Almighty, which art, and wast, and art to come; because thou hast taken to thee thy great power, and hast reigned (Revelation 11:16-17).

We see the raptured saints that have been an integral part of these proceedings fall prostrate again before the throne. Their worship in heaven is almost divine. God is the center of their attention and His throne is never far from any part of the story. They worship God because they see His sovereignty in every scene. The cry of a true saint of God is always, *"Thy kingdom come."* Finally, after long years, even millenniums, the day has come. They can see His kingdom rising from the ruins of judgment and tribulation.

> *And the nations were angry, and thy wrath is come, and the time of the dead, that they should be judged, and that thou shouldest give reward unto thy servants the prophets, and to the saints, and them that fear thy name, small and great; and shouldest destroy them which destroy the earth. And the temple of God was opened in heaven, and there was seen in his temple the ark of his testament: and there were lightnings, and voices, and thunderings, and an earthquake, and great hail* (Revelation 11:18-19).

The closing of this chapter is absolutely breathtaking. The nations of the earth are ripe for judgment, and they know it. They are angry because of the wrath of God. This is such an incredible closing of the seven years. The dead are going to be judged, and rewards are going to be given unto His prophets and all His saints. Anyone whose faith was a faith of righteous fear and loving obedience is going to be rewarded. Now read this statement that I have never seen before in Scripture; *"...and shouldest destroy them which destroy the earth."* This earth is God's creation, and the abusers of His beautiful universe will pay a heavy price.

And now the grand closing: *"the temple of God was opened in heaven."* No human being has ever entered this temple. Solomon built its counterpart, but this is the heavenly type of which Solomon's temple was but a shadow. The doors are wide open and the implication is that finally His created family, redeemed and glorified, will have eternal access. In the temple is the *"ark of His testament."* The Bible we have is but the copy of the eternal book that is in the temple. Even the natural world responds with sounds of *"voices, thunderings, an earthquake, and great hail."* These expressions of nature are the first sounds of a purified universe.

Conclusion

We must leave this beautiful story, return to the beginning of the seven years and view it again from the casting out of the devil from his mid-air kingdom down to the earth. The Lord intends for us not to let this scene slip from our view while we go back to take another look at these same dark seven years. Shortly, we will see those doors to the heavenly temple opened for eternity and all of His saints welcomed.

THE DEVIL GETS THE BOOT

W e are back at the time of the Rapture and the beginning of the Seven Years of the Great Tribulation. This next presentation of these same seven years deal almost exclusively with the devil, his designs, and his judgments. The Lamb of God and our Heavenly Father were center stage in the previous picture from chapter four verse one to chapter eleven verse nineteen. The Father's throne was the backdrop, and the Lamb of God was the source of all the action. The twenty-four elders that John saw around the throne presented a picture that symbolizes the multitude of saints raptured up out of a sin-cursed earth that is ripe for judgment. We watched the Lamb open the seven-sealed book and saw its action of judgment. We can clearly say that the Son of God, seen as the Lamb slain, is the Father's star character for all Seven Years of the Great Tribulation, as viewed in the first story.

Now, we must return to look again at the same seven years. This presentation will focus on the devil getting his hour in the spotlight and his final demise. God the Father always acts with judicial perfection. No man or created being will be judged unfairly. Satan walked into the garden disguised as a beautiful creature and lied and beguiled his way into possession of this created world. He must be judged, but his judgment must be of the order and method that is so complete that there can be no appeal. When this hour is finished, Satan will be seen not by his imitation of beauty but by his evil heart.

He will never have a second chance to prove his godhead when this display of his real nature is finished.

This is Satan's greatest effort to produce a masterpiece of a false godhead or trinity of beings. There has been many such trinities as this in the world of paganism. I have never viewed a pagan temple that did not have three altars. He originally said, *"I will ascend into heaven, I will exalt my throne above the stars of God: I will sit also upon the mount of the congregation, in the sides of the north: I will ascend above the heights of the clouds; I will be like the most High"* (Isaiah 14:13-14). He never reached that goal. He tried but failed, and the Son of God saw him fall. Jesus said, *"I beheld Satan as lightning fall from heaven"* (Luke 10:18). When the Son of God said *"like lightning,"* He was expressing the intensity of this action. This historic act by the Father was meant to display to the heavenly angels His sovereignty, and to make plain the extent of His judgment of Satan, and those

Satan walked into the garden disguised as a beautiful creature and lied and beguiled his way into possession of this created world.

angels that fell with him. This had to be one of heaven's saddest but brightest days. Now, the time has come to conclude the fall of Satan from the proximity of God's throne to the earth. His next fall will be by judgment from the earth to the bottomless pit and then out of the bottomless pit to the Lake of Fire for eternity. The present world-wide struggles in the spiritual realm are the pre-war of this coming worldwide war on a scale seen only in the Book of Revelation. It really is a grand scene and will be life changing for this universe.

Satan's hatred for Godly people is legendary. Nothing in his actions is more visible than his hatred for the coming Rapture of the saints. Satan will do everything in his power to delay this event, but the saints will be forever beyond his reach. The seed of the woman has always presented the greatest challenge to Satan. He remembers too well the words of the Father in the garden after man's fall. The great Creator spoke to Satan personally, *"And I will put enmity between thee and the woman, and between thy seed and her seed; it shall bruise thy head, and thou shalt bruise his heel"* (Genesis 3:15). He has already suffered a deadly blow—Calvary and the empty tomb—but his final judgment is at the door. When he sees that raptured multitude fly past him upwards through the air, it will be reckoning day. The raptured saints will be the crowning multitude of the seed of woman. As soon as they pass him in the sky, the angels will prepare for the battle that lands Satan earthbound and unable to ever approach God's throne again. Satan will be limited to casting blasphemy from the earth to the shouting multitude around the Father's glory. Viewing Satan in this reduced position is one of the remarkable parts of this chapter. Everything he does for the rest of the seven years of the Great Tribulation will be from a limited capacity, and then he will be cast into the bottomless pit.

> *And there appeared a great wonder in heaven; a woman clothed with the sun, and the moon under her feet, and upon her head a crown of twelve stars: And she being with child cried, travailing in birth, and pained to be delivered* (Revelation 12:1-2).

This is the most remarkable picture of the church of Jesus Christ found in the Scripture. John is viewing this church in its two-fold existence, both the organized and compromising church, and the remnant church of victory and quiet triumph. Everything in Revelation after chapter four verse one cannot be seen as historic or some event of the past but as future prophecy, beginning with the day of the Rapture and right into the future fulfillment of all things. The promises to the seven churches were stated seven times *"to the overcomers."* What is about to happen cannot include anyone but overcomers and cannot exclude even one of these overcomers. A great woman clothed with the sun is the outwardly visible church. She is rich, powerful, dominating, and pregnant with *"man child."* The twelve stars in her crown demand that she is either Israel or the church. But she cannot be Israel because Israel is in total unbelief, except for a remnant, until the end of the Tribulation Period. There are other proofs in this chapter that this is the church.

Israel's past has no record or period of time when she was like the sun or had the moon or darkness under her feet. It seems completely out of context to try to turn this picture back to prove that it is the people of Israel. The church has been the one entity that has done so much to spread sunshine into the night. With all her failures—and there are many—the church still has had a multitude in her ranks that shined for Christ like the midday sun. The moon or the darkness of sin, which this idea of *"under her feet"* represents, has been defeated and cast out millions of times by His saints. Israel has a glorious future, but her past is filled with more defeat than victory. It was the leaders of Israel that consented—even demanded—that the Son of God be put to death or crucified. No, Israel is not the image of the sun with her feet on the moon. It represents His church, the greatest institution of human history. This is not a put down of Israel as a nation or as His chosen family. Israel is the apple of the Father's eye, and her future is bright with promise.

There have been many from within Israel that have been both Israel and the church. They should be included in this *"sun-clothed woman."* There were many faithful saints among this nation that were called His church in the Old Testament. Remember the church in the wilderness: *"This is he, that was in the church in the wilderness with the angel which spake to him in the mount Sina, and with our fathers: who received the*

The angels will prepare for the battle that lands Satan earthbound and unable to ever approach God's throne again.

lively oracles to give unto us" (Acts 7:38). Godly men and women of Israel have carried the great burden of the kingdom and should not be treated lightly. Multitudes of them will be represented in the twelve of those twenty-four elders seen in Revelation chapter four. The prophet Malachi spoke of the saints of both Testaments that were called his jewels, *"And they shall be mine, saith the LORD of hosts, in that day when I make up my jewels; and I will spare them, as a man spareth his own son that serveth him"* (Malachi 3:17). These great saints should be included with this sun-clothed woman, not just as Israel but as saints of God. It is certain that Israel's prophetic place is on the horizon.

The greatest purpose of the church—this sun-clothed woman—is to produce a Rapture-ready bride to reign on this earth with Christ and to be His forever. Our mission is not just converts but saints set free from all worldly entanglement and ready at a moment's notice to meet the Lord. This second verse that speaks of a man-child must be the most beautiful statement identifying that remnant within the bosom of the whole—the real company of saints—found in this great Bible we love. These are not just church members, pew warmers, religious folks, but the company of the sanctified, *"pained to be delivered"* and ready to go at any minute. Apostle Paul said, *"For what is our hope, or joy, or crown of rejoicing? Are not even ye in the presence of our Lord Jesus Christ at his coming"* (1 Thessalonians 2:19). *"Whom we preach, warning every man, and teaching every man in all wisdom; that we may present every man perfect in Christ Jesus"* (Colossians 1:28). Again He said, *"For I am jealous over you with godly jealousy: for I have espoused you to one husband, that I may present you as a chaste virgin to Christ"* (2 Corinthians 11:2). There is a Rapture-ready Bride within the church, and that Bride is ready to leave this world.

And there appeared another wonder in heaven; and behold a great red dragon, having seven heads and ten horns, and seven crowns upon

*his heads. And his tail drew the third part of the stars of heaven, and
did cast them to the earth: and the dragon stood before the woman
which was ready to be delivered, for to devour her child as soon as it
was born* (Revelation 12:3-4).

The devil could not be described in more graphic terms to fit the
occasion. He is already gathering his worldwide government before
the Rapture because he is seen wearing the types of his governmental powers on his head before he is cast out. When someone tries to
make this a historic event concerning Israel and the birth of Jesus
Christ and His ascension, it really makes for a theological difficulty.
This is future prophecy and not something that happened before
John received this prophetic revelation. The devil is very close to having these government powers in place and, as seen in this chapter, he
must have the world ready before the Rapture. The world is either
ready—or very close to ready—for a master politician to put the One
World governmental powers in place. Russia, Turkey, Libya, Iran,
and Iraq, as well as the rest of the Middle East and the nations of
Europe, all appear perfectly aligned. Everything is waiting for the
Rapture of His chosen saints.

Fallen angels or demon spirits are presently organized for Satan's
control. There is an all-out assault on the present church world—
especially the idea of the Rapture. Never have evil spirits been more
animated to destroy. The church universal is full of unbelief and
unprepared for this Bride within, called a *"man child,"* to disappear.
This company is called the *"man child"* to illustrate the masculine
purity and the future role of *"elders."* To call the Bride a *"man child"*
is no different than to call her *"elders."* Much of the religious world
is already joining Satan's One World church and will be ready to
serve him as he establishes the worship and mark of his Antichrist.
These demons are presently active as the Rapture is preparing to

occur because they are resisting every idea connected to the *"man child's"* escape. These spirits are also busy preparing the religious world for the church of the Antichrist.

Along with the preparation for their new world religion is their assault on truth, especially the truth of the Bride's Rapture. Notice how this dragon, Satan stands on guard before the entire church world to defeat the remnant within from their glorious victory. Satan has marshaled an army of Rapture haters and truth deceivers to fight the remnant within the organized church world. The church is full of all descriptions of doctrines contrary to the great hope of our removal to His presence. They will lose their chosen war because the Lord Himself will come down from heaven to assure the ultimate victory. Satan will actually set up a guard of millions of fallen angels to try to fight against the ascending saints. The Lord of the hosts, a multitude of Cherubim, and angels will join the triumph as the saints ascend right through the multitudes of evil spirits. Devils will be scattered everywhere in awesome defeat.

> *And she brought forth a man child, who was to rule all nations with a rod of iron: and her child was caught up unto God, and to his throne. And the woman fled into the wilderness, where she hath a place prepared of God, that they should feed her there a thousand two hundred and threescore days* (Revelation 12:5-6).

The term *"man child"* could not represent the overcoming saints better. These are not the wimpy believers cowering in defeat and hardly able to mutter a weak *"Hallelujah."* The saints that go up in the Rapture are soldiers of the cross, firebrands plucked out of worldliness, and strong in the joy of full surrender to Jesus Christ. These will include the great missionaries that invaded foreign lands and fought back demons of hate, godly women that were prayer warriors in the

House of God, and gospel preachers that refused the compromise of big-time religion. They will be a victorious company that the devil cannot intimidate. We will win this coming battle.

This *"man child"* brought forth by His church will be destined to rule this world with a rod of iron during the Millennium. Israel will rule the land of promise, all the geographical area promised to Abraham. They were never destined nor promised to rule the world. That promise is to His church, always has been and always will be. That is settled. This one truth guarantees that this woman and her victorious son is His church. Christ will be King of Kings over the created universe, Israel will rule under Him in her promised kingdom, and the Bride will rule under Him over the whole world.

The greatest purpose of the church—this sun-clothed woman—is to produce a Rapture-ready bride to reign on this earth with Christ and to be His forever.

"And the woman fled into the wilderness" is an appropriate picture of the darkness that will descend on the church world. Most church members are not prepared for the Rapture and for what will happen if they miss it. They who willingly become martyrs will be able to prepare in repentance and wash their garments in the blood of the Lamb. Most of the liberal world will descend into the One World church. They will serve the One World church and then be destroyed with His Antichrist. A multitude of those that missed the Rapture will repent and have some degree of protection for a short time. The Antichrist and his One World church will persecute the saints who refuse their new religion. Many will die as martyrs and become a part of the Tribulation saints, as we saw in chapter seven.

> *And there was war in heaven: Michael and his angels fought against the dragon; and the dragon fought and his angels, And prevailed not; neither was their place found any more in heaven* (Revelation 12:5-6).

A celestial battle will follow this great Rapture of the *"man child."* Satan was cast into the midair long ago and has ruled from this advantaged spot. But now Michael, that great archangel, will gather the army of assigned angels to his leadership, and they will engage in a war of the spirit world. Satan and his fallen angels and Michael and the holy angels will meet in the air. There have been many engagements in this realm but none to compare with this war. Michael has won many times, but Satan was always left to fight another day or hour. This time Satan will be cast out of the midair and down to the earth, and there will be no more room for Satan in God's heavenly realm. He will never ascend again to accuse the chosen before the Father.

He and every angel that fell with him will at this moment of future fulfillment be removed from the spirit realm down to the limited focus of this earth. They are stripped of their right to appear before God and limited to be revealed only in their totally depraved nature or appearance. Today, they can act paranormally and take on angelic beauty and even appear as angels of light. Their light or angelic form will be stripped from them when they are cast down to this earth. All the beauty of their created presence will be lost and they will appear as their true character of darkness and lostness now represents. They will have great power to deceive and even perform miracles, but their miracles will be distinctly satanic and ugly. Their God-given creative beauty is forever removed.

And I heard a loud voice saying in heaven, Now is come salvation, and strength, and the kingdom of our God, and the power of his Christ: for the accuser of our brethren is cast down, which accused them before our God day and night. And they overcame him by the blood of the Lamb, and by the word of their testimony; and they loved not their lives unto the death. Therefore rejoice, ye heavens, and ye that dwell in them. Woe to the inhibiters of the earth and of the sea! for the devil is come down unto you, having great wrath, because he knoweth that he hath but a short time (Revelation 12:10-12).

The results of this great victory against Satan and his hosts are breathtaking. For at least six thousand years he has terrorized this world. His position in the midair gave him great advantage, and he has used it to the maximum. *"As the prince of the power of the air,"* he has been able to move swiftly and cunningly against the saints. This victory against

Most church members are not prepared for the Rapture and for what will happen if they miss it.

Satan is first announced from a *"loud voice in heaven."* There is no question but that the host of angels have longed for this day. The universe cannot experience the ultimate kingdom of God until this day of victory has arrived. The casting out of Satan starts the process of his final judgment. His end is in the making once he loses his midair occupation. It's his beachhead, and without it he's doomed.

The one source of victory over Satan, Christ's blood, is once again remembered, and it applies especially to those who defeat Satan after the Rapture. The traditions I was taught in my early years of church life said that no one could be saved after the Rapture. Of course, the Bible is literal, and literal truth allows no such teaching. That certainly is not to say that missing the Rapture is anything less than a disaster. How to be saved after the glorious Rapture is clearly described in verse ten: *"and they loved not their lives unto the death."* This proves that the only hope of salvation for those who accept Christ as Savior is to be ready to lay down their life and suffer the hell of Satan's fury. Today you can be saved unto life, but then you will be *"saved unto death."*

All the heavens, the raptured saints, and the host of angels rejoice, but are perfectly aware of what this casting out of Satan means to the earth. The devil is cast out and comes down to the earth, and *"he knows he has but a short time."* This is the first moment in biblical history that Satan knows and accepts that his defeat is absolute. The vicious battle he fights from this point to the return of Christ to the earth is guaranteed to be the act of a desperate being. I have read of men that knew a battle was lost, so they would wade into the enemy camp with an abandonment that made them almost invincible. This is the picture we get of the devil, and the earth will pay a price during his parting anger.

And when the dragon saw that he was cast unto the earth, he persecuted the woman which brought forth the man child. And to the woman were given two wings of a great eagle, that she might fly into the wilderness, into her place, where she is nourished for a time, and times, and half a time, from the face of the serpent. And the serpent cast out of his mouth water as a flood after the woman, that he might cause her to be carried away of the flood. And the earth helped the woman, and the earth opened her mouth, and swallowed up the flood which the dragon cast out of his mouth. And the dragon was wroth with the woman, and went to make war with the remnant of her seed, which keep the commandments of God, and have the testimony of Jesus Christ (Revelation 12:13-17).

The Devil immediately acts to manifest the final expression of his wrath on the left behind of the church world that did not give their immediate allegiance to the New World religion. There has never been an attack against the Bible-believers—those who have repented—as there will be after the Rapture. It is all-out war and utter destruction in the devil's mind, and he has nothing to lose that isn't already lost. He will persecute the world because he hates everything that speaks of the Creator, but he will especially persecute the woman who was once called *"a woman clothed with the sun."* The saints within her company are no longer visible but have been raptured. In this vision, she is now nothing but a hated and persecuted crowd. She lost her glory when this *"man child"* was caught away.

Satan's attack will be violent, but the Lord will not forsake those that claim His name. It appears that a supernatural provision is made for those willing to suffer the great wrath of Satan. Believers will learn of a hiding place—a wilderness, a place of Spartan living—a safe place from the Antichrist. Until the first three and one half years are complete, there will be a great victory provided by the Lord for some of the saints. The earth will provide supernatural action to defeat Satan as he attacks this remnant of the woman. During two thousand years of church history, many saints have defeated and frustrated the devil. Hatred for every expression of the true church has been the favorite mindset of this enemy of righteousness. This sun-clothed woman has redeemed millions from his clutches, and he will hate the last expression of her very existence.

The picture of the saints of God on earth during the Tribulation Period should leave no doubt of redemption being available while the Bride is rejoicing in heaven. The greatest reason that men should literally sacrifice all they are to be a part of the Rapture is not to escape the Tribulation but to be part of His Bride for eternity. Going in the Rapture has been reduced to the fear of being lost rather than the glory and joy of being His Bride. We must change this mindset and return to the great challenge of a church getting ready to reign and share His eternal kingdom. The greatest burden of each saint should be the Kingdom of God on earth. The Lord taught us to pray *"Thy kingdom come,"* but all that the majority of Christians can talk about is leaving this earth. We leave for one reason only, and that is to get ready to return and reign with Him.

Conclusion

The reason Satan hates this woman is because he has determined to rule this earth, and the Bride of Christ—the overcomers—will accomplish what he has failed to accomplish. His effort to rule this world has always turned to despair and sorrow. He now knows that we will rule, and this earth will become a garden. Satan's attack on the remnant saints, who have repented, kept the commandments, and have His testimony, is proof that he knows our future. He will fight to the finish, and in the end, he will be finished. Satan will develop his false trinity and leave his ugly mark right down to the end. Let's view the False Christ and the False Prophet that he will present to the world.

THE NASTY ASSYRIAN IS A BEAST

The Antichrist will be the most vicious beast that has ever been known by man or that has been revealed to this world. His lineage from the Assyrians could not be more fitting. They were evil, and they enjoyed being evil. They treated their enemies or captives in the vilest fashion that our human imagination could think. The ruins of their ancient palaces are filled with grotesque carvings in stone as a testimony to the evil ingeniousness of their character. They were, in life and in battle, a foretaste of what the Antichrist will be as the final dictator for Satan. The prophets have made it clear that the Antichrist will be an Assyrian.

A prophet named Isaiah spoke of this future beast that attacked and destroyed the northern kingdom of Israel. *"O Assyrian, the rod of mine anger, and the staff in their hand is mine indignation. I will send him against an hypocritical nation, and against the people of my wrath will I give him a charge, to take the spoil, and to take the prey, and to tread them down like the mire of the streets"* (Isaiah 10:5-6). Then, Isaiah gave another part of the prophecy that is yet to be fulfilled. *"That I will break the Assyrian in my land, and upon my mountains tread him under foot: then shall his yoke depart from off them, and his burden depart from off their shoulders"* (Isaiah 14:25). This has never been fulfilled so we know it is about the future Antichrist. He spoke of this Assyrian in clear end-time chronology to leave no doubt as to His meaning. *"And the LORD shall cause his glorious voice to be heard, and shall shew the lighting down of his arm, with the indignation of his anger, and with the flame of a devouring fire, with scattering, and tempest, and hailstones. For through the voice of the LORD shall the Assyrian be beaten down, which smote with a rod"* (Isaiah 30:30-31). The final Antichrist of this thirteenth chapter of Revelation must be that Assyrian. Even Micah spoke of his death in the gate of Nimrod, which is none other than Ancient Babylon being revisited at this very hour.

To add to the prophetic miracles that are occurring all over the world, this Assyrian beast represents an unspeakable mystery that can finally be understood. Except for a few historians and the people of Assyrian lineage, nobody in prophetic literature even considered that there were Assyrian people alive right up to this very point in history. Almost as mysterious as the Jews but completely off the radar, the Assyrians—as a distinct people—have survived the centuries with clear unmistakable identity. Living mostly in their own conclaves, they have survived great odds to now surface in northern Iraq and other nations where they have fled. For them to presently be involved in uniting their own culture and to be a voice in the new Iraq government cannot be less than perfect planning on the part of our Creator.

The Antichrist will be the most vicious beast that has ever been known by man or that has been revealed to this world.

There are very distinct, positive plans for the future of the Assyrians in the Bible. Indeed they will produce the Antichrist, but this should not and does not indict the present Assyrian people as bad themselves. The Antichrist must arise from a culture and a people that pledge allegiance to the God of the Bible, which the Assyrians do and have done since the day of Jesus Christ. Daniel said, *"Neither shall he regard the God of his fathers, nor the desire of women, nor regard any god: for he shall magnify himself above all"* (Daniel 11:37). But a much greater future awaits this ancient culture. During the Millennium, there will only be three nations in the Middle East. Assyria will be one of them. This would suggest that at some point the northern part of Iraq and Iran, all or much of the southern part of Turkey, Syria, and at least part of Jordan, will be the Assyrian nation. *"In that day shall Israel be the third with Egypt and with Assyria, even a blessing in the midst of the land."* (Isaiah 19:24).

Much bigger and broader than the ancient lineage is the connection of the coming Antichrist to Satan. He will be the slickest masquerader ever produced by Lucifer. The making of this evil character has been centuries in Satan's planning. He is not a flash in the pan, but a well-prepared imitation. He will have a partner in the False Prophet

Much bigger and broader than the ancient lineage is the connection of the coming Antichrist to Satan. He will be the slickest masquerader ever produced by Lucifer.

that will probably imitate all the works of the Holy Spirit. He should be called the false anointed one. Under Satan's tutorage, these two personalities will finalize a one world religion that cleverly unites all religions together.

No group of religious people are better at doing the devil's work than those that have slipped into compromise and deception. There are many among the evangelicals and Charismatics who are deeply involved with the Catholics in putting the finishing touch on Satan's future church. If she is not already, she will soon represent the final version of the *"moon-clothed woman with the sun under her feet."* Remember the church in the previous chapter is pregnant with the *"man-child"* (Revelation 12:5), even as the massive organizations are slipping into vile deception. God has a people hidden in many quarters of the world awaiting the call from the sky. We will learn more about this woman riding the beast in chapter seventeen.

> *And I stood upon the sand of the sea, and saw a beast rise up out of the*
> *sea, having seven heads and ten horns, and upon his horns ten crowns,*
> *and upon his heads the name of blasphemy. And the beast which I saw*
> *was like unto a leopard, and his feet were as the feet of a bear, and his*
> *mouth as the mouth of a lion: and the dragon gave him his power, and*
> *his seat, and great authority. And I saw one of his heads as it were*
> *wounded to death; and his deadly wound was healed: and all the*
> *world wondered after the beast* (Revelation 13:1-3).

The Middle East is clearly the geographical center of the rising Antichrist. The United Nations of Europe will slowly connect with the Middle East as the revived Roman Empire regains its footing in the needed order. Iraq had to become a democracy in its own unique style because the Antichrist will begin by flatteries not by military powers, *"And such as do wickedly against the covenant shall he corrupt by flatteries"* (Daniel 11:32a). The Antichrist, an Assyrian by nationality, will be connected to the ancient city of Babylon and that nation. Rising out of the sea as he appears certainly ties him closely to the Mediterranean Sea and the political powers within its vicinity. He quickly unites the political powers and becomes the leader of the emerging Roman Empire but especially its ancient eastern wing. His rise to power and his coalition of political partners will be blasphemous in nature and will bear a decidedly anti-Israel and anti-Christ tone.

All the power of the past world empires of Biblical order will be united in this last worldwide kingdom. The lion was Babylon, the bear was the Medes and Persian and the leopard was Greece. Everything embracing them geographically will be gathered together in this last one world order; Satan will manifest great authority and evil powers in the appearance of this beastly personality. Many government personalities are already using strange methods of the occult in deceiving the masses. Satan can transform a dull person into a magnetic persona that suavely moves undiscerning people. The Antichrist will be the ultimate "Dale Carnegie" type individual. The New Age has become extremely adept in personality transformation, and the Antichrist will be their master personality.

Supernatural signs will become a way of the one world government to control and deceive. Adolf Hitler turned Germany into a nation of beasts, and he was certainly a precursor of the final beast. One of the heads of Antichrist's kingdom will be wounded to death, and a miraculous recovery will occur. He will perform such a display of strange powers

The Middle East is clearly the geographical center of the rising Antichrists kingdom.

and religious miracles that he will dazzle the world, and they will wonder after him. The world has developed a cultic mindset over the last few decades. Rock stars, best-selling authors, movie stars, and many personalities are practically worshipped and thronged at public events. All of this is in preparation for the final event of human deception.

> *And they worshipped the dragon which gave power unto the beast: and they worshipped the beast, saying, Who is like unto the beast? who is able to make war with him? And there was given unto him a mouth speaking great things and blasphemies; and power was given unto him to continue forty and two months. And he opened his mouth in blasphemy against God, to blaspheme his name, and his tabernacle, and them that dwell in heaven* (Revelation 13:4-6).

Finally, Satan has accomplished the one thing his heart has been set on. The world sees his creation of the false Christ—the Antichrist—whom the world believes to be the long awaited "messiah." Every religion has a distant hope of the final answer to the world's problems. The Christian world has the expectation of the return of Jesus Christ. The Jews are still expecting their Messiah. The Muslims expect their Allah. Each religious entity is expecting their own redeemer, and Satan will reveal himself as the great sovereign one that can unite all religious hope in one great person, his false Christ. The display of religious powers will be so paranormal and dazzling that the world will worship the one viewed as the creator of such seeming perfection. Satan will revel in his glory.

The blasphemy coming from the Antichrist's mouth will be awesome. This will not be the blasphemy of the ugly, but the blasphemy of the distorted beauty. The entire religious world is already glorying in statues, icons, and art forms of different expressions.

Satan gets his worship, but it's at the tip of a sword.

The choreographed dance is one of the church world's darkest deceptions. Statues that are proclaimed as anointed—especially where grace is reportedly connected—have already been accepted in Charismatic circles. Millions follow apparitions of Mary. Some writers are describing visions and dreams of incredible creatures and experiences. All kinds of extra-biblical occurrences are preparing the way for religious blasphemy. To assign anything to God that is clearly of the occult is blasphemy. To claim to be God is the worst form of blasphemy, but to claim to be the Son of God is a dark hideous form of blasphemy.

Satan especially blasphemes everything that is heavenly about God the Father. When the Father and the Lamb sent angels to cast him out of heaven, he lost all ability to travel in the stratosphere of God's domain. Notice that he blasphemes God, His name, His heavenly tabernacle, and those that dwell in heaven. He certainly hates the Father—the Sovereign God—because he is now forbidden to appear in God's presence. Satan has sought to replace God with himself, but he has completely failed, and nothing but hatred can now find expression in his disappointed heart. The tabernacle of God is the grandest location in the entire universal system. It is glorious, even beyond words. Paul saw it and was left speechless. Satan has visited it at every opportunity permitted by the Father, but now it can only be a distant dream to Satan. He blasphemes it with vileness, along with everyone that dwells in this matchless place.

> *And it was given unto him to make war with the saints, and to overcome them: and power was given him over all kindreds, and tongues, and nations. And all that dwell upon the earth shall worship him, whose names are not written in the book of life of the Lamb slain from the foundation of the world. If any man has an ear, let him hear. He that leadeth into captivity shall go into captivity: he that killeth with the sword must be killed with the sword. Here is the patience and the faith of the saints* (Revelation 13:7-10).

Satan will be restricted to the earth, and his last recourse against God will be to attack all that worship or name His name. In the previous chapter, some repentant saints were protected for the first three and a half years; but during the last half of the seven years, they will be open season. No living soul will be protected from the anger of this Beast in the last three and one half years. Believers will die by the millions. Jews will be slaughtered mercilessly. The world will be subject to Satan's final rage.

Multitudes will escape his fury by turning to Antichrist in worship and adoration. Unless they have turned wholly to Christ and had their names written in the Book of Life, *"all that dwell on the earth"* will not have any power to resist. Satan gets his worship, but it's at the tip of a sword. The Bible calls Satan *"the god of this world"*

(2 Corinthians 4:4). This last one-world system will give Satan one short window of opportunity, and he will ride the glory to his own destruction. John was so moved by this revelation of Satan's final days that he paused to say, *"If any man have an ear, let him hear."*

The Antichrist, an Assyrian by nationality, will be connected to the ancient city of Babylon and that nation.

The results of evil are always the same. There is no capacity for sin to continue on its present course. This universe was created in moral order, and everything else is out of order. Sin and rebellion cannot survive anymore than a building engulfed with flames. Sin destroys itself. The words, *"He that leadeth into captivity shall go into captivity,"* is a perfect example. There is no power in evil to survive. The patience of God's saints is to watch sin as it is destroyed and know that "right always prevails." Learn, dear souls, to turn from sin as you live holy and set apart.

And I beheld another beast coming up out of the earth; and he had two horns like a lamb, and he spake as a dragon. And he exerciseth all the power of the first beast before him, and causeth the earth and them which dwell therein to worship the first beast, whose deadly wound was healed (Revelation 13:11-12).

Satan cannot present himself as God unless he has all the appearances of the Biblical picture of God. He must produce a false messiah and that false messiah must have a shadow spirit or person to imitate the Holy Spirit. This second beast is an imitator of the Holy Spirit and serves this false Antichrist like the Holy Spirit served Jesus Christ. This beast comes up out of the earth. He is demonic and either possesses a man or takes on the form of a man (I suspect it is the latter). The phrase, *"two horns like a lamb,"* is a masterful play on words. Lambs do not have horns, but this beast is lamb-like in outward demeanor but vicious in character. His false piousness will capture the world for the Antichrist. That same spirit is already being manifest in false prophets and prophetesses all over the world.

His first action is to bring glory and honor to the first beast and enlist the world to worship the Antichrist. He does not take the honor for himself but perfectly imitates the experience of Pentecost. Most of our world has rejected the Pentecostal model given in the Book of Acts, which has created a vacuum for this false beast. The healing of the deadly wound on the first beast becomes a rallying cry. This is a clear imitation of what happened in the first century church when the Spirit of God used the church to powerfully call the world to honor the Lord Jesus Christ and His redeeming sacrifice. The false prophet will bring the world to the feet of this false messiah, and they will worship him as the "Christ."

And he doeth great wonders, so that he maketh fire come down from heaven on the earth in the sight of men, And deceiveth them that dwell on the earth by the means of those miracles which he had power to do in the sight of the beast; saying to them that dwell on the earth, that they should make an image to the beast, which had the wound by a sword, and did live. And he had power to give life unto the image of the beast, that the image of the beast should both speak, and cause that as many as would not worship the image of the beast should be killed (Revelation 13:13-15).

People always resist the thought of actual miracles coming from the devil. Men are inherently superstitious and see nothing but good in unexplainable occurrences. Discerning the false from the true is almost totally missing from today's world. While the Bible makes it plain that Satan and his trinity will not deceive everyone, it does make it clear that there will be a majority that falls at Satan's feet.

The miracles will be spectacular, even to the point of causing fire to fall from the heavens in a dazzling display of paranormal powers. This second beast will declare the glory of this new "christ" and will deceive the world into making a great image in his likeness. Twice this false spirit has invoked the miracle of the first beast. His wound has become a redemptive event and his resurrection from the wound the

Discerning the false from the true is almost totally missing from today's world.

proof of his authenticity. The One World Religion will be the tool of this vicious man/beast. He will use all the powers of the church world to impose his will on the world. The total political, total religious, and total economic world will be united for a short time. It will be an awesome unity that tramples the world under its feet.

Something happens that is even more ominous. The false spirit moves upon the image and gives it life. The image takes on human characteristics and powers, and it becomes a worldwide display. Such overwhelming manifestation comes from this beastly image that its presence is dazzling. Men and women will swoon just to look on this image and will go into estatic states of euphoria. The fleshly pleasure from this image will be an experience of religious glory. Healing will occur on a worldwide basis as television, Internet, and radio carry the message to the world. The false church will call it a worldwide revival.

> *And he causeth all, both small and great, rich and poor, free and bond, to receive a mark in their right hand, or in their foreheads: And that no man might buy or sell, save he that had the mark, or the name of the beast, or the number of his name. Here is wisdom. Let him that hath understanding count the number of the beast: for it is the number of a man; and his number is Six hundred threescore and six* (Revelation 13:16-18).

A worldwide revival where everyone is first invited and then, secondly, required to attend will become a universal event. The church will not allow anyone to resist. The new trinity will proclaim itself "the way," and every belief contrary to "the way" will be proclaimed as heresy. All heretics—all those that resist the worldwide phenomenon—will be enemies of the church or the state and must recant, repent, or die. To assure repentance there will be issued a *"mark"* of conversion that all can read. The economic world will be totally supportive. The church will be in charge of the *"mark"* because it will be their "mark" of faith and devotion. It will be required worldwide and will be displayed with great joy and devotion.

The world is presently preparing for such economic control. The thieves of the world have contrived a multitude of ways to steal wealth and even identities. This is forcing the world to prepare for a perfect plan of protection. That

This universe was created in moral order and everything else is out of order.

protection will soon become control. The policy that says, *"no man might buy or sell without the mark"* will be instituted to protect the economic system but will quickly become the tool of the church. It will be instituted as a sacred bond between the world and this great image. The promise of protection will be attached. It is actually going to be an extension of the many religious trends that are growing in frequency.

"Here is wisdom ... it is the number of a man." Nothing reveals the Antichrist better than this statement. Unbridled flesh, the raw appetite of the Adamic nature, and the wildest possible life of sin is what the *"mark"* of the Antichrist will represent. The land will be full of pedophiles, animalistic sexual exploits, sado-masochism, and deeper and deeper vileness will continue until human flesh is worse than the worst beast. It will all be manifest with complete religious acceptance. To take the mark will be like becoming a human animal.

Conclusion

The Antichrist and the false prophet will give the devil his masterpiece of deception. Satan knows he has but a short time, so it will be an all-out war. When this deception is complete, it will then turn on its head and God will expose and judge. Satan always overplays his hand. He is an idiot god and will finally be cast into the bottomless pit, but his final destination will be the Lake of Fire. His two beasts will go directly to the Lake of Fire at the end of these seven years. When the world sees Satan cast into the bottomless pit, and his false Christ, and false prophet cast into the Lake of Fire, the world will know that the reign of wickedness is over. The picture of total victory for righteousness and the kingdom of the Father and His Christ is quickly coming into view.

THE LORD'S KIN AT THE WEDDING

In the midst of the greatest judgment in human history—the ultimate and final judgment—God the Father does not forget His chosen Children of Israel. In fact, He could never forget because His promises to Abraham are set in stone and cannot be altered. I pity the man that attacks Israel or even one of Abraham's sons or daughters many generations removed. In chapter seven, after the Rapture of the Bride, the Lord took notice of a chosen remnant and sealed them for His witness to their own nation and people. These were righteous men and women by their own testimony, but were not born again until after the Rapture. They missed being Rapture-ready because they were looking for a future Messiah, and not trusting in the true Messiah whom their leaders had missed two thousand years ago.

Jesus Christ became their Savior and Lord as they took notice of the Rapture and the resurrection of the dead. They saw thousands of open graves across the land of Israel, and they knew that the Wedding Supper that David had so beautifully prophesied was now in preparation in the city in the sky. Very simply, they exchanged the orthodoxy of their tradition for the redemption of their redeemer. This is the very basis of why they were sealed, one hundred and forty-four thousand strong. The blood of Christ alone is the salvation of every soul, and there can be no seal without His blood and His Spirit. While they could not be part of the bride, they could be among the guests of the Groom.

David profiled this wedding in beautiful form. *"Thy throne, O God, is for ever and ever: the sceptre of thy kingdom is a right sceptre ... All thy garments smell of myrrh, and aloes, and cassia, out of the ivory palaces, whereby they have made thee glad. Kings' daughters were among thy honourable women: upon thy right hand did stand the queen in gold of Ophir. The king's daughter is all glorious within: her clothing is of wrought gold. She shall be brought unto the king in raiment of needlework: the virgins her companions that follow her shall be brought unto thee"* (Psalms 45:6,8-9,13-14). The Bride will have her guests, and the Groom His guests, but the Queen is that treasured one whom David saw dressed *"in gold of Ophir."* Malachi called her his *"jewels."* This one hundred forty-four thousand saved Jews missed the Rapture of the Bride, but will be among the guests of the Groom at the Wedding.

After this chosen company joins the wedding party that is completely removed from the events on earth, a foreboding of the last sorrows is heavy on earth. An angel flies in the midst of heaven, preaching the everlasting Gospel. The very phrase, "everlasting Gospel," reminds the world that there is still a choice. A warning follows that Babylon—the worldwide city that has become the center to the Antichrist's pride—has fallen. This little clip of news will be like the end of a dream. The whole world will be tied economically to the success of this city. Then we see the warning to the inhabitants of the world not to take this mark of the Antichrist. The entire world is close to a meltdown and those that choose the Father and the Lamb will be those full of patience and faithfulness. There will be no cheap Christianity.

This chapter ends with all the evidence of a concluding story with climactic excitement. The Lamb of God is about to reap the final harvest. The coming seven last plagues and seven vials will certainly conclude God's wrath. The wine press of wrath has appeared to be full at so many points of history, but it is now overflowing. The end of this great future story is near.

And I looked, and, lo, a Lamb stood on the mount Sion, and with him an hundred forty and four thousand, having his Father's name written in their foreheads. And I heard a voice from heaven, as the voice of many waters, and as the voice of a great thunder: and I heard the voice of harpers harping with their harps: And they sung as it were a new song before the throne, and before the four beasts, and the elders: and no man could learn that song but the hundred and forty and four thousand, which were redeemed from the earth (Revelation 14:1-3).

The sorrows of Israel as a nation and of all the Jewish people worldwide during this seven years is called "Jacob'sTtrouble." The Old Testament prophets did not fail to warn them of this end-time scenario when they would be hated with a vengeance. This number of one hundred and forty-four thousand will serve as a clear message to all Israel that they are not forgotten in their trouble. This sealed number will certainly oppose the covenant that Jewish leaders make with the Antichrist, but they will be treated as fundamentalists and rejected. As for the greater number, the Jewish world will follow the liberal vein of their religious leaders.

The Bride will have her guests and the Groom His guests but the Queen is that treasured one that David saw was dressed "in gold of Ophir."

When these Bible-believing Jews have finished their purpose and have left an unmistakable witness before the world—while protected from the Antichrist—we now see them *"before the throne and before the four beasts and the elders."* The Son of God will be standing on heavenly Mount Zion when they arrive in the city of heavenly Jerusalem. They were sealed on earth with the *"Father's name"* in their forehead. Throughout the years, the Jews have often been tattooed or stamped to expose them to hatred and even death, but this time the seal is for protection. The Father and the Lamb will show the world the special position the Jewish people hold in the Father's heart, and He will do it right in the face of their enemies, including Satan and his false trinity. What a witness of God's love for His own. While billions of Gentiles are dying and even millions of Jews, these will be God's remnant from His own chosen family for His own precious Son.

Glory erupts in heaven when this company arrives at the welcome center. The Lamb's voice is as the *"voice of many waters,"* and joining Him are the heavenly hosts of Cherubim, Elders, and innumerable angels. We see *"harpers harping with their harps"* in the welcoming throne as the sealed number begins to sing. It's their song, and no one else can join. They are only the firstfruits of the Jews saved out of the Tribulation Period, for there will be others. These arrive early to be guests at the Lamb's wedding, and all the great heavenly hosts welcome them. The wedding ceremony can now proceed because the Lord has furnished heaven with His guests. The Bride's guests arrived in chapter seven as the multitude *"out of the great tribulations."* They too missed the Rapture, but washed their garments in the blood of the Lamb.

> *These are they which were not defiled with women; for they are virgins. These are they which follow the Lamb whithersoever he goeth. These were redeemed from among men, being the firstfruits unto God and to the Lamb. {redeemed: Gr. bought} And in their mouth was found no guile: for they are without fault before the throne of God* (Revelation 14:4-5).

The uniqueness of these children of Israel is beautiful. They are holy men and women, abandoned to their keeping of the commandments of God. Once they received the revelation that Jesus Christ was indeed the Messiah, they were committed wholeheartedly to Him. The Father proved this by placing His seal on their foreheads and protecting them from the Antichrist. Now that they have joined the Lamb of God in the heavenly city, they almost become His shadow. As His guests at the wedding, they serve Him in the preparation of His star-studded event. The tables must be prepared, the banquet meal readied, and the banquet hall arrayed that will be fit for a king. Much is to be done, and these redeemed souls find joy in serving the One that was so long rejected by God's chosen people.

In their mouths is nothing but praise to the One for whom they have longed for over many millenniums. This sealed company rejoices greatly because they know well what is occurring on earth to the Jewish world, and the reality of their escape brings nothing but joy. The words of Daniel are especially real to them. *"And I heard the man clothed in linen, which was upon the waters of the river, when he held up his right hand and his left hand unto heaven, and sware by him that liveth for ever that it shall be for a time, times, and an half; and when he shall have accomplished to scatter the power of the holy people, all these things shall be finished. And I heard, but I understood not: then said I, O my Lord, what shall be the end of these things? And he said, Go thy way, Daniel: for the words are closed up and sealed till the time of the end. Many shall be purified, and made white, and tried; but the wicked shall do wickedly: and none of the wicked shall understand; but the wise shall understand. And from the time that the daily sacrifice shall be taken away, and the abomination that maketh desolate set up, there shall be a thousand two hundred and ninety days"* (Daniel 12:7-11). These chosen and sealed are those wise souls that Daniel prophesied about: *"but the wise shall understand."*

And I saw another angel fly in the midst of heaven, having the everlasting gospel to preach unto them that dwell on the earth, and to every nation, and kindred, and tongue, and people, Saying with a loud voice, Fear God, and give glory to him; for the hour of his judgment is come:

and worship him that made heaven, and earth, and the sea, and the
fountains of waters (Revelation 14:6-7).

The one hundred and forty-four thousand witnesses are now
with the Lamb, so another witness, this time an angel, takes their
place proclaiming the Gospel. The Bible names this Gospel the *"ever-*
lasting gospel." Calling it *"everlasting"* does two things. It is the one
Gospel—the Gospel of Christ—and not some special message. There
is only one saving message. Second, it shows the fact that grace is
still available and that the Father and the Lamb are still ready to
save. Nothing is more named and proclaimed during these seven
horrible years than the availability of saving truth. Anyone that tries
to prove that salvation is unavailable during this judgment time
must discount the literal truth of this book. This angel is careful to
traverse the heavens and herald his message to every nation.

Can you comprehend that while hell is spewing its venom on the
earth an angel supernaturally circles the earth following, no doubt, the
path of the sun. This angel will preaching the glorious Gospel of our
Lord Jesus Christ? This angel will prepare a pulpit in the sky and will
preach to the multitudes. Knowing the superstition of men, the world
will certainly hear this message, though it will be unheeded by most.
Satan's trinity will be producing their own message of deception, so
the contest will be between truth and evil. The message will be simple,
"Fear God and give glory to Him." Satan is endearing himself to be worshipped, and this angel is warning that it is the great God alone that
should be worshipped.

And there followed another angel, saying, Babylon is fallen, is fallen,
that great city, because she made all nations drink of the wine of the
wrath of her fornication (Revelation 14:8).

This comes as unusual news. In the midst of the angels preaching and the devil roaring out his blasphemy, the alarm is heard, *"Babylon is fallen, is fallen."* The world will know that Babylon is the world capital proclaimed by the subjects of the One World Order. This probably suggests that the contest between the three major cities is in loud debate. The One World Church will call Rome the *"Eternal City,"* but the One

The Bible names the Gospel the "everlasting gospel." Calling it "everlasting" does two things. It is the one Gospel—the Gospel of Christ—and not some special message.

World Government will call Babylon the *"Eternal City."* At the very minimum the Jews will protest that Jerusalem is the *"Eternal City."* The storm is gathering between the factions of this unified One World crowd that call themselves the One World Order.

And the third angel followed them, saying with a loud voice, If any man worship the beast and his image, and receive his mark in his forehead, or in his hand, The same shall drink of the wine of the wrath of God, which is poured out without mixture into the cup of his indignation; and he shall be tormented with fire and brimstone in the presence of the holy angels, and in the presence of the Lamb: And the smoke of their torment ascendeth up for ever and ever: and they have no rest day nor night, who worship the beast and his image, and whosoever receiveth the mark of his name (Revelation 14:9-11).

This is the voice of the third angel in this fourteenth chapter. There will be four more for a total of seven. The Antichrist's kingdom is in high gear, and millions have joined his cause. Repentant Jews and Gentiles are being martyred. Fear is gripping the world like a raging storm. The mark is visible in every community, every business, and every newscast. Those with the mark will show their colors with pride and taunt those that try to hide.

The third angel, apparently also flying through the heavens, begins to warn the world of the worship and the mark of Satan. This mark is a lifestyle—it is a paradigm shift—and the world must know the truth of what they are receiving. The devil wants no false worshippers. Men are not encouraged to take it just to eat. It will be a baptism into Satanism of the darkest nature. The angel messenger proclaims a very clear message, "Take this mark and its eternal damnation." Neither Satan nor the Lamb will allow any turning back. The world does not want to hear about Hell and most ministers have removed it from their theology. This angel will leave no question.

> *Here is the patience of the saints: here are they that keep the commandments of God, and the faith of Jesus. And I heard a voice from heaven saying unto me, Write, Blessed are the dead which die in the Lord from henceforth: Yea, saith the Spirit, that they may rest from their labours; and their works do follow them* (Revelation 14:12-13).

There is no question that men and women are being converted to Christ, but it's a sacrifice unto death. It has always required much patience to be a faithful saint. Millions have been slain in brutal style, but the Antichrist will reinvent the horrors of brutality. The angel does not explain the kinds of death that men will endure, but he does glory in their obedience. To look at the suffering that even angels dare not describe, while showing the saints facing it patiently, is a delight.

The fourth angel—only called *"a voice from heaven"*—speaks and tells John to write. While John is instructed to write the whole book, this special instruction emphasizes his duty. The death of these martyrs is so remarkable that the message is, *"Blessed are the dead which die in the Lord."* Their sacrifice is the ultimate price because the death they face could not be more severe. The price of missing the Rapture is really beginning to show. There is a clear promise that their reward will be remarkable, because they count Christ worthy of whatever horrors and pain that Satan can inflicts.

> *And I looked, and behold a white cloud, and upon the cloud one sat like unto the Son of man, having on his head a golden crown, and in his hand a sharp sickle. And another angel came out of the temple, crying with a loud voice to him that sat on the cloud, Thrust in thy sickle, and reap: for the time is come for thee to reap; for the harvest of the earth is ripe. And he that sat on the cloud thrust in his sickle on the earth; and the earth was reaped* (Revelation 14:14-16).

This passage is preparatory for the coming war that we call the Battle of Armageddon. I call it a war because it will last weeks, if not months. The Son of God/Son of Man has been called a Lamb during the entire Tribulation period. This scene reveals the Lamb as the warrior, riding a cloud to descend upon the earth. The golden crown shows us that this describes Christ, as He will appear after the wedding feast and is now crowned Kings of Kings. The sickle in His hand shows great victory over the Antichrist as He reaps the closing harvest of wickedness. Heaven is rehearsing for the final victory of the Lamb of God and the Kings of Kings. The temple is open in heaven, and priestly angels that serve in the temple appear to be active as the end nears. All of the heavenly hosts know well that the Father has given the Son all power to judge and reconcile the earth. They appear both encouraged and excited that the Lamb is going to gain victory over all the wickedness of humankind. His second coming is with ten thousand times ten thousand of both angels and saints, *"And Enoch also, the seventh from Adam, prophesied of these, saying, Behold, the*

Lamb cometh with ten thousands of his saints, To execute judgment upon all, and to convince all that are ungodly among them of all their ungodly deeds which they have ungodly committed, and of all their hard speeches with ungodly sinners have spoken against him" (Jude 1:14-15).

Jesus spoke of this day and the triumph that will occur: *"Immediately after the tribulation of those days shall the sun be darkened, and the moon shall not give her light, and the stars shall fall from heaven, and the powers of the heavens shall be shaken: And then shall appear the sign of the Son of man in heaven: and then shall all the tribes of the earth mourn, and they shall see the Son of man coming in the clouds of heaven with power and great glory. And he shall send his angels with a great sound of a trumpet, and they shall gather together his elect from the four winds, from one end of heaven to the other"* (Matthew 24:29-31). The harmony of the entire Bible with the Book of Revelation is remarkable.

> *And he that sat on the cloud thrust in his sickle on the earth; and the earth was reaped. And another angel came out of the temple which is in heaven, he also having a sharp sickle. And another angel came out from the altar, which had power over fire; and cried with a loud cry to him that had the sharp sickle, saying, Thrust in thy sharp sickle, and gather the clusters of the vine of the earth; for her grapes are fully ripe. And the angel thrust in his sickle into the earth, and gathered the vine of the earth, and cast it into the great winepress of the wrath of God. And the winepress was trodden without the city, and blood came out of the winepress, even unto the horse bridles, by the space of a thousand and six hundred furlongs* (Revelation 14:16-20).

This is the awesome judgment of the living wicked. The White Throne Judgment is the time of the second death, when the wicked dead will be resurrected with a body that is fully alive and totally depraved, prepared to sustain the torment of the Lake of Fire for eternity. That judgment is after the one thousand year reign of Jesus Christ on earth. This judgment is for the living wicked who have taken the mark of the Beast and are Satan worshippers. This is the sixth angel in this chapter, and there will be no more. The fact of seven angels would suggest that the number of seven really is a greater number, seven being the type of the whole. These are angels prepared unto judgment, and it is biblically clear that such a time means a multitude of angels sharing in the triumph of righteousness over wickedness.

The seventh angel coming out from underneath the altar added great weight to this hour of exceeding wrath. All the burden of Christ's shed blood is upon that altar in the temple. It is total redemption, and connecting the altar with the angel and the sickle is awesome. This last half of the fourteenth chapter is not suggesting this judgment as already occurring but in preparation to occur. The fifteenth and sixteenth chapters actually bring this hour to fruition, but the process is in motion from the

All of the heavenly hosts know well that the Father has given the Son all power to judge and reconcile the earth.

temple in heaven to the scene on earth. The temple, which the angel comes out of, is the temple in heavenly Jerusalem, but the actual judgment is near earthly Jerusalem, where the great army of the Antichrist is planning its attack strategy.

This great battle will not be in Jerusalem but in Megiddo, north of the city. The Antichrist's army will stretch from the Sea of Galilee to the outskirts of the city. This Scripture suggests that very fact: *"And the winepress was trodden without the city."* The battle is clearly the battle of Armageddon, and the slaughter of this army will be spectacular. The army of the Antichrist suggests that he is beyond insanity in his fury and intends to obliterate the city that has so plagued his greatest dreams. Rome will have been destroyed at this time, and the Antichrist wants no competition for his capital of Babylon. Included with his love of Babylon will be his hatred of Israel. This is the battle in which he intends for Jerusalem to be no more.

Conclusion

The next chapter will bring us to the fullness of the rage of Antichrist and the judgment of Jesus Christ. There is great preparation by the beast to succeed, but the Son of God has already won the victory at Calvary.

THE SEVEN ANGELS OUT OF THE TEMPLE

The central court of God's kingdom—the most majestic place in the entire universe—is the temple of God in heavenly Jerusalem. As David suggested, there are many palaces in God's city. The temple, where God's throne and altar are located and where Christ sits at His right hand, is the most holy and grand. This temple has been given little attention in Scripture because the Bible focuses primarily on redemption. God's eternal glory and riches do not need defending because He exists in a realm outside the limits of our understanding.

This eternal temple is the central focus point of chapters fourteen, fifteen, and sixteen of Revelation. The last expressions of judgment to finish the seven years of Great Tribulation flow directly from this temple. This has never occurred, or if it did, it was not so stated. God's great angelic hosts have certainly been active and powerful forces when prior judgments occurred. We remember the angels that went into Sodom and Gomorrah, brought Lot out and then directed fire and brimstone on the city. These angels were mighty to judge, but they were never described as being temple angels or priestly angels. It is very clear in these three chapters that there are angels that serve in the temple of God. Such angels would have exceptional knowledge of the holiness and awesome purity of Jehovah, and now they are directing this last wrath.

I have personally come to believe that this is a distinct order of angels. They should be called the Melchizedek priesthood. There are clearly five orders of angels: Archangels, Cherubim, Seraphim, priestly angels, and servant angels. These seven angels that are seen in these chapters are of the order of priestly angels. Melchizedek was the high priest of their order and descended to minister to Abraham and to serve him communion in the prophetic assurance of the coming Christ. This order of the priesthood is higher in authority than the Levitical priesthood because it is a heavenly order. This is the reason why Jesus Christ was a priest after the order of the Melchizedek priesthood and not the order of the Levitical priesthood. *"For it is evident that our Lord sprang out of Juda; of which tribe Moses spake nothing concerning priesthood. And it is yet far more evident: for that after the similitude of Melchizedek there ariseth another priest, Who is made, not after the law of a carnal commandment, but after the power of an endless life. For he testifieth, Thou art a priest for ever after the order of Melchizedek"* (Hebrews 7:14-17).

God's eternal glory and riches do not need defending or even glorifying because He exists in a realm outside the limits of our understanding.

This heavenly temple is as superior to Solomon's temple as the city of the heavenly Jerusalem is superior to earthly Jerusalem. Solomon's temple was worth billions of dollars and was absolutely the richest temple or structure ever built. Yet it pales before God's temple. The New Jerusalem actually incorporates the temple and has been merged to become the home of the bride for eternity. The temple and New Jerusalem are now a part of each other. The priestly angels have performed their rites in this temple since they were created, a length of time that we have no means to measure. The overcomers—the elders that will become His army, His kings, and His priests—will soon be His Bride. As His Bride, we will be pillars in His eternal temple. *"Him that overcometh will I make a pillar in the temple of my God, and he shall go no more out: and I will write upon him the name of my God, and the name of the city of my God, which is new Jerusalem, which cometh down out of heaven from my God: and I will write upon him my new name"* (Revelation 3:12).

Establishing that the temple of the Heavenly Father is the center of this activity, elevates the proceeding to a superior level. This is not just tribulation, but this is the ultimate judgment time. This is a heavenly order that we are viewing, and it will occur exactly as described. The temple in heaven is where the eternal recordings are located of which our Bible is a perfect revelation. It is called the "tabernacle of the testimony" or the temple where the Bible, God's Testimony, "is preserved."

This heavenly temple is as superior to Solomon's temple as the city of Heavenly Jerusalem is superior to earthly Jerusalem.

> *And I saw another sign in heaven, great and marvellous, seven angels having the seven last plagues; for in them is filled up the wrath of God. And I saw as it were a sea of glass mingled with fire: and them that had gotten the victory over the beast, and over his image, and over his mark, and over the number of his name, stand on the sea of glass, having the harps of God* (Revelation 15:1-2).

These seven priestly angels, united together to begin the proceedings, are seen by John. It was an awesome display of power and authority. The attire of their priestly garments from this majestic temple—the very central location of the Father's throne and dwelling—were beyond description. John did not try to describe them. This is probably the same scene Paul said, *"It was not lawful to explain"* (2 Corinthians 12:4). Paul mentioned that this scene is reserved for the occasion that John is writing about and cannot be told until we view it on the day of fulfillment. It was God's rule of disclosure. Those temple angelic priests in their attire have never been seen except in John and Paul's revelations, but we will see them at the right moment.

They have in their possession *"the last plagues"* to fill up the wrath of God. Sin has done its damage beyond explanation. Human suffering because of sin is an incomprehensible mountain of sorrows. Every wrecked life, every broken home, every soul destined for the Lake of Fire, and every sorrow is contained in the winepress. It must be accounted for in the last expression of wrath. Even the sorrows of Christ's life and death, and His sacrifice to redeem will be accounted in those final acts of cleansing and purification.

The temple in heaven is where the eternal recordings are located of which our Bible is a perfect revelation.

Yet again, souls have repented. Desperate men and multitudes have gotten the victory over the devil and his beasts. These are additional Jews, another group separate from the one hundred and forty-four thousand. The one hundred and forty-four thousand were sealed and protected but these additional jews were saved and unprotected. They have paid the price of the Antichrist's wrath and have overcome by the blood of the Lamb. This Scripture named four forces of the Antichrist attack. *"The beast, his mark, his image, and his number"* are each listed as what these saints had defeated. To win against these powers certainly deserves God's wonderful attention.

And they sing the song of Moses the servant of God, and the song of the Lamb, saying, Great and marvellous are thy works, Lord God Almighty; just and true are thy ways, thou King of saints. Who shall not fear thee, O Lord, and glorify thy name? for thou only art holy: for all nations shall come and worship before thee; for thy judgments are made manifest (Revelation 15:3-4).

Their song clarified their identity as *"Born Again"* Jewish converts and clearly *"Born Again"* by the Blood of the Lamb. They sang both the song of Moses and the song of the Lamb. These saints are the fruit of the labors of the one hundred and forty-four thousand. Their witness to the Jewish world has had its effect, and a number worthy of mention in this book cannot be ignored. The Jewish people have proven by their history that when they set themselves to a task it will be finished. The devotion of this redeemed was such that the Antichrist and his powers could not defeat them. As they began to glorify the Lord and exalt His name, their love for Him shined.

Jewish worship has always been of this higher order. Their devotion to the truth during their First Testament was so pure that a Biblical scribe would destroy their work if they found an error. The name of God could never be fully spelled out; one letter was always left out. If they had to cease from their work, they would wash thoroughly before they returned. The temple was furnished with lavers to wash their hands and feet when entering to worship. This same level of devotion shows up in their words of praise. *"For thou art holy"* was more than words, but rather their sense of how truly majestic the Lord is. They knew that the day was near when their nation would be finally ready to honor the Lord as they had learned.

> *And after that I looked, and, behold, the temple of the tabernacle of the testimony in heaven was opened: And the seven angels came out of the temple, having the seven plagues, clothed in pure and white linen, and having their breasts girded with golden girdles* (Revelation 15:5-6).

When the Scripture says, *"Behold the temple of the tabernacle of the testimony in heaven was opened,"* there is so much more than open doors. Everything of God's majesty and holiness is suddenly in full view. Everything that He is—His glory behind the walls of this eternal temple that the human family has never seen—will progressively come into view. This is the beginning of the full revelation of God, His center of command, and the glory in whose presence the angels have worshiped. How to describe such splendor is beyond the knowledge and words of any human mind. This final judgment of the seven last plagues and vials of wrath is so wrought with the pure holiness of God that it will close the chapter of human sin.

It is hard to put into proper words a description of these angels of this priestly order, the order of Melchizedek. These seven angels are clearly clothed in the attire of priests. They are not simply priests, nor are they merely angels, but they are angels of a priestly order. They are clothed in pure white linen and have great plates of golden girdles. They are priests that have cared for God's eternal temple where worship is not a distant experience but a personal encounter with the Father Himself. The glory of these angels cannot be less than that of an archangel or Cherubim. Worship is their character. The unction of God is their function. To involve these angels in judgment is to lift judgment to the highest level. Their will be judicially perfect and there will be no appeal when they are involved.

> *And one of the four beasts gave unto the seven angels seven golden vials full of the wrath of God, who liveth for ever and ever. And the temple was filled with smoke from the glory of God, and from his power; and no man was able to enter into the temple, till the seven plagues of the seven angels were fulfilled* (Revelation 15:7-8).

Now the picture widens as one of the living creatures, a Cherubim, gets involved in the process. Cherubim are the keepers of holiness in the earth. These awesome angels know every act of rebellion or disobedience in this earthly realm, and their involvement with the seven angels should put this world on notice. These Cherubim possess the authority and powers to deal with sin, and they have prepared seven vials full of wrath to pass to these angels of the priestly order. Their business has been worship, but not that worship which will be blended with utter correction and retribution against the vileness that has invaded God's created world. The vials containing this correction are clearly establishing the highest level of righteous wrath. This is the level of pure wrath against the blasphemy of the Antichrist's kingdom.

Jewish worship has always been of this higher order. Their devotion to the truth during their First Testament was so pure that a Biblical scribe would destroy their work if they found an error.

The God they serve is not the god of this earth or the false god Satan, but the true God who *"liveth forever and ever."* These angels—both the cherubim and the priestly angels—have one purpose. They are directed to the coming kingdom of righteousness and the full preparation of this earth for that righteousness. They are servants of God, but they are also servants of the elders soon to be His Bride. The Bible informs us that angels stand in awe of the righteousness by faith and the everlasting gospel and desire to look "into" our redemption story. They must know that preparing this world for His righteous kingdom brings the day closer when it all will be an open book. Opening up the temple in heaven for the final drama is awesome news to these heavenly beings.

Conclusion

The progression from chapter six to this chapter has been truly awesome. When Jesus called it the *"Great Tribulation,"* He placed it on a level by itself. He said, *"For then shall be great tribulation, such as was not since the beginning of the world to this time, no, nor ever shall be. And except those days should be shortened, there should no flesh be saved: but for the elect's sake those days shall be shortened"* (Matthew 24:21-22). It is of such a day that the length of time must be cut short to preserve the earth from a total holocaust and obliteration. Sin will get its due reward and every unrepentant sinner will pay the price. This sixteenth chapter before us will finish the total cleansing of sin and all its consequence, and like a sunburst at midnight, the earth will spring forth into an eternal garden.

16

DRINKING THE VIAL OF GOD'S WRATH

It is fitting to believe that Satan was a temple priest or a priestly angel because his Biblical description was that of a musically talented creature. He was God's music-maker and probably His music-minister. A music-maker in heaven would certainly be associated with the Father's temple, and the worship in that temple would be to the Father.

Thus saith the Lord GOD; Thou sealest up the sum, full of wisdom, and perfect in beauty. Thou hast been in Eden the garden of God; every precious stone was thy covering, the sardius, topaz, and the diamond, the beryl, the onyx, and the jasper, the sapphire, the emerald, and the carbuncle, and gold: the workmanship of thy tabrets and of thy pipes was prepared in thee in the day that thou wast created. Thou art the anointed cherub that covereth; and I have set thee so: thou wast upon the holy mountain of God; thou hast walked up and down in the midst of the stones of fire. Thou wast perfect in thy ways from the day that thou wast created, till iniquity was found in thee. By the multitude of thy merchandise they have filled the midst of thee with violence, and thou hast sinned: therefore I will cast thee as profane out of the mountain of God: and I will destroy thee, O covering cherub, from the midst of the stones of fire (Ezekiel 28:12-16).

The fact that it is now angels from the heavenly temple that are ministering judgment makes this completely understandable. Now, the faithful angels that were not deceived by Satan have become God's angels to direct judgment on this false kingdom. Saints are going to judge the world and the fallen angels that tried to deceive us. The purpose of our Father is to employ those angels, who were attacked by Satan before he was cast out, to direct the source of judgment on Satan's earthly kingdom. God's judgment is always personal and direct.

This last period of the seven years is reserved for the judgment of the Antichrist kingdom. Those that have taken the *"Mark of the Beast"* are beyond the pale of repentance. Salvation is no longer an option to them. The seven vials of wrath, which are poured out by these angels, are only for the kingdom of the devil worshippers. This multitude has heard many witnesses of God's wrath and His wonderful Gospel. They heard the angels flying through the midst of heaven shouting out the everlasting Gospel. They knew it was for them. The one hundred and forty-four thousand Jewish witnesses have spread the truth far and near. The two prophets have performed miracles—true miracles—and Satan's own evil crowd could not kill them until they finished their prophecies. These Satan worshippers saw them die and lay in the street with decomposing bodies but also saw them resurrected and ascended to God. Even then, they would not repent; and now they cannot repent.

The cup of wrath is full. Those marked by the beast will have become so loyal to Satan and his kingdom that they can march to death for him with absolute sadistic joy. I have seen people so controlled by unclean spirits that they would destroy the righteous with delight. The deception in this story will be on a level never before experienced. Miracles will be freely performed for those marked by the Antichrist. They worship the devil, and the frenzy of their worship will be such an altered state that the human becomes divine-like on a dark, evil scale. Witchdoctors have walked in fire without the smell of smoke on their bodies. They can walk on sharp objects and never suffer injury. If Satan can empower a statue and cause fire to rain down from heaven, his miracle will be spectacular and convincing—although always dark and foreboding.

The entire earth, where those with the mark of the Antichrist dwell, will suffer the effect of these vials of wrath. Each and every sin must be accounted for, and the price of the sin must be required from the hands of wicked men. In a small way, that is already occurring. *"The way of transgressors is hard"* (Proverbs 13:15b). *"For they have sown the wind, and they shall reap the whirlwind"* (Hosea 8:7). There is no such thing as a happy sinner. They must cover every sin with

the faithful angels that were not deceived by Satan have become God's angels to direct judgment on this false kingdom.

another sin to survive. Now, total restitution is occurring on this entire globe. To worship the devil is to commit an abomination against God. Nobody has the created right to choose the devil. It is not a right, but it is a choice and it is insanity.

Blasphemy is the character or culture of those with the mark of the beast. It is not just a tattoo or a stamp, it is a nature, a character one receives from the devil. The number "666" has always been a toy to the wicked world. They are so enamored by it that they constantly play games with it. Book, movies, and all kinds of talismans are produced to try to laugh it all away. Their laughter becomes more insane the closer we get to the final hour. This crowd will laugh at it all until the fire and brimstone of the Lake of Fire drowns it out. They will not be laughing as they are falling into the flames. They are so blinded by the devil that only then will the reality of it become real to them.

And I heard a great voice out of the temple saying to the seven angels,
Go your ways, and pour out the vials of the wrath of God upon the
earth. And the first went, and poured out his vial upon the earth; and
there fell a noisome and grievous sore upon the men which had the
mark of the beast, and upon them which worshipped his image
(Revelation 16:1-2).

Notice that the great voice came out of the heavenly temple. The Son of God sits at the Father's right hand, and it will be His duty to speak. He speaks with a commanding voice, and the heavenly angels move instantly to obey. Jesus Christ is Lord of the Sabbath or Lord of hosts (Romans 9:29). At this point, the work is a swift action, and the whole universe immediately feels the effect. Wherever there is a Satan worshipper there will be a flood of results from each of the vials. The earth will reel and rock with sorrows. This time, it's the worshippers of Satan that suffer. The wicked have mocked the righteous and sought in every way to defeat them and even rejoice at their pain. It's always easy to identify the unrighteous even when they act religious. They have no conscience when they impose their ugliness on the righteous.

The first vial is *"noisome and grievous sores."* Noisome means a sore that is not just of the flesh but also something that affects the whole person. It's like leprosy or rabies that ravages the emotional being, and it is grief to every fiber of the body. We are speaking of pain that borders on insanity. Pain for which there is no cure or remedy. Devil worshippers have boasted of their love of Satan and treated truth with utter disgust. This judgment will finally cause them to see the depth of what Satanism really represents. These sores will mark every Satan worshipper. They will not be able to hide. Those that have refused the mark of the Antichrist will finally see Satan's folly for its real sorrows.

And the second angel poured out his vial upon the sea; and it became as the blood of a dead man: and every living soul died in the sea. And the third angel poured out his vial upon the rivers and fountains of waters; and they became blood (Revelation 16:3-4).

The blood of dead men or dead animals has always been a loathsome thing. To think of blood literally being poured out into every sea of the world, until there are no uncontaminated waters, appears impossible. Blood quickly becomes the source of disease and dreaded plagues. Everything in the sea dies, and both the surface of the waters and the shores become a place of horrible stench and death. Finding the necessity of sustaining life becomes dangerous and almost impossible. The population of scared, sick, and angry lives will only serve to multiply their sorrows.

This pouring out of blood on the sea will be followed in kind with the pouring out of blood upon every river, spring, and fountain of waters. They all begin to produce nothing but blood. Nothing is more necessary to life than water, and to be deprived of it is misery. This replacing of water with blood places life on the edge of total despair. Disease will literally wipe out millions in a very short time. Men will seek water in almost every possible place only to be taunted by the flow of blood that carries with it an odor of rotten flesh.

And I heard the angel of the waters say, Thou art righteous, O Lord, which art, and wast, and shalt be, because thou hast judged thus. For they have shed the blood of saints and prophets, and thou hast given them blood to drink; for they are worthy. And I heard another out of the altar say, Even so, Lord God Almighty, true and righteous are thy judgments (Revelation 16:5-7).

An angel begins to praise the Lord for His righteous judgment.

Nothing is truer about the holiness of God than that He will exact absolute righteous justice. The world has forgotten this truth. The God of love without justice has become a modern theme, but it is a musky love that only deceives and destroys. It has no kinship to the true holiness of God. Every soul will spend eternity in the joy or sorrow of his or her obedience or disobedience. The blood of the Lamb cleanses from sin but never covers sin. God's imputed righteousness transforms the soul. This angel is named the *"angel of the waters."* Every act of nature is the natural working of the God of the natural world. The Father and the Lamb direct the great host of angels, and the entire universe is sustained by their powers. Therefore, it is beautiful to speak of angels as part of His natural laws. This angel was certainly an active part of this transformation of the waters into blood.

There is a remembrance at this time of every saint and every prophet of God that this world has ever despised. Satan and the spirit of Antichrist have never ceased to attack, terrorize, and destroy every saint and prophet since Pentecost. Millions have been martyred and continue to die in many parts of our world. Most of today's ministers in rich nations are so complacent that suffering is unknown. During the time of God's wrath, the saint or servant of God that refuses to conform to the modern way will be tried and tested. After the Rapture, there will be no lasting safe place for those that repent and become His saints. This angel of the waters speaks volumes to these saints and prophets that have suffered so greatly. This should be encouraging to us to know that His angels are keeping record of every cross we bear.

Not only the angel of nature, but also the angels from the altar— priestly angels—know of the suffering of the saints. As the first angel speaks praise to God for His righteous vengeance on our behalf, another altar angel chimes in his excitement on the saints' behalf.

John said, *"I heard another* [angel] *out of the altar"* that was defending the righteousness of God acting in our behalf and for our defense.

> *"And the fourth angel poured out his vial upon the sun; and power was given unto him to scorch men with fire. And men were scorched with great heat, and blasphemed the name of God, which hath power over these plagues: and they repented not to give him glory"* (Revelation 16:8-9).

These angels out of the temple of God are certainly powerful angels. The earth and every element of nature respond to them as if these actions were a second nature. The truth is that nature was pure in creation, and not one action of the natural earth was harsh or destructive. Every earthly storm full of fury is the result of sin and the satanic influence on the universe. That was not so in the beginning. Now, the response of

The God of love without justice has become a modern theme, but it is a musky love that only deceives and destroys.

nature is a preparation for a total renewing and cleansing. The earth is groaning to be renewed, and the response to these angels is evident of that groaning for relief. Paul said to the Roman believers, *"Because the creature itself also shall be delivered from the bondage of corruption into the glorious liberty of the children of God"* (Romans 8:21).

This fourth angel pours his vial of wrath upon the sun. He had the power to change the natural habits of this awesome body, and the heat of the sun increases dramatically. It's clear that the sun takes on a personality of its own at the action of God's angel and treats the people of the earth according to their evil nature. The pain from the scorching of the sun only affects those that worship Satan and have taken the *"mark of the beast."* Men are literally scorched by the sun and begin to blaspheme God for their suffering. Being beyond repentance and greatly in love with Satan and his Antichrist, every act of the Father makes them even more vicious. They will not repent because they cannot repent. They are actually double doomed as the servant of Satan to suffer on earth and in the Lake of Fire.

> *And the fifth angel poured out his vial upon the seat of the beast; and his kingdom was full of darkness; and they gnawed their tongues for pain, And blasphemed the God of heaven because of their pains and their sores, and repented not of their deeds* (Revelation 16:10-11).

Once the city of Babylon is fully rebuilt and the Antichrist takes his government center to this ancient city, the population will explode. The most vicious of the Antichrist's central leadership will make this geographical area their home. By the time of this scriptural fulfillment, very close to the end of the seven years, Satans capital will certainly be located in Babylon. This vial of wrath will be directed to the seat of the beast. It cannot be any other city than this ancient rebuilt city where Nebuchanezzar ruled, Darius captured, Alexander the Great died, and where the Antichrist now reigns. God's wrath will thrust this entire region into a blackness and darkness that is worse than pain. The evil of Satan's literal presence, the anger of the Antichrist at the resistance of his One World Government, and the wrath of God makes this area a moral, spiritual, and emotional wilderness.

The city will become the center of blasphemy. Rallies and marches will keep the tension of military control at the highest possible level. Anger against the sovereign God will cause such an immoral baptism of filth that peace cannot exist. Without any degree of restraints, homosexuality, lesbianism, and all different forms of sexual conduct will be open in the street, in the parks, and in every order of life. When you take total chaos and thrust it into utter darkness, that chaos explodes. This darkness will include a total blackout of electricity and all power sources. The angel will simply speak, and all the electrical grids of the world will suddenly be shut off, putting the whole Antichrist kingdom into a blackout state. Their only response will be to blaspheme God.

> *And the sixth angel poured out his vial upon the great river Euphrates; and the water thereof was dried up, that the way of the kings of the east might be prepared. And I saw three unclean spirits like frogs come out of the mouth of the dragon, and out of the mouth of the beast, and out of the mouth of the false prophet. For they are the spirits of devils, working miracles, which go forth unto the kings of the earth and of the whole world, to gather them to the battle of that great day of God Almighty* (Revelation 16:12-14).

This angel's activities help confirm the activity of the previous angel. The Euphrates River flows right through southern Iraq near the city of Babylon. During Nebuchadnezzar's reign, it flowed in and out under the walls of the city. Very likely, the Antichrist will once again divert the river to flow through the heart of Babylon. The river will be a living source to the massive population that will live in Babylon at its peak. Suddenly, the river is dried up. The population will quickly become desperate, and rage will fill the city. With the darkness of the previous vial and the sudden desperate search for a solution to the water problem, the Antichrist must divert the attention of his subjects to avert an uprising.

The unholy trinity will probably declare an emergency and set their sights on Rome and Jerusalem and, with a charge of conspiracy, excite his kingdom for the coming battle against the Jews. Each member of the satanic trinity is said to produce a spirit ready to work miracles and convince the world to help eliminate Rome and

Jerusalem from the face of the earth. By this time the One World Religion has become an enemy to the Antichrist crowd. These spirits literally go out to the kings of the earth, working miracles, showing occult powers, and drawing the armies of the world to Armageddon. There is an apparent suggestion that they are actually targeting God Himself as they prepare for this battle.

> *Behold, I come as a thief. Blessed is he that watcheth, and keepeth his gar-ments, lest he walk naked, and they see his shame* (Revelation 16:15).

This is a beautiful statement that John inserts into the middle of this prophecy. No person living before the Rapture has to endure the hell that is coming on this earth. John's statement is a warning and an invitation. This was written for the benefit of readers and students of the Bible or anyone reading this Scripture and these comments. We must escape this coming darkness. Here is a warning to be ready. This statement is given for everyone who would believe during this time of Tribulation, and for us today. Because of the imminent return of Christ, we must be prepared by totally surrendering to Christ and putting on the clothes of His righteousness, which is the wedding garment.

> *And he gathered them together into a place called in the Hebrew tongue Armageddon. And the seventh angel poured out his vial into the air; and there came a great voice out of the temple of heaven, from the throne, saying, It is done. And there were voices, and thunders, and lightnings; and there was a great earthquake, such as was not since men were upon the earth, so mighty an earthquake, and so great. And the great city was divided into three parts, and the cities of the nations fell: and great Babylon came in remembrance before God, to give unto her the cup of the wine of the fierceness of his wrath. And every island fled away, and the mountains were not found. And there*

fell upon men a great hail out of heaven, every stone about the weight of a talent: and men blasphemed God because of the plague of the hail; for the plague thereof was exceeding great (Revelation 16:16-21).

The Battle of Armageddon is at hand. At this point, the armies of the world are gathering in northern Israel. The spirits from the unholy trinity are demonically inspiring the world for this fateful effort to destroy Jerusalem. They will have accused Israel and the Jews of many atrocities that they probably had nothing to do with. Jerusalem will be hated and constantly attacked for the entire second half of the seven years. When the image of the Antichrist was erected in their temple, he broke the covenant with the Jews. Since then, the Antichrist has slaughtered every Jew he could find or capture, who would not submit to worshipping Him as Messiah.

The seventh angel sets up the closing scene of this chapter. When his vial is poured forth into the air, a great voice from God's temple in heaven cries forth, *"It is done."* An earthquake, the greatest in the history of the earth, will occur. Babylon will be greatly affected with the city being divided into three parts. This earthquake is worldwide, and all the great cities of the world will be destroyed. It will be a worldwide calamity. No doubt there will be a financial collapse that has the world economy in shambles. Islands are said to disappear, which suggests great tsunamis from the worldwide upheaval. The text says, *"Every island fled away."* This event suggests that the earth's trauma from this earthquake will cause the mountains to disappear and the earth to return to its pre-flood condition. The Father is in control, and the calamities are actually restoration of the earth. While at the same time it means total destruction for the Antichrist kingdom.

God is remembering Babylon for all of her blasphemies, idolatries, and her hatred for His saints. Babylon gets the ultimate judgment, *"the fierceness of His wrath."* When the Antichrist leaves Babylon to fight in Megiddo, which the Bible calls Armageddon, Babylon will be lying in ruins. The Antichrist will be angry and vicious. He will be close to losing his mind in his final wrath. He will return to the city when he loses the Battle of Armageddon and will perish in the gates of the city. Micah prophesied this moment nearly three thousand years ago: *"And they shall waste the land of Assyria with the sword, and the land of Nimrod in the entrances thereof: thus shall he deliver us from the Assyrian, when he cometh into our land, and when he treadeth within our borders"* (Micah 5:6). We will see the destruction of this city in chapter eighteen.

Conclusion:

The final acts of these seven vials of judgment are hailstones raining down upon the Antichrist kingdom. The hailstones will kill anyone that is unprotected because of their enormous size and weight of one talent (75 pounds). The armies of the world will already be gathering in northern Israel and this hailstorm will be rained on the Antichrist worshippers wherever they are at that time. Houses will be crushed, cars and military vehicles will be destroyed, along with their occupants. What a final carnage of terror and sheer calamity to end the pouring out of the seventh vial of wrath on the Antichrist world. The seventeenth chapter is the story of the Antichrist and his One World Religion and its final destruction.

17

A RELIGIOUS SYSTEM SATAN LOVES

The unthinkable is at hand. God has become the final toy of the world's religious leaders. His name is no longer important. The only important thing is unity. To them the only unpardonable sin is to believe that the Bible is the infallible Word, and the only God to hate or reject is the God of the Bible. To finish the vision that the Lord Jesus Christ gave to John the Revelator, we must see this One World Religion as it helps empower Satan and the Antichrist for their evil part. In the book of Zechariah, we see three evil women representing the political, economic, and religious systems as they unite to deliver the world over to the Antichrist. Zechariah described his vision, *"Then lifted I up mine eyes, and looked, and, behold, there came out two women, and the wind was in their wings; for they had wings like the wings of a stork: and they lifted up the ephah* [The third woman is in the ephah] *between the earth and the heaven. Then said I to the angel that talked with me, whither do these bear the ephah? And he said unto me, To build it an house in the land of Shinar* [Babylon]*"* (Zechariah 5:9-11a).

The religious system described in Zechariah's prophecy is the One World Religion we read about in Revelation seventeen. The Holy Scripture has perfectly foretold of this One World Religion that would give credibility and power to the One World political system. This religious system or its primary leader is called a beast and/or a false prophet. Here is John the Revelator's first description. *"And I beheld another beast coming up out of the earth; and he had two horns*

225

like a lamb, and he spake as a dragon" (Revelation 13:11).

Several functions of this religious order are clearly described. Please note carefully how important these actions are in promoting this New World Political System or New World Order. The One World Religion has the same power and authority as the One World Political Order and is the authority that requires the people to worship the Antichrist. The head of this religious order will resurrect the

To finish the vision that the Lord Jesus Christ gave to John the Revelator, we must see this One World Religion as it helps empower Satan and the Antichrist for their evil part.

Antichrist after he is slain with a sword. This will be a kind of mimic of the resurrections of Jesus Christ. This religious giant will also have power to animate a statue of the Antichrist and cause the statue to speak and pronounce judgment. The New World Religious Order will be the force behind the mark of the Beast and will require all to receive this mark.

Since the mark of this Beast (666) is a religious mark identifying the person as a worshipper of the new godhood of Satan, no person can be redeemed or saved after receiving this mark. They are lost forever. *"And the beast was taken, and with him the false prophet that wrought miracles before him, with which he deceived them that had received the mark of the beast, and them that worshipped his image. These both were cast alive into a lake of fire burning with brimstone"* (Revelation 19:20).

This New World Religion is called *"The Great Whore."* The description of this false religion becomes even more graphic as the picture unfolds. It is called a beast or false prophet in the previous explanation. After receiving power from the Antichrist and great acceptance and worship from the world population, this New World Religion becomes a mammoth force, and is seen riding on a *"scarlet-coloured* beast, full of names of blasphemy" (Revelation 17:3). John gives us this vivid description.

> And there came one of the seven angels which had the seven vials, and talked with me, saying unto me, Come hither; I will shew unto thee the judgment of the great whore that sitteth upon many waters: With whom the kings of the earth have committed fornication, and the inhabitants of the earth have been made drunk with the wine of her fornication. So he carried me away in the spirit into the wilderness: and I saw a woman sit upon a scarlet coloured beast, full of names of blasphemy, having seven heads and ten horns. (Revelation 17:1-3).

Please note her characteristics and vileness. This religious whore is a great fornicator and is guilty of changing, twisting, and debauching the Word of God. God has pronounced judgment on anyone who adds to or subtracts from the Word of God. "For I testify unto every man that heareth the words of the prophecy of this book, If any man shall add unto these things, God shall add unto him the plagues that are written in this book: And if any man shall take away from the words of the book of this prophecy, God shall take away his part out of the book of life, and out of the holy city, and from the things which are written in this book" (Revelation 22:18-19). This is one of the ultimate sins already dominant in the church world. She is rich, but spends her riches on herself. She is proud and worldly and decks herself with costly jewels. She drinks from a golden cup, but its contents are vileness and abomination. She is also the mother of harlots, and all her offspring are as wicked as herself. There are many different religious ideas that unite with this mother of harlots. Her greatest hatred is for the true believers who hold to the Holy Bible and its infallible truths. She is drunk with the blood of murdered saints.

Nothing is as vile as religion that has lost its way and departed from purity and holiness. There have been many dark moments in the past when this has happened. Jesus came in a time when the Jewish religion was a botched form of greed and selfishness. He walked into the temple with a whip and drove out the temple-evangelists. The Reformation came after a thousand years of Madonna-worship, indulgences (buying sin-rights from the priest in advance), and distorted communion. Again, the Holy Spirit drove out the priest and the pope, and then the gospel was heard by millions. Even the Reformation leaders became almost as vile as the system they replaced. Very soon religion will be more vicious and vile than ever before, and multitudes will either worship a false god or will be tortured and slain. The Son of God will arrive on schedule to cleanse this earth of the last religious deception, and He will be installed as King, Prophet, and Priest.

This chapter must be seen as part of this entire seven years of the Great Tribulation. From chapter six to sixteen, this prophecy of a One World Religion overshadows and functions in the midst of all else that is occurring. In fact, this One World Religion is developing today and is practically ready for the seven years to begin. The Antichrist spirit is overspreading almost everything that is occurring and will be the tool of the Antichrist himself. The second beast in Revelation chapter thirteen is the mastermind of this religious system. Do not confuse this chapter with chapter eighteen. This chapter is about *"Mystery Babylon,"* or a religious form of Babylon, while chapter eighteen is about the literal city of Babylon, the physical capital of the Antichrist himself.

The main purpose of this chapter is to show the judgment of the false religious system (The Great Whore) that is serving the Antichrist. No description in this book is more direct and revealing than this woman and the beast she rides. The idea of every symbolic name in the Bible is to express the character of that person. The woman is the One World Religious system of every apostate or pagan religion united together. The ecumenical system of the World Council of Churches is preparing this whore/woman at the present. The term "woman" is the biblical type of religion.

This harlot system has induced the world into a false religious mindset. Instead of Godly saints that serve and honor the Father and Jesus Christ, this One World Religion has duped the world so far beneath truth, the infallible Bible, that it's all an apostasy. Apostasy means a religious idea that claims to be right but lives so far from right that there is no Biblical identity. Very simply, apostasy is the loss of Biblical identity and Biblical obedience. A person that does not live by the totality

Nothing is as vile as religion that has lost its way and departed from purity and holiness.

of Scripture, obeying all truth, does not have the right to claim Christianity. This One World System will go even further than that. It unites all religions, paganism, animalism, New Age, occultism, etc., into a single package and claims that all gods are actually part and the total of each other. It is the darkest religious order of human history. It is a whore, a debauched religious order.

The kings of the earth—rulers of the many levels of governments, dictators, or presidents—will all love this emerging system. The One World Order of religions will unite with this One World Order of government, and the two will support and unite the One World Order of the economy. All of them will be rich together for a brief period. This unity will fall apart, as it appears, because a rift will start over three major cities: Babylon, Rome, and Jerusalem. Other cities will likely be a part of this rift over prestige, wealth, and political advantages. They will all be drunk with lust, power, pleasure, and wealth. The world population will join both the love of money and pleasure and then the rift of cultural pride and political advantage.

This woman sits astride the political system identified with the exact order of the Antichrist kingdom. The religious order will combine many religious ideas from the different religions united together, and probably incorporate many new imaginations of religious concoctions. All of it will be blasphemous against God and the truth. The image of the Antichrist erected in the Jewish temple will certainly be to blaspheme the Bible, the infallible Word of God. This kind of deception is already happening in much of the church world.

> *And the woman was arrayed in purple and scarlet colour, and decked with gold and precious stones and pearls, having a golden cup in her hand full of abominations and filthiness of her fornication: And upon her forehead was a name written, MYSTERY, BABYLON THE GREAT, THE MOTHER OF HARLOTS AND ABOMINATIONS OF THE EARTH. And I saw the woman drunken with the blood of the saints, and with the blood of the martyrs of Jesus: and when I saw her, I wondered with great admiration* (Revelation 17:4-6).

The true faith of Christ will always be simply held, simply obeyed, and simply presented to the world. It's easy to see when religions go amuck. False religion must present itself in the flash and grandeur of the world to cover up its emptiness. When religion must dress its leaders in scarlet color and deck them with gold, you know they have lost the way. The Lord Jesus Christ left us the Biblical example of the Biblical faith. This New World Religion joined to the political pomp will always follow the wealth and the lifestyle of fornication and abominations. At this point, the religious leaders will be so wealthy that she will dazzle the carnal church world to her feet.

God hates religion that has lost its humility and simplicity. Religion that is all flesh, wholly given to building grand cathedrals, controlling the governments, and flashing its wealth is an abomination to God. God Himself calls this whore system, *"Mystery Babylon."* Why does He call it *"Mystery Babylon"*? Babylon is the seat of Satan, and *"Mystery Babylon"* is Satanism or Babylonianism dressed up in a mystery form to hide its true nature. When paganism can incorporate itself with Christian concepts and ideas, you have a mystery form of Babylon. The name *"Mystery Babylon"* is perfect in describing the emerging One World Church.

And she is drunk with her slaughter and hatred for the true saints of God. Millions of saints have been martyred since Pentecost in A.D. 33. God has always had a pilgrim church that is true and devoted to Holy Scripture as its one and only way. There has been some form of *"Mystery Babylon"* since the first century of the church world. At times, the slaughter of saints has been a catastrophe. No time in history will match what is about to happen. The seven years of Tribulation will witness this One World Church baptizing the world with the slaughter of Bible-believers. The entire crowd in Revelation chapter seven verses nine through seventeen was martyred by this religious Babylon. This One World Religion is drunk with the murder of anyone professing Biblical Christianity.

> *And the angel said unto me, Wherefore didst thou marvel? I will tell thee the mystery of the woman, and of the beast that carrieth her, which hath the seven heads and ten horns. The beast that thou sawest was, and is not; and shall ascend out of the bottomless pit, and go into perdition: and they that dwell on the earth shall wonder, whose names were not written in the book of life from the foundation of the world, when they behold the beast that was, and is not, and yet is. And here is the mind which hath wisdom. The seven heads are seven mountains, on which the woman sitteth. And there are seven*

kings: five are fallen, and one is, and the other is not yet come;
and when he cometh, he must continue a short space
(Revelation 17:7-10).

This woman is marvelous to behold. She is rich, powerful, and
universal. She holds sway over the whole earth and is an intimate
part of the Antichrist government. Her wealth, her power, and her
incredible religious facade create a picture of genuineness and great-

The true faith of Christ will always
be simply held, simply obeyed, and
simply presented to the world.

ness. Any person that has an air
of being religious will love this
developing system. John is fasci-
nated by this whore of religion
"with great admiration." The angel
now rebukes him for being so undiscerning. John only saw the outward sight and not the inward deceit and destruction, and that's
often how people look on the religious façade that fills our world
already.

John is allowed to hear the mystery of this woman, both for him
and the true church. She is a mystery, as the spirit of iniquity has
always been a mystery. No one will ever truly understand Satan's
scheme without spiritual discernment, which most of the world does
not have. Wickedness in religion is the worst kind of wickedness and
the most impossible to understand. This woman is the most deceived
form of religion ever witnessed. In this picture, the beast she rides
reveals more about her than all else. This beast is the Antichrist government that is busy uniting the world as seen in Revelation chapter
thirteen. Governments have been deceived in giving full power to this
final form of human government. This woman and her One World
Church are helping the Beast create the One World Government. Both
the woman and the Beast are using each other to their own benefit.

This Beast is a great demon spirit, a fallen angel that had been assigned into the bottomless pit but now possesses the *"Man of Sin,"* the Antichrist. Again, we have reference to the deadly wound the Beast received but had been miraculously healed in order that he may deceive the world. The angel reminds John that this Beast will go into perdition at the close of this seven-year period. The scene of this miraculous recovery will be so spectacular that the world which has not been converted and sealed will be instantly deceived and will glorify this great religious person and event.

The angel gives us a bird's eye view of one geographical tidbit to help us discern. *"The seven heads are seven mountains on which the woman sitteth."* It's agonizing to read Catholic materials and see the fear they have of an Antichrist taking control of the church. Bible-believers that adhere only to Scripture see the presence of the Antichrist all the way back hundreds of years. It is correct to say that discerning Catholics and discerning believers see the same prophecy occurring shortly. The city of Rome will be a focal point of the coming One World Church and will be united with the government of this world with even stronger ties than presently in force.

History is replete with great governments that have ruled the known world. This Scripture speaks of five governments, before the Roman government, that ruled as John was receiving this vision. Rome was the sixth, and one more is the beast upon which this woman is riding. Anyone that knows history should recognize this prophecy and vision and then know that the Book of Revelation is a masterpiece, not just of end-times prophecy, but also of history or, better stated, His-story.

> And the beast that was, and is not, even he is the eighth, and is
> of the seven, and goeth into perdition. And the ten horns which
> thou sawest are ten kings, which have received no kingdom as
> yet; but receive power as kings one hour with the beast. These
> have one mind, and shall give their power and strength unto

the beast. These shall make war with the Lamb, and the Lamb shall overcome them: for he is Lord of lords, and King of kings: and they that are with him are called, and chosen, and faithful (Revelation 17:11-14).

The configuration of the coming One World Government system has been described in different ways. I do not believe anyone can perfectly pre-form the governments, as they will fulfill these verses. It will be the revival of the ancient Roman system, especially the eastern configuration, but lines will be crossed. The Antichrist comes out of the Assyrian people, but they are scattered over several eastern countries. The seventh and eighth are connected. Maybe this is because the seventh is killed and resurrected. When he is resurrected, he will be possessed by the spirit from the bottomless pit and will be a living beast of a man.

All the governments are now ready to give complete power to the Antichrist. Each of them will be given certain rights and positions of power and will have their moment in the sun. They are now uniting themselves, and the object of their unity is rejection of the Lamb of God. They will have developed a hatred for God the Father and God the Lamb, and this world will unite to establish the one loved "woman," the harlot church. There will be a readiness to march and destroy Jerusalem because this city will have become intimately connected to Jesus Christ, the Lamb of God.

And he saith unto me, The waters which thou sawest, where the whore sitteth, are peoples, and multitudes, and nations, and tongues. And the ten horns which thou sawest upon the beast, these shall hate the whore, and shall make her desolate and naked, and shall eat her flesh, and burn her with fire. For God hath put in their hearts to fulfill his will, and to agree, and give their kingdom unto the beast, until the words of God shall be fulfilled. And the woman which thou sawest is that great city, which reigneth over the kings of the earth (Revelation 17:15-18).

Once the world is united with the Beast, it will appear that he is close to his ultimate dream. The angel clearly said that the world population is committed to him: *"The waters which thou sawest, where the whore sitteth, are peoples, and multitudes, and nations, and tongues."* But something happens that causes the One World Order to hate the One World Church. We can do nothing but speculate what may cause this sudden split. I believe Babylon will declare itself The Eternal City, which Rome has long ago declared for herself. The woman rides the beast and the beast uses her until she is no longer needed. The Antichrist hates Jerusalem, but the False Prophet loves Jerusalem. Now, the rift over the three cities must be settled.

Before this army is prepared to attack Jerusalem, the Antichrist and his government decide to destroy Rome. The Antichrist strips the world church of her glory and her wealth, and sets a torch to Rome and burns the city to the ground. Sages within the Catholic system have prophesied that this will occur. One prophet, now labeled a saint, sets the very next pope as the occupant of that city when it will be burned.

Conclusion

The perfect Revelation of God cannot but fill our heart with rejoicing. False religion has plagued the world. Any system that creates its own theology or that builds a wall with a part of truth cannot stand the test of time in doing God's business. The pilgrims and the pilgrim church have been hated and chased to death but have continued until this hour. Now, we see that religion that unites itself apart from infallible truth will finally be destroyed by the very powers they promoted and served. God will actually use the Antichrist army to destroy the false church illustrated by the whore woman. She is the perfect illustration of what God thinks about religions that have left the Bible behind.

THE LAST HOORAH OF BABYLON

Jerusalem and Babylon are often named in the Bible. These two cities are totally opposite from each other. One is the city of our God, the Creator and Sovereign, and the other has been Satan's capital since the book of Genesis. Satan is the father of lies, and his first lie was, and his last lie will be centered around his chosen capital. Babylon is where Satan began his thrust to win the hearts of men, and he will finish his reign as the god of this world in that same city. The Bible is too precise and too perfect to consider anything different.

Mystery Babylon of chapter seventeen is Babylon's religious counterpart. Satan himself engineered the moving of his religious system in literal Babylon to the chief city of mystery Babylon (Rome). It was a clever move, and the center of religion in Rome allowed Babylon to fade from the radar. For hundreds of years strange mysteries of a religious nature have flowed almost continually out of Rome. At the same time a cloud of evil has hung over Babylon. Evil spirits have come and gone from this mystery center, while her counterpart, Rome, has sought to fill the world with her doctrines. Most Bible scholars have forgotten the place that this wicked city of literal Babylon holds in Biblical truth. It must be revived and rebuilt for Satan's Antichrist so that God can vent righteous wrath upon the seat of Satan.

The war in Iraq has allowed this city to become available for her future role in God's finished work of judgment. Today, millions of dollars are being appropriated to restore the city. The government and the province of Al Hillah, where Babylon is located, are already talking of tourism and expansion as they plan Babylon's future. Officials at the United Nations have talked of moving their headquarters to Baghdad or Babylon. Such talk would have been unthinkable before the removal of Saddam Hussein. The country of Iraq, the very center where the Garden of Eden was located and where Adam and Eve were placed and died, is presently the center of the world's attention. To even think that this is an accident would be careless.

Babylon will become the capital of the Antichrist and his One World Order. The name Babylon is the genesis of Satan's earthly kingdom. Evil men have spoken of this city with great interest. Nebuchadnezzar built his capital there and made it one of the great wonders of the world.

> Babylon will become the capital of the Antichrist and his One World Order.

Alexander the Great fought his way to the city, capturing every kingdom he passed, and died in the city itself. In 1997, the Rolling Stones named their last album, "Bridges to Babylon." Babylon is a fitting namesake to rock and roll music. This city is slowly etching its name into the human mindset. It will soon leap its way into the hearts of the multitude.

To talk about prophecy without mentioning the name of Babylon is impossible. To talk about Jerusalem without naming Babylon is like the positive of an electrical current without the negative of conductivity. God will judge the source, and Babylon is the world's source of all vile human government, education, and religion. Every basic language structure on this earth was imparted to that multitude building the Tower of Babel. It is only after that city is judged that God will restore a perfect single language to all mankind. God's plan is perfect, the Bible has revealed it, and the Lamb will finish it in perfect redemption of this earth. Before the earth can be recreated in holiness, every source and expression of sin must be perfectly judged.

> *And after these things I saw another angel come down from heaven, having great power; and the earth was lightened with his glory. And he cried mightily with a strong voice, saying, Babylon the great is fallen, is fallen, and is become the habitation of devils, and the hold of every foul spirit, and a cage of every unclean and hateful bird. For all nations have drunk of the wine of the wrath of her fornication, and the kings of the earth have committed fornication with her, and the merchants of the earth are waxed rich through the abundance of her delicacies* (Revelation 18:1-3).

For a city to be heralded for its greatness—as we find in this chapter—it must have a breathtaking past, a beautiful history, and be an exceptionally great city in the coming events of end-time prophecy. To take the Book of Revelation literally you must take the city of Babylon literally. Mystery Babylon is made a type by the use of the word *"mystery"* (Revelation 17:5). The word *"mystery"* does not appear in this chapter. This chapter also changes scenes from chapter seventeen. We have already seen Mystery Babylon burned, so this city must be different. Chapter seventeen deals exclusively with religion, and this chapter deals exclusively with merchandise and the fornication of lust for things and wealth. The Antichrist will build his kingdom with the lust of things and pleasure.

Time wise, this entire chapter is synonymous with the seven years we have seen in the two different views since chapter six. The period of the Great Tribulation is the timeframe for this total picture of prophetic events. We must keep laying each aspect of this period on top of the seven-year period. It is like a multiple story building with each floor laid over the previous floor. All events are occurring either partially or fully over the same time period. The Antichrist will establish his kingdom in Babylon at the beginning of the seven years and most of what he does will be announced from within this wicked city.

We hear the angel's announcement of Babylon's destruction at the beginning of this chapter because the Father and the Lamb have had it prophetically planned since the day Nimrod formed the city for Satan. When the devil is part of an operation, its failure is already guaranteed. The city has been nothing but a source of hatred and rebellion against God from its foundation. Evil spirits have ascended and descended to these earthly staging grounds and even into the bottomless pit from where a multitude of them were loosed in chapter nine. The city has been filled with foul spirits and unclean creatures since the beginning.

Every evil idea had its beginning in Babylon. I have studied the names of gods and goddesses and there is none that cannot be traced back to their genesis in Babylon. Inanna and Isis of Babylon became the multiple goddesses of history. Indeed, all nations have drunk of her fornications and idolatries. Governmental systems that seek to contain, harness, and control the lives of people have all had their beginning in Babylon. Education by the elitists to create a controlling upper class of people was founded in Babylon. The world has drunk deeply of the culture of lust from the spirit of this ancient city, and this has become the spirit of the present world.

And I heard another voice from heaven, saying, Come out of her, my people, that ye be not partakers of her sins, and that ye receive not of her plagues. For her sins have reached unto heaven, and God hath remembered her iniquities. Reward her even as she rewarded you, and double unto her double according to her works: in the cup which she hath filled fill to her double (Revelation 18:4-6).

The cry from the mighty angel of the Lord is both for us today and a warning for the world's population of those coming seven years. Babylon is the ultimate picture of worldliness when it reaches its peak of deception. Worldliness has been the enemy of righteousness since the first sin in the Garden of Eden. We are constantly warned of the power of the world to destroy faith. You cannot love the Lord and love the world at the same time. The fornication of Babylon is not just sexual sins but rather the drunkenness of being captured by the world's lust and desires. When this mighty angel said, *"Come out of her my people, that you be not partakers of her sins,"* he was calling us from living for this world unto holy living—living for the things of the Lord.

When the devil is part of an operation, its failure is already guaranteed.

In his epistle to the saints, the same John that received this great revelation wrote, *"Love not the world, neither the things that are in the world. If any man love the world, the love of the Father is not in him. For all that is in the world, the lust of the flesh, and the lust of the eyes, and the pride of life, is not of the Father, but is of the world. And the world passeth away, and the lust thereof: but he that doeth the will of God abideth for ever"* (1 John 2:15-17). He was the perfect apostle to speak those words because he had heard this warning from the Lord. He knew what the spirit of Babylon and its lust for the world was sure to do to those captured by its powers. This angel warned that anyone caught up in this worldly bondage was also going to receive of her plagues. This chapter documents those plagues, and every saint must take heed.

Babylon—the seat of Satan—is the Biblical type of living for the things of the world and becoming deceived by its occult indulgences.

This revelation story is the final look at what Babylon has accomplished since her origin in southern Iraq in the valley first known as Sumer. Her sins have never failed to capture multitudes. Now, they have reached into heaven and God says, "It is enough." Nothing escapes the knowledge of God and His hosts. Every sin is recorded, and no sin can escape unless the blood of Jesus has washed it away. The Father's recording angels are perfect, and all human actions are recorded. This is also true of the spirit world as it is of the human world. Every deed of the fallen angels is carefully recorded, and they will be judged.

The judgment of Babylon is a double judgment. The spirits of the world have hated the saints who have refused their influences. Millions have been persecuted, often to death. Others have had their lives pursued like animals, often killed by the most vicious methods. Babylon has always hated the saints of God. During these dark years, she will increase her hatred and will attack with fury. But God has it all recorded. Soon, the city of Babylon and all who have loved her, supported her, and did her bidding will share her sorrows. She, and all of hers, will experience a double judgment, double of everything she has measured out to others.

> *How much she hath glorified herself, and lived deliciously, so much torment and sorrow give her: for she saith in her heart, I sit a queen, and am no widow, and shall see no sorrow. Therefore shall her plagues come in one day, death, and mourning, and famine; and she shall be utterly burned with fire: for strong is the Lord God who judgeth her. And the kings of the earth, who have committed fornication and lived deliciously with her, shall bewail her, and lament for her, when they shall see the smoke of her burning, Standing afar off for the fear of her torment, saying, Alas, alas, that great city Babylon, that mighty city! for in one hour is thy judgment come (Revelation 18:7-10).*

The world of Babylon—including all of her children for the millenniums of her years of influence—has always been proud, haughty, and arrogant. These verses describe her perfectly. All of her adherents have indeed acted as queens, believing that they are at the top of the heap and not much is under them. Because of her pride, her destruction will come like a storm. The whole of Babylon and her world will be judged in such a whirlwind that she will have no escape. She will suddenly see how irrational all of her wisdom has been.

The mighty men of the earth who have grown wealthy by her trades will suddenly see it all begin to crumble. The worldly crowd loves the world and all its expressions of worldly living because it represents wealth and prestige to them. When it suddenly starts the downward spiral, their wealth will vanish. A man worth billions will become

Nothing escapes the knowledge of God and His hosts. Every sin is recorded, and no sin can escape unless the blood of Jesus has washed it away.

a pauper in a matter of hours as the stock market crashes. When Babylon starts her free fall, every city in the world will experience the exact same decline. Economic disasters of the past will pale by significance. This is not a national crisis but a world crisis. It will be apparent that there will be no recovery.

And the merchants of the earth shall weep and mourn over her; for no man buyeth their merchandise any more: The merchandise of gold, and silver, and precious stones, and of pearls, and fine linen, and purple, and silk, and scarlet, and all thyine wood, and all manner vessels of ivory, and all manner vessels of most precious wood, and of brass, and iron, and marble, And cinnamon, and odours, and ointments, and frankincense, and wine, and oil, and fine flour, and wheat, and beasts, and sheep, and horses, and chariots, and slaves, and souls of men. And the fruits that thy soul lusted after are departed from thee, and all things which were dainty and goodly are departed from thee, and thou shalt find them no more at all. The merchants of these things, which were made rich by her, shall stand afar off for the fear of her torment, weeping and wailing, And saying, Alas, alas, that great city, that was clothed in fine linen, and purple, and scarlet, and decked with gold, and precious stones, and pearls! For in one hour so great riches is come to nought. And every shipmaster, and all the company in ships, and sailors, and as many as trade by sea, stood afar off (Revelation 18:11-17).

This picture of material destruction is almost beyond words. Wealth and pleasure are the twin companions of Babylon, and all of her world of lust and satisfaction. Take away a lost man's wealth, and those things that are pleasurable to him and he has nothing. The world does not live in the things that are eternal so when wealth and pleasure are gone, they become empty souls. No wonder this angel adds the *"souls of men"* to its list of merchandise that Babylon trades. The world always steals the soul in its process of deception. The reason a wealthy person, who has suddenly lost it all, goes berserk is that the soul had already been forgotten in the race for wealth. Blessed is the person that sees this truth before it is too late.

Watching this crowd standing afar off, as Babylon and her cities of the world burn, is a perfect picture of regrets. Wealth is the most slippery possession in this universe. It can vanish in a night or in one fleeting accident. Trying to comprehend how so much wealth and pleasure suddenly goes up in smoke is a stretch. Connected to this disaster is the ransacking of Rome and the torching of the world church. The Antichrist—as a tool of Satan—shares the same tendency toward viciousness and self-destruction. God's hand of judgment is supernaturally involved, but I also believe the devil and his cohorts will be prone to terrible vengeance on all who stir their anger. In one hour of catastrophe the world slips into an irrecoverable collapse.

> *And cried when they saw the smoke of her burning, saying, What city is like unto this great city! And they cast dust on their heads, and cried, weeping and wailing, saying, Alas, alas, that great city, wherein were made rich all that had ships in the sea by reason of her costliness! for in one hour is she made desolate. Rejoice over her, thou heaven, and ye holy apostles and prophets; for God hath avenged you on her* (Revelation 18:18-20).

At the peak of the Antichrist's kingdom, Babylon will be the most glorious city of human history. United to every major hub of the world via satellite, Internet, and all modern communication, it will appear a world of propriety has been born unparalleled. Conferences of major corporations will occur by the link of technology, and billions of dollars will slip between banks and corporate headquarters. Men and women will have the ability to make millions, even billions, daily. Sexual pleasures will be exchanged like smiles. But suddenly, billionaires cannot buy hamburgers. They will weep with the multitude as the entire economy explodes and cities are burning like trash piles. *"Weeping and wailing,"* they will cry for the return of such glory.

But God has His saints who have escaped to His presence, and the angel calls for their rejoicing. *"Rejoice over her, thou heaven, and ye holy apostles and prophets,"* says the angel. The saints, prophets, and the apostles begin to fill the heavens with praise. The great wealth of heaven that will soon descend down upon this earth causes all the destruction occurring to be no more than refuse. Those saints and prophets have suffered much waiting, watching, and enduring of the hatred of the false wealth and false pleasures, knowing it was but insatiable lust. This world looks beautiful only to those whose eyes have never seen the promises of the Lord. The great crowd of saints will rejoice as Babylon burns.

The angel declares that Babylon and her world system will be no more. The very geography of Babylon will be cursed and given over to destruction and the Lake of Fire. The angel will declare that music will never again be heard in Babylon because its music was the devil's false and deceiving lyrics.

> *And a mighty angel took up a stone like a great millstone, and cast it into the sea, saying, Thus with violence shall that great city Babylon be thrown down, and shall be found no more at all. And the voice of harpers, and musicians, and of pipers, and trumpeters, shall be heard no more at all in thee; and no craftsman, of whatsoever craft he be, shall be found any more in thee; and the sound of a millstone shall be heard no more at all in thee; And the light of a candle shall shine no more at all in thee; and the voice of the bridegroom and of the bride shall be heard no more at all in thee: for thy merchants were the great men of the earth; for by thy sorceries were all nations deceived. And in her was found the blood of prophets, and of saints, and of all that were slain upon the earth* (Revelation 18:21-24).

The end of the world system of greed and control is finished. The elite of all human plans has paid the price of selfishness and rebellion. Daniel prophesied of this hour as perfectly as possible. *"Thou sawest till that a stone was cut out without hands, which smote the image upon his feet that were of iron and clay, and brake them to pieces. Then was the iron, the clay, the brass, the silver, and the gold, broken to pieces together, and became like the chaff of the summer threshingfloors; and the wind carried them away, that no place was found for them: and the stone that smote the image became a great mountain, and filled the whole earth"* (Daniel 2:34-35). It is amazing that

Nebuchadnezzar—the great dictator of Babylon—is the very man that dreamed the dream that Daniel interpreted. God has never given the devil anything but time. Now, his time is finished.

Conclusion

The mystique of Babylon has never failed to capture the entertainers, the liberal educators, and the greedy dictators. It has always represented the worst of human nature. Satan made it his capital, with Nimrod as his servant. The culture of this city, most often unrecognized by the supporters, has possessed the great majority of the human family. God's kingdom cannot appear until Babylon disappears. This city is one city, but its influence is worldwide and that power to capture will end as the final Antichrist is judged and assigned to the Lake of Fire. As the final judgment arrives, a multitude, along with the beast, his companion beast, and the devil will be judged together for eternity.

A WEDDING YOU CANNOT AFFORD TO MISS

At this point, the Antichrist kingdom is in ruins. Babylon is burning with fire, and the headquarters of the One World Religion has been destroyed. The Antichrist is seething with hatred, and his false trinity is using the last ounce of their powers to gather an army for a last-ditch stand. The chosen location is Megiddo in northern Israel, and Jerusalem is bracing for an all-out war. The Jews who have not been killed have retaken Jerusalem and are preparing for the greatest battle of their existence. The army of the Antichrist is massive and Israel knows they will either be victorious or the ancient city will be no more. The massacre of the smaller cities in northern Israel has already cost many Israeli lives. The whole area stretching into Lebanon, Syria, and Jordan is an incredible war camp and nobody gives Israel an ounce of hope. the odds are hundreds-to-one in favor of this army of beasts.

While this is happening on earth, in heaven, the elders, the saints redeemed during the tribulation years, Jewish believers of the one hundred forty-four thousand, and their converts, the host of angels, Cherubim, the great God and His Son, are all preparing for a wedding in the sky.

All judgments are complete except those that will occur when the Son of God descends with His army of the redeemed. Before that army leaves heaven, the Son of God must take His Bride unto Himself and prepare for His Millennial reign on planet Earth. The

Son of God is the Eternal Creator, and when He descends He will revolutionize this universe with righteousness and the very nature of God. Planet earth will quickly become a garden of rare beauty and prosperous to the fullness intended in creation.

As heaven prepares for the wedding of all eternity, rejoicing turns God's city into a holy celebration. The banquet is being prepared, flowers fill every nook and corner, angels busy themselves with the banquet meal, and others set the table with spotless care and expensive ware. This transpires while the Bride waits in perfect peace. Multitudes of Cherubim and Seraphim are worshipping the Father and the Lamb. They are filling all heaven with their music. The Bride in waiting has her own song and music echoes across the towering walls of this heavenly city. The redeemed Jews also have their unique song and their singing is like the echo of angels as they celebrate their love for a Messiah so long rejected.

Satan's trinity is well connected to the spirit realm and they know what is happening in the heavens. This dark threesome is in continuous troubling conversation with their generals and commanders. The army is massive, but they are a very disturbed multitude. They can be united only by occultic deceptions and constant debates made horrendous by the many language barriers. Hatred for every living Jew and any semblance of Biblical Christianity is the one power and idea that holds back total revolt. They are one in purpose only because the condition of the present Antichrist kingdom is chaos, and there is nothing else to dream about but war on Jerusalem.

Before Christ's army leaves the heavenly city, the wedding of Christ and His Bride will transpire. The Psalmist David was given a peep into this royal ceremony. First, he spoke of this coming King

Messiah and declared Him with a glorious sense of His lofty stature. Here is his description of our future Groom, *"My heart is inditing a good matter: I speak of the things which I have made touching the king: my tongue is the pen of a ready writer. Thou art fairer than the children of men: grace is poured into thy lips: therefore God hath blessed thee for ever. Gird thy sword upon thy thigh, O most mighty, with thy glory and thy majesty. And in thy majesty ride prosperously because of truth and meekness and righteousness; and thy right hand shall teach thee terrible things. Thine arrows are sharp in the heart of the king's enemies; whereby the people fall under thee. Thy throne, O God, is for ever and ever: the sceptre of thy kingdom is a right sceptre"* (Psalm 45:1-6).

David's description of the throne and the kingdom of Christ is too high to even consider and causes me to marvel at our Father's gift. Jesus Christ is very God—already a King—and grace pours from His life. He is majestic in humility, mighty in battle, and truth is the essence of His person. He came from a throne and is destined to return to a throne with everlasting victory in His right hand. He will be the Bride's everlasting companion in a spiritual union where marriage is but a shadow.

David's description of the Bride is awesome. She is not the product of a mixed multitude. The present church world treats the Bride like she is a loose knit bunch of church members that make it in by the skin of their teeth. The great voices of the past church world adhered to strict Biblical interpretation and saw a very different truth. The brideship of Christ must be seen as a coveted promise for those willing to forsake all and follow Christ. David clearly shows the distinction between the Bride or Queen and the guests at the wedding. *"Kings' daughters were among thy honourable women: upon thy right hand did stand the queen in gold of Ophir. Hearken, O daughter, and consider, and incline thine ear; forget also thine own people, and thy father's house; So shall the king greatly desire thy beauty: for he is thy Lord; and worship thou him. And the daughter of Tyre shall be there with a gift; even the rich among the people shall intreat thy favour. The king's daughter is all glorious within: her clothing is of wrought gold. She shall be brought unto the king in raiment of needlework: the virgins her companions that follow her shall be brought unto thee. With gladness and rejoicing shall they be brought: they shall enter into the king's palace"* (Psalm 45:9-15).

These words are written in a complex manner, but carefully show this Queen dressed in the extravagant gold of Ophir. She stands forth among the virgins, the daughter of Tyre with her gift, and the multiple kings' daughters. This special Bride and Queen is dressed and prepared in raiment of needlework to be brought unto the King Himself. Not only is she attired in raiment of needlework, but also she is all-glorious within. Twice it was declared that her clothing is of wrought gold. All of this beauty is a work of grace and redemption that the King Himself wrought for her when He stepped out of eternity to enter the winepress of wrath as our sacrifice for sin. What a picture of the Bride shortly to be celebrated in the banquet hall of the heavenly city of Jerusalem, God's mountain of holiness on the sides of the north.

And after these things I heard a great voice of much people in heaven, saying, Alleluia; Salvation, and glory, and honour, and power, unto the Lord our God: For true and righteous are his judgments: for he hath judged the great whore, which did corrupt the earth with her fornication, and hath avenged the blood of his servants at her hand. And again they said, Alleluia. And her smoke rose up for ever and ever. And the four and twenty elders and the four beasts fell down and worshipped God that sat on the throne, saying, Amen; Alleluia (Revelation 19:1-4).

The judgment of this *"Great Whore"* of a One World Religion takes front page as this chapter unfolds. Nothing in human history has done more damage and nothing is more assuredly the tool of Satan than false religion. It's practically impossible to debate the world's problems with a critic without them speaking of the damage religion has caused, and they are right. But, in every case the damage is the work of some false expression of religion, never the real church and Biblical truth. Satan, being religious himself, has always clothed his dark deeds in some religious garb for maximum damage. The Book of Revelation clearly shows that the Father and the Lamb hate a religious mixture and any form of a false church.

Jesus Christ is very God—already a King—and grace pours from His life. He is majestic in humility, mighty in battle, and truth is the essence of His person. He came from a throne and is destined to return to a throne with everlasting victory in His right hand. He will be the Bride's everlasting companion in a spiritual union where marriage is but a shadow.

Revelation chapter nineteen is a triumphant chapter and begins with the destruction of the false religious orders united into one massive religious whore. It is amazing to see how the religious world was allowed, even directed by the Lord, to create this great system representing all false systems into one, so the Lamb could pour His wrath on them in total destruction. The blood of millions of the true saints is avenged in one great moment. Every organization that is guilty of defying truth, that has fought genuine saints, and has caused harm or martyrdom will be brought into this whoredom and will be destroyed.

Alleluia and praise is heard from the twenty-four elders that first appeared before God's throne at the Rapture in chapter four. They are joined by the living creatures, cherubim, because this is the church's triumph of the ages. Nothing has been such a pain as the tares growing among the wheat. The saints are rejoicing because the fires of judgment have cleansed the world of false religion that has been described as the opium of the people. Cherubim join this celebration because their mission has always been to protect holiness and defend the earth. They have borne the great challenge of judging the false and protecting the real, and they have had no rest. They join the saints, now elders, as cause for great rejoicing has filled God's universe.

> *And a voice came out of the throne, saying, Praise our God, all ye his servants, and ye that fear him, both small and great. And I heard as it were the voice of a great multitude, and as the voice of many waters, and as the voice of mighty thunderings, saying, Alleluia: for the Lord God omnipotent reigneth. Let us be glad and rejoice, and give honour to him: for the marriage of the Lamb is come, and his wife hath made herself ready* (Revelation 19:5-7).

The call for celebration comes directly from the Throne of God. The Father and the Lamb have been at the very center of every event in this Book. Every voice from an angel, an elder, or Cherubim had support and direction from the throne. The great happenings of judgment or redemption were never accidents or some momentary decision, but a course in prophecy set by the Creator in ages past. The whole design of this book flows out of the previous sixty-five books of the Bible, and this is a culmination of them all. It's God's Masterpiece of end-time events and all is on schedule. The Father had planned His day for His Son to be united with His Bride and the time is here in this text. A voice calls out, *"Praise our God, all ye his servants."*

All of creation begins to praise the Lord. Thunderings now become praise instead of the voice of a storm. These sounds begin the rejoicing because the false religion is judged and the true religion triumphs.

The false bride married to Antichrist has to be divorced, because her marriage was an act of fornication, the love of flesh, and it has ended in God's purge of uncleanness. The result of this purge has prepared the way for the royal marriage of God's Son to His chosen Bride. God's Son has always been the joy of heaven and the praise of all righteousness. For the time of this celebration to begin, He fills the heavenly sphere with exceeding joy. The Father was the Master Giver that sacrificed His own Son that this day could be possible. The words most fitting from the Heavenly Hosts are *"the Lord God omnipotent reigneth."*

Then the voice from out of the Throne speaks again, *"Let us be glad and rejoice, and give honour to him: for the marriage of the Lamb is come."* From the Revelation of the glorified Christ in chapter one, every event and occurrence in this book has been directed towards this wedding and the wedding company's destination in the city prepared as a *"Bride adorned for her husband."* The wedding and the city of New Jerusalem is the crowning joy of this book and indeed of the entire Bible. The Father's plan for His Son is the final honor for His sacrifice of redemption. The Bride for His Son is the highest honor for the saints that give a total surrender of themselves to the Kingdom of God. The proclamation, "the Marriage of the Lamb," is one of the Father's grandest revelations in Holy Scripture. It was in His heart when He placed the first man and woman in the garden.

> *And to her was granted that she should be arrayed in fine linen, clean and white: for the fine linen is the righteousness of saints. And he saith unto me, Write, Blessed are they which are called unto the marriage supper of the Lamb. And he saith unto me, These are the true sayings of God. And I fell at his feet to worship him. And he said unto me, See thou do it not: I am thy fellowservant, and of thy brethren that have the testimony of Jesus: worship God: for the testimony of Jesus is the spirit of prophecy* (Revelation 19:8-10).

The relationship of this Bride to the Lord Jesus Christ is what the Father intended for all mankind. We were created to be His intimate family, to live in a splendor that every king has labored to create. Fellowship between God and man was ordained to give Him pleasure and great joy, and for a short time, He and Adam walked together in the great expanse of gardens and prosperity. Daily, as the afternoon began to merge with the evening, the Father would step down from His eternal city and meet Adam and Eve in the splendor of their surroundings. The singing and laughter was no doubt the joy of angels and cherubim alike. Darkness fell when man sinned, and God spoke of another day when the intruder would be finished and truth would prevail. This wedding is the day that God spoke of in the shadows of Adam's failure.

The Bride *"hath made herself ready."* No wonder the Bible says, *"For many are called, but few are chosen"* (Matthew 22:14). This Bride is the chosen out of all church history, both the First Covenant and the Second. They gave themselves totally, they were the overcomers, and their reward is the highest honor of human history. This voice out of the throne spoke to John and said, *"Blessed are they which are called unto the Marriage Supper of the Lamb"* (Revelation 19:9). This company will be made up of martyrs that laid down their life with joy: prophets and pastors, elders, and elect ladies. These are the souls that have clearly paid the price of their cross, forsaken all to follow Jesus, and never complained that their cross was too heavy. These saints will be pillars in His temple. As citizens of New Jerusalem, they will eat of the tree of life in the midst of the paradise of God. They will wear crowns, sit on thrones, eat the hidden manna, have a new name, possess the Morning Star, and hear the Son confess their name to the Father. They are royal sons and daughters, the Bride of the Lamb.

The Bible could well have given us many more details about this wedding, but the event is so royal that its language was never meant for the ears of carnal men. The elder that gave John the message of the wedding was quick to stop John from worshipping him. God chose an elder to speak of this wedding because it is an affair of Christ and redeemed men. Angels were not allowed to talk of this special time for Him and His saints. The elder said to John, *"I am thy fellowservant, and of thy brethren that have the testimony of Jesus: worship God: for the testimony of Jesus is the spirit of prophecy"* (Revelation 19:10b).

> *And I saw heaven opened, and behold a white horse; and he that sat upon him was called Faithful and True, and in righteousness he doth judge and make war. His eyes were as a flame of fire, and on his head were many crowns; and he had a name written, that no man knew, but he himself. And he was clothed with a vesture dipped in blood: and his name is called The Word of God. And the armies which were in heaven followed him upon white horses, clothed in fine linen, white and clean* (Revelation 19:11-14).

The Lamb has received His Bride, and the earth must become their redeemed possession. The army in heaven includes all His saints: every redeemed soul, the elders of chapter four, the Tribulation saints of chapter seven, the one hundred and forty-four thousand of His Jewish kin and their converts of chapters fourteen and fifteen, and the two witnesses of chapter eleven. The Antichrist's army is as prepared as the Antichrist crowd can obtain. The Lamb must lay aside the appearance of death and take up the office of the *"Word of God."* The *"Word of God"* rides a white stallion and His army rides white horses with Him.

This is the Battle of Armageddon. Every title that has prepared Christ for this great moment rides with Him on His white stallion. He is *"Faithful and True."* It is righteousness alone that He comes to establish. The judgments of this descent of Christ are to establish the purity of the Father on this earth. Almost all wars have been the result of the anger, vindictiveness, and lust of mankind; but this is a holy war to cleanse the earth of the last vestige of carnal men and their carnal pursuits. The armies of the Antichrist were slain on the battlefield of Armageddon, but their politicians, their supportive trainees, and those that handle the logistics of shipping the war machinery must be dealt with in the countries of the world. This army that rides with the Son of God will be fully prepared to take possession of the earth for the great victor that rides the white stallion.

His appearance is the rendering of all He will represent as King of Kings over all God's created world. We saw Him as a Lamb slain during the entire seven years of tribulation, but now the new appearance must match the new challenge. He is coming to perfect a world, transforming it from human government to divine government. The omniscient, all-knowing, all wisdom, revelation of the eternal Son of God is breathtaking. He is wearing the crown of all crowns—the final crown of all kingdoms—because He alone will rule the world in righteousness. He has a name that is His final name—the total of all His names—because He is the Son of man perfected, and the Son of God accepted by the entire universe.

While His glory is that expression of total triumph over all the results of sin and redemption, He will still bear the remembrance of sin. His vesture, a small part of His matchless robe, is dipped in blood. Eternity, though high and exalted above all the pains of sin and rebellion, will forever remember His sacrifice. Coupled with the vesture dipped in blood is His name, the *"Word of God."* One God-man, Jesus Christ, is the eternal manifestation of the Father's spoken Word as well as the fullness of His sacrifice.

His army is fully ready and armed with His authority. This is the first time in Revelation that His saints are called His army. They became His elders when they were raptured. They are His Bride at this moment of descent to the earth, but will not be called such until after the Millennium. They must serve as His army, then as His kings and priests, and then they will enter the nuptial city to celebrate eternity and begin their reign as His chosen Bride, basking in His glorious city and His glorious presence forever.

> *And out of his mouth goeth a sharp sword, that with it he should smite the nations: and he shall rule them with a rod of iron: and he treadeth the winepress of the fierceness and wrath of Almighty God. And he hath on his vesture and on his thigh a name written, KING OF KINGS, AND LORD OF LORDS* (Revelation 19:15-16).

This expression of the Word of God as a sword proceeding from His lips is heaven's best rendering of the infallible Bible. All judgment—every act of divine reckoning—must proceed from the Word. The Holy Bible contains the exact words of the Son of God, who is the Word Incarnate. You cannot separate the Word of God in its written form from the Word of God in person. When this world gets this manifestation of the Lamb of God made up of the Word of God—descending and revealing—the entire universe will bend, bow, and surrender to His mastery. This Word becomes a rod as it proceeds from His mouth and the rule and reign of this earth yields tenderly into His hands. The Word is a fury towards sin, and a shepherd's rod towards a yielding populace of the earth's redeemed. The Word has entered the winepress and flows out of the winepress as righteousness to rule the world. The Word is fury to the wicked, but joy to the righteous.

The vesture dipped in blood is inscribed with words of His majesty. The strength of a man is in His thigh and the Son of God is the ultimate Son of Man. Both His vesture and His thigh are inscribed with the words, "King of Kings and Lord of Lords." Every glory that has been manifest of the Son of God comes to be revealed as He descends to finish the Antichrist's kingdom and to establish God's kingdom on earth. There can be no failure or mistakes. Every name of authority is now perfected in one great person as God ordained. The Son of God is returning to earth, this time to conquer in righteousness.

> *And I saw an angel standing in the sun; and he cried with a loud voice, saying to all the fowls that fly in the midst of heaven, Come and gather yourselves together unto the supper of the great God; That ye may eat the flesh of kings, and the flesh of captains, and the flesh of mighty men, and the flesh of horses, and of them that sit on them, and the flesh of all men, both free and bond, both small and great. And I saw the beast, and the kings of the earth, and their armies, gathered together to make war against him that sat on the horse, and against his army. And the beast was taken, and with him the false prophet that wrought miracles before him, with which he deceived them that had received the mark of the beast, and them that worshipped his image. These both were cast alive into a lake of fire burning with brimstone. And the remnant were slain with the sword of him that sat upon the horse, which sword proceeded out of his mouth: and all the fowls were filled with their flesh* (Revelation 19:17-21).

It's all over except for the clean up. The first act after He descends is for an angel to call for the fowls of the air to gather together to devour the flesh of this slaughtered army of deceived and angry worshippers of Satan. The angel calls the fowls to *"the supper of the great God."* God is so very patient, but when the axe falls it will be final. Even during these seven years of the Great Tribulation, men have had invitation after invitation to repent. Nobody will go to hell but those that deserve to go to hell. The mercy of God will guarantee this fact.

I marvel at an army so blatant that they can look up at the heavens that are filled with saintly warriors led by the Eternal Son and still propose to fight. They saw Him and His great redeemed hosts and sent out the call, "Fight them, fight them." Surely, He will laugh at their ignorance before He speaks the final words. To consider such a scene is almost like heaven itself. The history of the war on God reads like a novel. If it could be called fiction, those that know God and His Word could easily understand it. But Satan is real, and his war against God is real, but it will end at the prophesied moment when Satan passes his last God's appointed privilege. The Father has always been in control. He is Sovereign.

Conclusion

The Beast of the Antichrist is taken, captured with his false prophet and all that are not slain by the sword. This whole Antichrist crowd is seen in this closing moment as worshippers, but worshippers of a masquerade under Satan's total mastery. The two beasts go straight to the Lake of Fire while his multitude of deceived followers are killed. They will be confined in hell until the resurrection of damnation and the White Throne Judgment.

The victory is complete. The earth is now ready to be blessed with the Millennial Kingdom. Sin and sorrow, pain and death, will give vent to the blessings of the Creator. Christ and His kings and priests will rule the natural people that have survived. The earth is going to explode in its creative wonders without the curse to impede its beauty. The Millennial Kingdom will be grand.

WHEN THE BOOKS ARE OPENED

The twentieth chapter of the Book of Revelation is full of the prophetic future. There are at least three movements of great significance in these fifteen verses. Each one is a major part of end-time events. Casting the devil into the bottomless pit where he is chained for one thousand years begins the peaceful and prosperous time of the coming Millennium. The final or complete finishing of the First Resurrection is of special importance. The company of kings and priests that will reign with Christ during this great period will be complete. No one, for which this time is planned, will be missing. Finally, the judgment of the wicked will close out the Millennium period and leave only New Jerusalem to enter earth's immediate sphere and inaugurate the eternal Brideship of Christ.

Of all the twenty-two chapters in Revelation, none places a more infallible guarantee on the authenticity of this book. Hell and the Lake of Fire were prepared for the devil and his angels. *"Then shall he say also unto them on the left hand, Depart from me, ye cursed, into everlasting fire, prepared for the devil and his angels"* (Matthew 25:41). Denying Satan's role in the world and its coming judgment would be to accuse God of being the source of all rebellion and wickedness. The presence of evil is everywhere and this chapter shows us its final demise. The very term "White Throne Judgment"—where the wicked will be judged—is etched in the minds of all Christendom. On the bright side, every Christian theology in the world testifies to the coming great resurrection of the saintly dead. Here is its grandest picture. In one chapter of this masterpiece is proof positive that the Book of Revelation must be reckoned with by all Bible-believers. This great book belongs at the completion of Holy Scripture. Do not doubt it. Read it and believe it!

The great Battle of Armageddon that occurred in the closing verses of chapter nineteen brings Israel—both as a nation and the individual Jewish person—into the middle of these two chapters. We know that this book was written and sent to the New Testament church, but we were warned to never forget the Jewish people. When Jesus Christ rides His white stallion into Jerusalem, He does so to the worship and praise of the entire Jewish world. They have seen His defense of Jerusalem when the Antichrist army was poised to march on the city. The one hundred and forty-four thousand Jews sealed out of the twelve tribes have been effective in proclaiming Jesus Christ as Messiah. The two prophets certainly accomplished their intent by proclaiming the Lord and His commandments. All Israel is saved, born again, the very day that the Lord arrives in the ancient city and the capital of Israel.

Both the First and Second Testaments confirm this marvelous Day of Triumph. Zechariah proclaimed, *"And I will pour upon the house of David, and upon the inhabitants of Jerusalem, the spirit of grace and of supplications: and they shall look upon me whom they have pierced, and they shall mourn for him, as one mourneth for his only son, and shall be in bitterness for him, as one that is in bitterness for his firstborn"* (Zechariah 12:10). They will see His scars and cry to Him, *"What are these wounds in thine hands? Then he shall answer, those with which I was wounded in the house of my friends"* (Zechariah 13:6b). The Apostle Paul was a diehard in his love and defense of Israel's future hope. He said, *"And so all Israel shall be saved: as it is written, There shall come out of Sion the Deliverer, and shall turn away ungodliness from Jacob"* (Romans 11:26). The City of

Jerusalem will become the capital of the Millennium kingdom, and the world's wealth will enrich the city beyond present understanding. This city is the one and only earthly city that can be called the "Eternal City."

The Bible is a Book of Books, and it talks about other books that are significant to God's total plan. The sixty-six books in the Bible are a perfect whole, with each book playing a very important part. The books united represent God's covenant with man. The First Testament is His covenant with Israel, as God the Father provided a temporary sacrifice while His entire universe waited for the day of His Son. The New Testament is the completed sacrifice, and His plan for the future. This masterpiece of Revelation is the comprehensive finality to all prophecies in both Testaments. It is perfectly chronological and ends exactly as the Father and His Son have planned. This chapter is the link between the seven years of the Great Tribulation and the New Jerusalem revealed in the last two chapters.

There is a central book called *"The Lamb's Book of Life."* It is the recorded list of the names of every redeemed saint. Nothing but the blood, the Lamb's blood, can merit a name to be written in this book. The Church of Sardis was promised that all overcomers would not have their names removed from the Lamb's Book of Life. *"He that overcometh, the same shall be clothed in white raiment; and I will not blot out his name out of the book of life, but I will confess his name before my Father, and before his angels"* (Revelation 3:5).

Even after the Rapture, the Blood of Christ will be redeeming repentant souls, and names will be written in this book. As the Beast of Antichrist is revealed, those that repent and have their names written in this book will be able to resist the Antichrist and refuse his mark. *"And all that dwell upon the earth shall worship him* (Antichrist), *whose names are not written in the book of life of the Lamb slain from the foundation of the world"* (Revelation 13:8). This book will be opened at the White Throne Judgment of the wicked. It appears that the Father will always make a final search in this book before a soul is cast into the Lake of Fire.

Another group of books appear in the Holy Bible. They are called the Books of Records of all our deeds. We see these books in this chapter. *"And the books were opened: and another book was opened, which is the book of life: and the dead were judged out of those things which were written in the books, according to their works"* (Revelation 20:12). We have no idea how many of these books there are, but they contain every deed, every work, every sin or righteous act committed by every living soul of all human history. The only acts of men not in these books are sins

The Bible is a Book of Books, and it talks about other books that are significant to God's total plan. The sixty-six books in the Bible are a perfect whole, with each book playing a very important part. The books united represent God's covenant with man.

that the blood of Jesus Christ has washed away. The saints will be rewarded for every good work on their record. The wicked will be rewarded with judgment for every sin in these books. Nothing can change one thing recorded, but the blood of the Son of God. Once your sins have been blotted out, those sins can never be recorded again. Even God has no memory of them: *"For thou hast cast all my sins behind thy back"* (Isaiah 38:17).

One more book is found in the Word of God that demands mention. It is called the *"Book of Remembrance."* It is mentioned in a lively passage from the Book of Malachi. *"Then they that feared the LORD spake often one to another: and the LORD hearkened, and heard it, and a book of remembrance was written before him for them that feared the LORD, and that thought upon his name"* (Malachi 3:16). The rest of this passage created a context for the understanding of this particular book. It is a First Testament reference to the Rapture and to the return of the saints to reign on the earth as kings and priests during the Millennium. This book is God's record being kept in the past, present, and right on into the future until the Rapture of the saints in chapter four of Revelation. These are His rapture-ready saints over whom His angels keep a constant watch and record. Those written in this book are His jewels, His future bride.

And I saw an angel come down from heaven, having the key of the bottomless pit and a great chain in his hand. And he laid hold on the dragon, that old serpent, which is the Devil, and Satan, and bound him a thousand years, And cast him into the bottomless pit, and shut him up, and set a seal upon him, that he should deceive the nations no more, till the thousand years should be fulfilled: and after that he must be loosed a little season (Revelation 20:1-3).

Before Christ suffered on the Cross and won the eternal victory, angels often came to each other's rescue when they were in battle against the devil or his unclean spirits. One angel stood toe to toe with the Prince of Persia and could not prevail until a second angel broke the stronghold. *"But the prince of the kingdom of Persia withstood me one and twenty days: but, lo, Michael, one of the chief princes, came to help me; and I remained there with the kings of Persia"* (Daniel 10:13). After Calvary, *"all power in heaven and in earth"* was assigned to the victorious Conqueror. This angel that descends to take hold of the devil himself, and to take him down into the bottomless pit is fully capable of the task. It has been millenniums since Lucifer was cast out of heaven, and began his reign in the midair. Now it is time for him to be chained and to taste his own defeat.

It is no wonder that Satan hates the Book of Revelation so intently. Little is said concerning Satan in the sixty-five books of the

Bible before we get to this masterpiece. From the Garden of Eden in Genesis to the book of Jude, he is always in the background working his dark deeds. The Bible is about redemption, so Satan is viewed as the foe. This great book fully exposes his character, his witty style, and his insane blasphemy. Fully exposed, Satan will now pay the price of his masquerade. This text uses every key name that represents his character. He is the dragon, the old serpent, the devil, and Satan. He has stood in the presence of the Father and the Son. He was originally created for their glory, but he rebelled. Because of his created glory, he has fought long and hard. Now he is bound and delivered into the pit under hell in the darkest and most painful spot in the realm of Sheol.

There will be no more deception for one thousand years. Then, there will be a short release for Satan. After that short span of time, Satan will be cast into the Lake of Fire. The King of Kings and His appointed saints will now govern the nations, where prosperity will abound and *"the plowman shall overtake the reaper"* (Amos 9:13).

> *And I saw thrones, and they sat upon them, and judgment was given unto them: and I saw the souls of them that were beheaded for the witness of Jesus, and for the word of God, and which had not worshipped the beast, neither his image, neither had received his mark upon their foreheads, or in their hands; and they lived and reigned with Christ a thousand years. But the rest of the dead lived not again until the thousand years were finished. This is the first resurrection. Blessed and holy is he that hath part in the first resurrection: on such the second death hath no power, but they shall be priests of God and of Christ, and shall reign with him a thousand years* (Revelation 20:4-6).

Immediately, the government of the world falls unto the King of Kings, and authority to govern in righteousness is fully established.

John said, *"And I saw thrones and those that sat upon them."* The state-ment here about the *"thrones"* refers back to chapter nineteen, verse fourteen and chapter twenty, verse four. Let's read these two verses together; *"And the armies which were in heaven followed him upon white horses, clothed in fine linen, white and clean." "And I saw thrones, and they sat upon them, and judgment was given unto them"* (Revelation 19:14, 20:4a). Clearly, the army of saints that descended with Him occupies these thrones. The Bible is full of promises that the saints will inher-it the earth, and that we will rule the kingdoms of the earth with our great Lord and King, Jesus Christ.

Carefully read verse four. The word *"they"* in the first part of this verse is the army of saints that were previously caught up to Him and His throne, and were present at the Marriage Supper of the Lamb, either as the Bride or guests of His Bride or the Groom, and are ready, as glorified saints, to reign with Him. They are an awesome company, fully united with the Word of God and King of Kings, and there is not a selfish thought in one heart among them. It is an army under His banner, and they are ready to rule a redeemed world, and set up a kingdom of righteousness. The world will become a garden.

But another company of saints suddenly joins the great army that descended with the Son of God. John said, *"And I saw the souls of them that were beheaded for the witness of Jesus, and for the word of God, and which had not worshipped the beast, neither his image, neither had received his mark upon their foreheads, or in their hands; and they lived and reigned with Christ a thousand years."* This group of victorious saints has not previ-ously appeared in this great book. They came through, either part or all of the seven years of the Antichrist's reign of terror. They could not have been the Tribulation saints of chapter seven or the Jewish saints of chapters fourteen and fifteen. This company paid the ulti-mate price and withstood the darkest time in human history. Now, they are seen resurrected and ready to join the army of saints and to *"reign with Him a thousand years."* They were all beheaded or martyred because they rejected the Antichrist and his mark, his worship, and his image.

The rest of the dead must wait until the end of the great Millennium reign without their resurrection or participation. John specifically states that this is the completion of the "First Resurrection." We watched as *"elders were seated on thrones"* in chapter four after the Pre-Tribulation Rapture up to heaven. We saw a company of Tribulation saints in chapter seven. We saw two witnesses ascend to heaven in chapter eleven, one hundred and forty-four thousand Jews in chapter fourteen, and a remnant of Jews in chapter fifteen. Now, we see another remnant just before the one thousand years of Christ's reign begins. This completes the First Resurrection.

A great blessing and honor is declared for every one of His saints that are a part of this First Resurrection. Their rewards will be different, but He gives them exactly the reward they have earned in their use of the talents and privileges. The saints of God will be held accountable to Him, the Lord of the church, and His records of our lives will include every action, attitude, and deed we have performed in His name or failed to perform because of indifference, disobedience, or laziness. It is beyond my imagination to grasp the extent of this coming day of rewards and celebrations. We are talking about millions of saints and the entire redeemed earth setting up a kingdom fit for the Great Son of God, and the Sovereign of this whole earth. The wealth of the earth will be totally the property of this great company of His glorified family.

There will be no crashes of the stock markets and no storms on the seas. The earth's curse will be lifted and all the animals will be peaceful pets. Lying and stealing is finished, and there will be no locks on doors or gates of this world. *"Nothing will hurt or destroy"* and perfect peace will reign in every heart. The lion and lamb will sleep together, and the nations will learn war no more. It's the Millennium of Jesus Christ and it will last one thousand years.

And when the thousand years are expired, Satan shall be loosed out of his prison, And shall go out to deceive the nations which are in the four quarters of the earth, Gog and Magog, to gather them together to battle: the number of whom is as the sand of the sea. And they went up on the breadth of the earth, and compassed the camp of the saints about, and the beloved city: and fire came down from God out of heaven, and devoured them. And the devil that deceived them was cast into the lake of fire and brimstone, where the beast and the false prophet are, and shall be tormented day and night for ever and ever (Revelation 20:7-1).

The natural people that survived the Seven Year Tribulation will reproduce great families. During the thousand years of blessing, they have never known temptation by Satan, and they will be given an opportunity to choose. Satan will be loosed for a short season and unredeemed hearts will yield to his lies and deception. The only possible way to understand this choice by the multitude is the old nature of self and sin. When you give unredeemed men an intriguing chance to do their own thing, seldom do they turn it down. Above all else, the self-nature is the sin nature. The greatest of sins is not to lie or cheat but to be selfish and self-centered. All sin begins with self, and that's all Satan needs to win a host of otherwise blessed people.

He deceived a great number identified as *"the sand of the sea,"* and they attacked the saints of God, and Jerusalem determined to take the reigns of government. Without question, it will be the power of wealth and control that Satan will use as his approach of deception. The saints will be totally in charge of government and the world's wealth during this Millennium. Although all will be blessed and prosperous, the unredeemed will serve them. This is the seed that Satan uses to gain their attention. We presently call it "class warfare." A lot of money only serves to make unspiritual people hungry for more. They attack the city of Jerusalem, and the Father acts to stop their insanity. Fire descends from heaven to destroy this great army of greedy and selfish souls.

Satan is taken, and this time he will be cast into the Lake of Fire. His Antichrist and religious false prophet are already there. He joins them to be tormented day and night forever and ever. Every character of evil that wicked men or angels possess will be the character of their resurrected bodies or entities in the case of angels forever. A brute beast will be full of hatred and will seethe in that hatred for eternity. The unclean will long to satisfy the urge of that uncleanness. The sexually perverted will be consumed with lust every moment forever.

And I saw a great white throne, and him that sat on it, from whose face the earth and the heaven fled away; and there was found no place for them. And I saw the dead, small and great, stand before God; and the books were opened: and another book was opened, which is the book of life: and the dead were judged out of those things which were written in the books, according to their works. And the sea gave up the dead which were in it; and death and hell delivered up the dead which were in them: and they were judged every man according to their works. And death and hell were cast into the lake of fire. This is the second death. And whosoever was not found written in the book of life was cast into the lake of fire (Revelation 20:11-15).

Between the one thousand year reign of our Lord and all of His saints and the descent of New Jerusalem and eternity will be this *"White Throne Judgment"* of the wicked. The wicked dead that have slept from the earliest death in Sumer or southern Iraq to the end of the Millennium reign must be judged. There will be death during the Millennium among natural people, and they must be judged. This *"White Throne Judgment"* is the last and final judgment of all the wicked and will be the last judgment for all eternity. This is an awesome event because the darkest characters of human history will be there. Millions have festered in their wrath and filth in hell fire. These souls have suffered an endless hell, and, now, they are resurrected to add darkness upon darkness. With damnable bodies united with their souls, they must be judged.

The dead, small and great, the great fearless dictators, the powerful kings and queens, along with the poor, wretched subjects of the great will be standing together on equal footing. Suddenly, the wealth of the rich has no bearing. Famous men and women will stand without applause. The glory of God in His holiness will be so awesome that even the earth and heaven stand back to let Him, the Great Jehovah God, be the absolute center of attention. The least sin will feel like the weight of the world. Conscience will strike terror in hearts of men as they tremble in guilt. Standing back or moving away from His presence will be impossible.

The books of works will cause every soul to search their whole life like a flash. Hidden sins will no longer be hidden. Angels will begin to name every soul and then read the list of sins that have never been exposed. Each sin will bear a penalty and the culmination of sins will leave souls hopeless for escape. The words missing on this day will be words proclaimed by the righteous and known to almost every soul that has lived. Mercy, forgiveness, grace, and redemption will be words of the past as death, sorrow, pain and a sense of being lost rules the day. Even when the sin debt is almost unknown, the search for the names in the Book of Life will still leave no hope. No one will be sadder than the moral and upright in life who have failed or refused to trust Christ for salvation. The good will perish right along with the worst.

The angels of God will discover every living soul. The sea will not be able to hide those consumed in its depth. Whether by fire or by other forms of death, the soul of man is like a falcon that when released cannot escape. Some think that to be cremated is to rob God of His justice, but they shall not escape. The Book of Life is there so that no one can be lost that was redeemed. God is perfect in judgment.

Conclusion

Death and Hell are now cast into the Lake of Fire. This death is not just to cease to live, but to cease to have one semblance of beauty. The sun will never shine again for those that enter this judgment realm. They will never hear the cry of a newborn baby or see the smile of choice loved ones. Everything God created to make life beautiful is forever removed. The wicked will remember when mercy was real and love was close, but will know that all is forever gone. The Lamb's Book of Life is the final act of this chapter. It towers above all that exists. It stands as the opposite of the Lake of Fire. To have your name in this book means "Life Everlasting."

21

A CITY TO PRICELESS TO VALUE

This earth is a beautiful creation. Men have built cities, parks, buildings, and campuses that are marvels of technology and splendor. The natural splendor of this earth is overwhelming. But never has this earth seen beauty as we are destined to view. Ancient Babylon was known as one of the wonders of the world. Chariots raced on and around the tops of its walls, and the Great Euphrates River flowed beneath its towering strength. Yet, when New Jerusalem descends out of heaven its glowing beauty will dazzle the world. Never has this world viewed anything so glorious and so massive. The streets of gold are the most common of all its riches. This city will actually be heaven on earth.

God Himself, in the excellent glory of His person, and His exalted glorified Son will dwell in the midst of this city. It will become a temple or a sanctuary of His sovereign presence, and worship will fill every beautiful inch. I cannot explain the presence of the Heavenly Father, but I can assure you that there are not human words to fully describe Him. He is awesome in holiness, and that characteristic will be the overarching expression of Him. No sin can live or even approach Him. His holiness is not acquired but issues forth from Him. He is the one and only source of all holiness, and it absolutely fills His person to overflowing. All that come near to Him will take on His holiness in them and reflect it throughout this matchless city.

The Son of God, in all His glorified manhood will, along with

His Father, be the Light of the city and of the new heaven and new earth. The brilliance of that Light will create a lighted world without shadows. Everywhere you look will be this brilliance of Light so remarkable that it will appear to reflect off and out of everything. It will be Light that forever and totally eliminates the presence of darkness so that the entire universe has a God-like splendor. The Son of God Himself is the source of this Light. When He said, *"I am the light of the world"* (John 9:5) it was a divine statement. When we see Him, there will be a satisfaction in us that forever fulfills the greatest hunger known to man. Every pain, sadness, or sorrow known to the human family is but a deep need to be filled with Him. In His literal presence is fullness of life, and we will never have emptiness again. *"For now we see through a glass, darkly; but then face to face: now I know in part; but then shall I know even as also I am known"* (I Corinthians 13:12).

God Himself, in the excellent glory of His person, and His exalted glorified Son will dwell in the midst of this city. It will become a temple or a sanctuary of His sovereign presence, and worship will fill every beautiful inch.

The massive walls of this city are fifteen hundred miles high and are created with jewels of great value and beauty. The city will be foursquare, equal on each side to its height. There will be three identical gates on each side of the city of the same height as the twelve levels of city walls. They will add splendor because they will be solid pearls polished to their highest perfection. There is nowhere in God's universe that this city will not be visible. The Bible does not tell us how it will be set in conjunction to the new earth, but it must be seen because within it is the source of all light and there is no darkness. The gates will bear the names of the twelve tribes of Israel, and the twelve foundations will bear the names of the twelve apostles. These twenty-four representations reflect the same complete type as seen in chapter four when the Rapture occurred. They are His raptured saints from the Old and New Testament. The number twenty-four is but a type of a multitude.

The *"new heaven"* assures us that the heavenly bodies, the weather patterns, and the very atmosphere will be purified unto perfection. The great planets, stars, and other celestial bodies will be the source of beauty and heavenly splendor that will make the sky above to glisten in perfect clarity. It will be picture perfect, and the weather will never be anything but the source of life. When it rains it will be like drinking water bathing His created world. Snow and ice flakes will fill His world with a carpet that delights His entire creation. The birds, earth animals, and the sea creatures will spend their lives in playful delight, and God's family will love every moment of it.

The earth will bring forth nothing but that which delights our appetites. Fruit trees will never bear imperfect fruit. The vineyards will provide its vintage flavors to man. The entire earth will be a garden and flowers will explode in their beauty. There will be nothing on the earth or produced by the earth but those things that man enjoys. The earth will be so pure that God Himself will find delight in a renewed fellowship with His family. He will walk among us as He visited Adam in the garden. Labor will be sweet and we will tend our gardens with delight. Every moment on God's earth will be like heaven.

This great chapter (Revelation twenty-one) is the single place in God's World that the *Book of Life* is called by its full title. John wrote as the Spirit gave witness, *"And there shall in no wise enter into it any thing that defileth, neither whatsoever worketh abomination, or maketh a lie: but they which are written in the LAMB'S BOOK OF LIFE"* (Revelation 21:27). Nothing on His earth, in His heaven, or in New Jerusalem will be unclean. Nothing that defiles can enter His eternity. The total culture and population will be His redeemed saints. Holiness will be the lifestyle and love will be the emotion that fills this universe and His holy city forever. Sinners that refused to repent and surrender only to Christ will already have been cast into the Lake of Fire.

> *And I saw a new heaven and a new earth: for the first heaven and the first earth were passed away; and there was no more sea. And I John saw the holy city, new Jerusalem, coming down from God out of heaven, prepared as a bride adorned for her husband. And I heard a great voice out of heaven saying, Behold, the tabernacle of God is with men, and he will dwell with them, and they shall be his people, and God himself shall be with them, and be their God. And God shall wipe away all tears from their eyes; and there shall be no more death, neither sorrow, nor crying, neither shall there be any more pain: for the former things are passed away* (Revelation 21:1-4).

There has been a long, continuing debate over the new heaven and new earth. Some say that everything passes completely out of existence and a new heaven and a new earth replaces it all. That is not Biblical, but it does no harm if you want to believe it. It will be so new that to call it anything less would be untrue. Everything that has defiled this earth shall be cleansed so that its newness will be just as real as if it really did pass totally from existence and will then be recreated. But the language of the Scripture in its perfect context teaches that it is made new by the Blood of the Lamb and is redeemed as all else is redeemed. *"...The earth abideth for ever."* (Ecclesiastes 1:4). *"For the earth is the Lord's, and the fulness thereof"* (I Corinthians 10:26). Sin never changed the fact that the earth belonged to God from the beginning.

As His judgment comes to bear on this earth, every imperfection caused by sin and its consequences will be cleansed and reversed to its original glory and perfection. *"And there was no more sea"* is the perfect rendering of the ending of the effects of the flood of judgment in Noah's day. To a great degree, the earth was turned upside down and it will return to its perfect topographical expanse. The stormy developments on the earth will cease. The ice caps in the North and South Pole will vanish, and the earth's relationship to the sun will return to its original perfection. It is well known that the great oceans were caused by God's flood, so their elimination is a natural result of the earth returning to its original created likeness.

When He was about to be crucified, Jesus promised that He would go back to heaven and prepare mansions for all His saints. *"Let not your heart be troubled: ye believe in God, believe also in me. In my Father's house are many mansions: if it were not so, I would have told you. I go to prepare a place for you. And if I go and prepare a place for you, I will come again, and receive you unto myself; that where I am, there ye may be also"* (John 14:1-3). When He ascended, He did not wait to do that hundreds of years into the church age. At the

The earth will bring forth nothing but that which delights our appetites. Fruit trees will never bear imperfect fruit. The vineyards will provide its vintage flavors to man. The entire earth will be a garden and flowers will explode in their beauty.

very least, He did it before John wrote this Revelation. John saw this New Jerusalem with it indisputable glory. Here is the description of the city found in this chapter and the next and last chapter of this book. The Son of God is the Creator of this city and its glory. John gives us a little taste of that glory, for this is only a little glimpse. John's description of the city said that it was *"prepared as a Bride adorned for Her Husband."* Our Lord made certain that this city would exceed our expectations and be His prize for His overcomers.

Dwelling in the midst of this city and of His own family will be the Father Himself. The Son of God loves His Father with a love that can only be called divine. Yet, this divine love has a component of manhood, because He was begotten of the Father in His earthly pilgrimage. This city is the Son's gift to His Bride. After He brings His Bride into the city, He proceeds to exalt His Father to be with Him and His Bride and to be their God. One of the greatest mysteries that we shall soon discover is voiced in words that show this future honor that the Son gives His Father. *"Then cometh the end, when he shall have delivered up the kingdom to God, even the Father; when he shall have put down all rule and all authority and power. For he must reign, till he hath put all enemies under his feet. The last enemy that shall be destroyed is death. For he hath put all things under his feet. But when he saith all things are put under him, it is manifest that he is excepted, which did put all things under him. And when all things shall be subdued unto him, then shall the Son also himself be subject unto him that put all things under him, that God may be all in all"* (I Corinthians 24-28). New Jerusalem will be the location of this grand moment.

Then, the Father shall proceed to *"wipe away all tears from their eyes."* Every memory of pain and loss must be forever eliminated. Memories of loved ones that refused to surrender to Christ, although we sacrificed much pain to win them, must be forgotten. That will be possible only because the Father removes them from our minds. The human soul and spirit is eternal and all our experiences are stored in both our mind and in our emotions. This is why our world carries so much pain from the abuse, unfair and unkind experiences, and is a world filled with sin and its consequences. Our God has a plan and the authority to execute. *"The former things are passed away."*

> *And he that sat upon the throne said, Behold, I make all things new. And he said unto me, Write: for these words are true and faithful. And he said unto me, It is done. I am Alpha and Omega, the beginning and the end. I will give unto him that is athirst of the fountain of the water of life freely. He that overcometh shall inherit all things; and I will be*

his God, and he shall be my son. But the fearful, and unbelieving, and the abominable, and murderers, and whoremongers, and sorcerers, and idolaters, and all liars, shall have their part in the lake which burneth with fire and brimstone: which is the second death (Revelation 21:5-8).

When the Father is speaking, the entire world must listen. He starts with, *"Behold, I make all things new."* That settles the entire debate about a new heaven and a new earth. The Father created everything that exists except His own self and His Divine Godhead. He does not replace heaven and earth, but makes them new. That could not be more exact. He commanded John to write, because these are His words, and they cannot be altered. After at least six thousand years of putting up with the devil and his destruction of everything beautiful, the Father lets us know that it is over. Everything is going to be beautiful beyond measure again. Hallelujah!

The Father does not end it with a new world. He affirms that indeed He is not just the Creator that He calls the *"Beginning,"* but He is also the *"Finisher."* He will conclude the whole finality of His universe. His unalterable plan is to satisfy the needs and desires of His created world and He promises that we will drink from the *"fountain of the water of life freely."* There is a powerful meaning in this promise. The very source of life is the fountain, and it will be the joy of all creation forever. There is no question but that He speaks of His Son, the Lord Jesus Christ. The life that we are going to inherit is eternal, complete, full, and divine. It flows from our Redeemer; and it will satisfy the spirit, soul, and our new body with endless joys and delights.

He immediately gives us another great promise. He tells us that we *"shall inherit all things."* The entire new heaven, new earth, New Jerusalem, and all that goes with this New World is going to be ours.

Notice that He adds that great phrase, *"he that overcometh,"* again. This word, *overcometh*, is in the Book of Revelation eight times. *"To Him that overcometh"* forever destroys the cheap theology of this generation. This cheap theology says, "just believe," and then offers no Biblical truth about responsibility and judgment accountability. It has done irrefutable damage to God's church, and payday will be heartbreaking to those that have carelessly believed such theology of cheap Christianity. Only the *overcomers* will inherit eternal life, and Christ has made overcoming a work of His marvelous grace and sanctification.

Now, the Father Himself clearly shows the end results of careless living. All of these words are character words that He declares will condemn you in this awesome day of no excuses. *"The fearful, and unbelieving, and the abominable, and murderers, and whoremongers, and sorcerers, and idolaters, and all liars"* is a list that appears as much like most churches as it does the world. The Blood of Jesus Christ does not cover unconfessed and unforsaken sins, regardless of how pious and religious an individual. This crowd of sinners will spend eternity in the Lake of Fire.

> *And there came unto me one of the seven angels which had the seven vials full of the seven last plagues, and talked with me, saying, Come hither, I will shew thee the bride, the Lamb's wife. And he carried me away in the spirit to a great and high mountain, and shewed me that great city, the holy Jerusalem, descending out of heaven from God, Having the glory of God: and her light was like unto a stone most precious, even like a jasper stone, clear as crystal; And had a wall great and high, and had twelve gates, and at the gates twelve angels, and names written thereon, which are the names of the twelve tribes of the children of Israel: On the east three gates; on the north three gates; on the south three gates; and on the west three gates. And the wall of the*

city had twelve foundations, and in them the names of the twelve apostles of the Lamb (Revelation 21:9-14).

John had received the last words before verse nine from the Father, Who was seated on His throne. Now, he receives it from one of the angels of the temple. This angel is one of the seven that had the seven last plagues. Those plagues will be history when we come to this moment in the fulfillment of this prophecy. This angel is now taking John on a tour of the future city of New Jerusalem. He calls the city, *"the bride, and the Lamb's wife."* This is beautiful language to describe a city that is part of our inhabitance because it is the nuptial chamber, the eternal dwelling place of Christ and His Queen. It was created to be personal, so perfect in its splendor that the city and Bride are named as one.

> *The New Jerusalem is the Son's gift to His Bride. After He brings His Bride into the city, He proceeds to exalt His Father to be with Him and His Bride and to be their God.*

John had to be transported *"in the spirit"* to be capable of viewing this marvelous sight. Flesh and blood cannot endure the transcending glory as this created city represents. We are not just speaking of gold, pearls, precious stones, and other earthly materials; but of the glory and majesty of His consuming likeness. The city is called *"holy"* because He recreates Himself into every inch of this towering place. It is actually a temple that is filled with His presence. Because it is seen descending, could we suggest that it is even now on a carefully course toward planet earth? As I just stated, the city is a great temple of His glory and His light. It glistens with a glory or splendor that can only be called His Shekinah. The brilliance of this great city will lighten the universe and no additional light will ever be needed.

The great walls of this city will probably be translucent, allowing the city's beauty to shine without or allowing those dwelling outside to see within. The twelve gates carved from pearls will be the most beautiful gates of eternity. They never close, but stand as a welcome to the saved of the earth to enjoy and delight themselves with God's glory within. A great angel will be God's porter at each gate; and the gates will bear the names of the twelve tribes of Israel, with each gate having a different name. I would imagine that the children of Israel would use the gates to enter and visit the city that bears their tribal names. These gates are perfectly placed with three gates on each side. The foundations of the city are named after the twelve apostles.

> *And he that talked with me had a golden reed to measure the city, and the gates thereof, and the wall thereof. And the city lieth foursquare, and the length is as large as the breadth: and he measured the city with the reed, twelve thousand furlongs. The length and the breadth and the height of it are equal. And he measured the wall thereof, an hundred and forty and four cubits, according to the measure of a man, that is, of the angel. And the building of the wall of it was of jasper: and the city was pure gold, like unto clear glass. And the foundations of the wall of the city were garnished with all manner of precious stones. The first foundation was jasper; the second, sapphire; the third, a chalcedony; the fourth, an emerald; The fifth, sardonyx; the sixth, sardius; the seventh, chrysolite; the eighth, beryl; the ninth, a topaz; the tenth, a chrysoprasus; the eleventh, a jacinth; the twelfth, an amethyst. And the twelve gates were twelve pearls; every several gate was of one pearl: and the street of the city was pure gold, as it were transparent glass* (Revelation 21:15-21).

Without argument, this city is too priceless to value. It is fitting that an angel of the heavenly temple is chosen to measure and give

John this walking view of this city of His Bride. As one of those seven angels of the temple, this angel knows every detail of this new temple. This City of New Jerusalem is a temple itself and will be united with the eternal temple from heaven. This is God's gift to the new heaven and new earth and to His Son's Bride. This description is just an earthly explanation of an indescribable city. The temple angel measures the city in John's presence. The golden reed suggests that these measurements are an eternal matter.

The city is a foursquare city. The width is exactly the same on all four sides and the height is equal. Twelve thousand furlongs is fifteen hundred miles. To imagine a city that is fifteen hundred miles square and fifteen hundred miles high that is surrounded by jasper walls is breathtaking. The highest mountain in the world is less than six miles high (Mount Everest - 29,035 feet) and the highest in America is less than four miles high (Mount McKinley - 20,320 feet). We are speaking of a city so massive that our minds can only imagine its grandeur. The city of New Jerusalem is 7,920,000 feet high compared to Mount Everest at 29,035 feet. This comparison makes Mount Everest appear to be nothing but a molehill.

The total wealth of this entire earth does not hold a light to the wealth of this new city. The gold that has been mined and minted during human history is minute compared to the gold in this city. It would not be enough to pave the streets of one level of this city and this will be a city of twelve foundations or levels. Each level will be one hundred and twenty-five miles high or 657,700 feet, over twenty-two times higher than Mount Everest. The height of the walls on each level is 144 cubits or approximately 226 feet. These walls are not provided to keep the glorified saints in or out. Nothing is more beautiful than the present massive stone walls of present day Jerusalem. These stone walls have a golden hue appearance as they are beautifully lit at night or in the sunshine. But the walls of New

Jerusalem will be primarily wrought of jasper stone. Jasper is a dark green semi-translucent to opaque form of semi-precious chalcedony. Its beauty is rare. It is readily comparable to a fine polish and has the physical properties of those of quartz. No one would think of building city walls out of jasper in our present world. The expense would be totally prohibitive to the richest person but certainly not to our Father. The entire walled structure of this city, all twelve levels, will be jasper and pure gold. It appears that the outside formation of these walls is jasper, with the interior of the walls being pure gold.

The foundations at each level are one hundred and forty-four cubits, which is approximately 226 feet high. These foundations are then garnished with twelve manners of precious stones. The first foundation is garnished with jasper on jasper. We can certainly expect that the garnishing jasper will be of a different shade as the jasper wall, which comprises the wall's structure. There are different colors of jasper depending on the location where it is mined. The second level will be garnished with sapphire stones. The color of a pure sapphire is sky blue; using it to garnish the jasper will be extraordinary. The third level will be chalcedony, which can be any color of the rainbow from pale blue to yellow, brown, or gray. The fourth level will be garnished with emeralds. The finest emeralds are more valuable than diamonds; they are magnificent gems of the most beautiful green color.

The stone used to garnish the fifth foundation is sardonyx or onyx. This stone varies in color; it may be translucent or opaque and is often striped. The sixth stone used for garnishment is sardius, possibly the red variety that is highly polishable and extremely beautiful. The seventh level is garnished with chrysolite, which is a form of topaz of Tarshish. The garnishment of the eighth level is beryl, which is actually colorless, but reflects a great variety of colors depending on foreign substances it contains. It is indeed a precious stone. The ninth garnishing stone on the ninth level of this city is topaz, which is called by some, the "gem of the setting sun." Sometimes, it is said to be the color of gold or peach. The tenth level is chrysoprasus, which is called the apple and is a light green variety of agate. It is a very rare stone.

The eleventh foundation of this magnificent city is jacinth. The jacinth is a red variety of zircon, which is found in square prisms of different shades. The last of the twelve levels is garnished with amethyst. This is a royal purple and a fitting crown for the city. Imagine the crown of this city of transparent purple quartz that is decorating the jasper translucent walls with the gold within reflecting throughout the foursquare city.

Beautify all of this with gates of pearl, each gate one pearl carved into form to be twelve matching gates into the city. Each gate will be fifteen hundred miles high. Glowing through each gate will be streets of pure gold. It is hard to imagine the beauty of a solid pearl gate set on the walls of this city. This city reflects the creative masterpiece of a Groom full of love for His eternal Bride.

> *And I saw no temple therein: for the Lord God Almighty and the Lamb are the temple of it. And the city had no need of the sun, neither of the moon, to shine in it: for the glory of God did lighten it, and the Lamb is the light thereof* (Revelation 21:22-23).

Here is a beautiful city, New Jerusalem, set at the center of a new heaven and a new earth. The city itself is called a *"Tabernacle."* It is also called a *"holy city,"* the *"Lamb's wife,"* and *"a bride adorned for her husband."* He now says, *"And I saw no temple therein..."* He is not saying there is no temple, but rather there is no need of a temple separate from this city. The picture is of the glory of the Father and of the Lamb of God. Their splendor transcends all the majesty of this great city and its wealth. They themselves will be the center of worship and of the Shekinah of God's glory. The eternal divinity of our God and the worship that centers in them will make all else seem as unimportant. It is a city so contained by God that all becomes worship and praise. The glory of the Creator will fill all of it to a total fullness. Our God and our Christ will become the essence of the temple themselves.

The created sun, moon, and stars are no longer of service to God's great universe. They have served their purpose. Now, the light of God is no longer shielded or manifested as a shadow. We have seen our Father and the Lord *"through a glass darkly,"* but now the darkness is gone, and His light breaks forth in its splendor. A world where the *"glory of God did lighten it"* seems like a dream. It is soon to be a reality. He says, *"The Lamb is the light thereof."* Calling Christ a Lamb at this time in our prophetic future is a reminder of Calvary's great accomplishment. There is no future without the cross. The very title, *Lamb,* is our reminder that there is no path to eternal bliss except by passing by the bloodstained hill outside and near Jerusalem's earthly walls.

> *And the nations of them which are saved shall walk in the light of it: and the kings of the earth do bring their glory and honour into it. And the gates of it shall not be shut at all by day: for there shall be no night there. And they shall bring the glory and honour of the nations into it. And there shall in no wise enter into it any thing that defileth, neither whatsoever worketh abomination, or maketh a lie: but they which are written in the Lamb's book of life* (Revelation 21:24-27).

We must understand that this city is the eternal reward of the Bride, but there is a world outside of this city where the saved that did not receive the reward of Brideship will live. The Apostle Paul tried to excite us to so follow Christ that we would inherit the highest honors. He stated, *"And be found in him, not having mine own righteousness, which is of the law, but that which is through the faith of Christ, the righteousness which is of God by faith: That I may know him, and the power of his resurrection, and the fellowship of his sufferings, being made conformable unto his death; If by any means I might attain unto the resurrection of the dead"* (Philippians 3:9-11). He also spoke of being "saved by fire" but losing your reward. *"If any man's work abide which he hath built thereupon, he shall receive a reward. If any man's work shall be burned, he shall suffer loss: but he himself shall be saved; yet so as by fire"* (I Corinthians 3:14-15). These great Scriptures in the Word of God make it absolute that the New World will be filled with the saved that failed to inherit a full reward. This should awaken the multitude that lives right and overcomes sin, but are too busy to be soul-winners and burden bearers in the kingdom of God.

The brilliance of the New Jerusalem will lighten the universe and no additional light will ever be needed.

This city of such wealth and splendor will become the delight of those that dwell on the earth. They will find joy in the light and reflection from this city, and they will walk in that light with joy. The great cities of the earth live and prosper with the view of bringing all their glory into this capital of the universe. Those living in the Bride's splendor will delight to welcome the earth's saved to visit in their mansions. That will become a joy to their past acquaintances that come to share their honor of being a resident in this golden city. Part of the Bride of Christ's honor will be to welcome and share this city with the earth's inhabitants. The gates of the city never close and there is no night. It will be one eternal day.

No one can enter this city but the saved, those written in the Lamb's Book of Life. The angels that stand in honor at every gate will recognize instantly the names of the Father's extended family as they come to delight in this golden city of priceless beauty.

Conclusion

This chapter is the highlight of the entire Holy Scripture. All that the Garden of Eden represented is completely fulfilled in this golden city. Everything Jesus died to accomplish is finished. There will never be another sinner nor will there ever be a need for another cross. The last words of the entire Revelation of Jesus Christ will now follow and men will be warned never to touch or change those truths contained in this Holy book.

THE GARDEN OF EDEN HAS RETURNED

22

The famous garden that the great Creator created in which He placed Adam and Eve disappeared in southern Iraq, which was originally called Sumer, approximately four thousand years ago. It is presumed that it was present and protected by the Cherubim of God until the great flood. Men were not allowed in this garden after the fall, lest they would eat of the fruit of the Tree of Life in the midst of the garden and then live eternally in their depraved state. *"And the LORD God said, Behold, the man is become as one of us, to know good and evil: and now, lest he put forth his hand, and take also of the tree of life, and eat, and live for ever: Therefore the LORD God sent him forth from the garden of Eden, to till the ground from whence he was taken. So he drove out the man; and he placed at the east of the garden of Eden Cherubim, and a flaming sword which turned every way, to keep the way of the tree of life"* (Genesis 3:22-24).

If there is a theme in this last chapter of Revelation and last chapter of the Bible, it must be the return of this incredible garden near the city of New Jerusalem that is certainly at the center of God's presence in the new heaven and the new earth. I have found that almost no attention has been given to this incredible truth. The original Garden of Eden had to have been the most magnificent garden ever created. Creating gardens has been a pastime and a joy of the rich and famous for millenniums. It seems to me that this lost centerpiece of human life has left a vacuum in the human family that has never found true satisfaction. This garden was so pristine and perfect that it invited the joy of fellowship between God and His choice creation. Because of its excellent beauty and the deep sense of the divine delight of the Creator, Satan chose it as his location of attack against God and man.

Even as Eve listened to Satan's lie, the River of Life was splashing in the background. When she looked upon the tree of good and evil, she well may have held in her hands the fruit of the Tree of Life. Her deception and then Adam's deception occurred within the reach of a life so perfect and full that the heart of a pure soul has never understood such foolishness. How could it have happened? The only possible answer is that our Creator gave this man He created absolute right of choice. He did not create a robot, but gave him the freedom to choose to choose to love. That day in the breathtaking garden, sorrow began that still rushes like a tsunami upon the whole of the human family and the created world.

If there is a theme in this last chapter of Revelation and last chapter of the Bible, it must be the return of this incredible garden near the city of New Jerusalem that is certainly at the center of God's presence in the new heaven and the new earth.

This great closing text reveals the final end of human misery and a total new beginning.

The Creator is going to move in with His redeemed family, the total curse will have been eliminated, and we will actually see the Father face-to-face. While the city of New Jerusalem will be the most magnificent creation of all eternity, the earth will have been recreated into the paradise of perfect bliss. It will be a worldwide garden, and nothing of disease, weeds, undergrowth, or destroying insects will be present to mar the beauty. If you can imagine the city of New Jerusalem set within and upon this garden-like world, and the beauty of both united to welcome all of His and the Lamb's family, you are beginning to get the vision. We will be so identified with Him that His family appearance will be written upon each countenance.

His entire cosmos will be filled with creative beauty. The only exception will be the Lake of Fire that will contain the wicked. The second death, the most dreadful indictment ever assigned, will have been finished and assigned to its victims and that multitude of the wicked will be cast into this eternal lake of brimstone. It will be in the vicinity of Babylon and large enough to contain every lost soul of all eternity. It will be possible for man to visit this site and forever remember the sacrifice of the Lamb that spared their souls that same fate.

Isaiah spoke of this dreadful place that would be visible forever. *"For as the new heavens and the new earth, which I will make, shall remain before me, saith the LORD, so shall your seed and your name remain. And it shall come to pass, that from one new moon to another, and from one sabbath to another, shall all flesh come to worship before me, saith the LORD. And they shall go forth, and look upon the carcasses of the men that have transgressed against me: for their worm shall not die, neither shall their fire be quenched; and they shall be an abhorring unto all flesh"* (Isaiah 66:22-24). Babylon has been the devil's capital since the day of Nimrod. He moved it to Rome nearly two thousand years ago, but only to deceive. The Antichrist will return this capital back to Babylon. Isaiah also spoke of this future judgment against Satan and clearly tied this location to Babylon. He saw, *"That thou shalt take up this proverb against the king of Babylon, and say, How hath the oppressor ceased! the golden city ceased...Hell from beneath is moved for thee to meet thee at thy coming: it stirreth up the dead for thee, even all the chief ones of the earth; it hath raised up from their thrones all the kings of the nations. All they shall speak and say unto thee, Art thou also become weak as we? art thou become like unto us? Thy pomp is brought down to the grave, and the noise of thy viols: the worm is spread under thee, and the worms cover thee ... How art thou fallen from heaven, O Lucifer, son of the morning! how art thou cut down to the ground, which didst weaken the nations! Yet thou shalt be brought down to hell, to the sides of the pit"* (Isaiah14:4, 9-12, 15).

Hell will rise up out of the heart of the earth to be joined with the Lake of Fire, and God will set a boundary around the ancient center of Satanism. It will become the final abode of Lucifer, the Antichrist, and the false prophet, along with his fallen angels and every wicked soul that rejected God's offering of grace. Babylon will finally become the desolation promised by the prophets of old. God the Creator will reward the wicked at the very center from which wickedness has charmed the earth.

Anyone that doubts the Book of Revelation must deny some of the plainest speech in the Bible. After John has finished viewing the city of New Jerusalem in the midst of the new heaven and new earth, his host who had taken him on the tour, spoke great words of warning. This angel that later identified himself as a fellow servant of Jesus Christ said to John, *"And he said unto me, These sayings are faithful and true: and the Lord God of the holy prophets sent his angel to shew unto his servants the things which must shortly be done"* (Revelation 22:6). The messenger continued his attention to John by prophesying of Christ. *"Behold, I come quickly: blessed is he that keepeth the sayings of the prophecy of this book"* (Revelation 22:7).

Before we review the verses individually, we must understand the warning in this book that speaks so loudly. The church world is full of religious people and leaders that either deny or ignore this "Masterpiece of Truth." The messenger to John pronounced by the voice of Holy Ghost prophecy that it is spiritual death to change or reject these words. *"And if any man shall take away from the words of the book of this prophecy, God shall take away his part out of the book of life, and out of the holy city, and from the things which are written in this book"* (Revelation 22:19). Jesus also said that the *"Scripture cannot be broken"* (John 10:35). It is time for the church and the church world to embrace this wonderful revelation within the Book of Revelation.

And he shewed me a pure river of water of life, clear as crystal, pro-
ceeding out of the throne of God and of the Lamb. In the midst of the
street of it, and on either side of the river, was there the tree of life,
which bare twelve manner of fruits, and yielded her fruit every
month: and the leaves of the tree were for the healing of the nations.
And there shall be no more curse: but the throne of God and of the
Lamb shall be in it; and his servants shall serve him: And they shall see
his face; and his name shall be in their foreheads. And there shall be no
night there; and they need no candle, neither light of the sun; for the
Lord God giveth them light: and they shall reign for ever and ever
(Revelation 22:1-5).

These verses continue the subject of chapter twenty-one. This
magnificent city of New Jerusalem is more than an ordinary city; it
is the temple of God and Christ. This temple is united with the city
of New Jerusalem, the home of Christ's Bride. God the Father is
moving the heavenly temple within the New Jerusalem and uniting
it all with His new creation. Our view of this eternal and glorious creation is certainly limited to human words and descriptions that
remind us of the Biblical warning, *"For now we see through a glass, dark-*
ly; but then face to face: now I know in part; but then shall I know even as also
I am known" (1 Corinthians 13:12). This is the grandest view ever
revealed, and from it we can catch a limited vision of our future.
Living for anything but our lord Jesus Christ and His eternal plans
is folly.

John is now allowed to view one of the most breathtaking aspects
of this city and the new world. The River of Life and The Tree of Life
is second only to the Father and the Lamb as the heartthrob of this
city. It is our substance of eternal life. While Adam and Eve were created to be eternal, the River of Life and the Tree of Life were the
source of that eternal life. It is in this eternal picture again as it was

in the beginning. We will live forever and the provision of that life is flowing directly out of the throne of God and of the Lamb. Our eternal life is not resident in His created family but in Himself and the Lamb of God. While this river is a literal river and this tree is a literal tree, the substance of both the river and tree is divine life, His divine life provided for His family.

This river will flow throughout this great and marvelous city and throughout the new earth. The original river in Eden divided into four streams and flowed far and wide to provide life for all of Adam and Eve's family. This river flowing from the throne of God shall certainly do no less but will be the joy of the whole universe. On either bank of this river will be the Tree of Life. The Bible is not speaking of one tree, but of one variety of multiple trees bearing multiple fruits. This tree will bear twelve manners of fruit and the fruit will be yielded and renewed monthly. Everywhere the river flows, the tree will line its banks and satisfy every eternal soul with life everlasting. The leaves of the tree will be filled with renewable nutrients that provide perfect substance for our glorified bodies.

The curse of sin is finished and the glorified saints will have perfect fellowship with their God and Father. It will be the joy of the earth to serve the Great Creator and His Son and to worship Him forever. The care of our mansions and the breathtaking gardens that fill the landscape will fill every saint with unfailing pleasure. Fellowship with other saints, viewing a dazzling world of exquisite beauty, and worshipping with the angels and great prophets will never allow for one moment of boredom.

There will never be a sunset. Artificial light will not be needed because this new world will be flooded with the light of the Lord God Himself. It will be a world bathed in the glory of the Eternal and filled with His presence forever and ever.

And he said unto me, These sayings are faithful and true: and the Lord God of the holy prophets sent his angel to shew unto his servants the things which must shortly be done. Behold, I come quickly: blessed is he that keepeth the sayings of the prophecy of this book. And I John saw these things, and heard them. And when I had heard and seen, I fell down to worship before the feet of the angel which shewed me these things. Then saith he unto me, See thou do it not: for I am thy fellowservant, and of thy brethren the prophets, and of them which keep the sayings of this book: worship God (Revelation 22:6-9).

The fact that an angel of God, charged with delivering this message of Jesus Christ, would interrupt this great revelation to emphasize the truthfulness of this masterpiece is thrilling. This messenger is not speaking for himself but by direct inspiration. These words are the words of God. Everything in this book is perfect, *"faithful, and true"* and cannot be denied or changed. The angel plainly says, *"The Lord God of the holy prophets sent* (me) *his angel to show unto His servants the things which must surely come to pass."* This book is either literal or all of Christianity is in trouble.

The statement that I have already quoted in the beginning of this chapter is a post-stated warning that carries the student or reader back to chapter four where the saints were caught up to the throne before the Great Tribulation. This is given to readers and students of this book so we do not wait to suffer through the great Antichrist period. Let's read that warning again. *"Behold, I come quickly: blessed is he that keepeth the sayings of the prophecy of this book"* (Revelation 22:7). The Lord did this very same thing in Matthew chapter twenty-four when He painted the picture of the dark Tribulation but ended with a route of escape. No believer has to endure the coming hell on earth. The Lord said the exact same thing to the church of Philadelphia, *"Because thou hast kept the word of my patience, I also will keep thee from the hour of temptation, which shall come upon all the world, to try them that dwell upon the earth"* (Revelation 3:10). When John could get his breath from what he had seen and heard, he fell down in front of this angel or messenger to worship. This walking tour of the city, plus the words of proof for all he had seen, left him in a rapturous mood. But the angel was more than an angel. He was a servant of the Lord, a fellow servant, a glorified saint, actually an elder participant in the grand events of God's kingdom. This certainly suggests that the saints of God in heaven are not there to picnic, but to worship and participate. This servant of God was quick to confirm that he was one *"of them which keeps the saying of this Book."* He adds, *"Worship God."*

> *And he saith unto me, Seal not the sayings of the prophecy of this book: for the time is at hand. He that is unjust, let him be unjust still: and he which is filthy, let him be filthy still: and he that is righteous, let him be righteous still: and he that is holy, let him be holy still. And, behold, I come quickly; and my reward is with me, to give every man according as his work shall be* (Revelation 22:10-12).

Now we get a warning on top of a warning. This Elder of the Lord (Let's call him that for the rest of this discussion.), plainly tells John that this book is an ironclad truth that cannot be put aside. The Book of Revelation has been on the shelf all the way back to the beginning of the dark ages. Too few of God's saints have dared to dig for the truths found in this Masterpiece. The Elder says something that is hair-raising: *"Seal not the sayings of the prophecy of this book: for the time is at hand."* If the time was at hand then, what would that Elder say today? This book is a "revelation, an unveiling," not a "concealing or a hidden thing."

The Elder then declares a warning that leaves no one innocent. *"He that is unjust, let him be unjust still: and he which is filthy, let him be filthy still."* Righteousness is not just a legalistic or a positional standing, but a literal transformation. We will be what we are now in our heart and present lifestyle when we stand before the Great Judge, unless you allow grace to transform you.

The declaration that follows the warning is exciting. The Lord to whom we relate is perfect in His sovereign being, and every fact of eternity is totally open before Him. When He comes, every saint of God will be rewarded. The reward is based on one thing alone - obedience to Him in our works. We will be rewarded, and every reward will be individually determined. We will get what our surrender and devotion to Him merits. The new heaven, the new earth, the New Jerusalem, and the Garden of Eden will not be a place of identical saints and rewards, but every person will be special. Every mansion will be different and every garden will be unique.

> *I am Alpha and Omega, the beginning and the end, the first and the last. Blessed are they that do his commandments, that they may have right to the tree of life, and may enter in through the gates into the city. For without are dogs, and sorcerers, and whoremongers, and murderers, and idolaters, and whosoever loveth and maketh a lie. I Jesus have sent mine angel to testify unto you these things in the churches. I am the root and the offspring of David, and the bright and morning star* (Revelation 22:13-16).

These closing truths of this great book are really breathtaking. Easy believism is the product of apostasy. It certainly never existed in the Bible. The elder is clearly caught up in the language and the message of our God and His Son. Right in the middle of these closing words, the Spirit takes this elder's lips and he proclaims the voice of the Sovereign One, *"I am Alpha and Omega, the beginning and the end, the first and the last."* Then, God says, *"Blessed are they that do his commandments.*" The promises are more than worthy of our total commitment. Every saint will enjoy the Tree of Life and have the right to either live in the city of His Bride or visit and enjoy the city.

As I said in the opening of this chapter, the Lake of Fire will be on earth for eternity and will be visible to be visited. The warning, "*For without are dogs,*" makes it clear that the judgment will forever be in the conscience of every saint. To forget the consequence of sin and its judgment would be unthinkable. The sacrifice of the Son of God will be an eternal matter, and we will never forget to worship our Savior. The glorified saints will possess in themselves the redemption of the Cross, and the glory of our new bodies will forever testify to the triumph of Calvary. This is why the Lord Jesus Christ is called the "Lamb" right down to the very last chapter.

Jesus Christ gave this book to John, through an array of angels and elders, for the church. It belongs to every church and every saint. It is our last "Will and Testament" and was always meant to bless and embolden the followers of our Lord Jesus Christ. The Lord said, "*I Jesus have sent mine angel to testify unto you these things in the churches. I am the root and the offspring of David, and the bright and morning star.*" What a love letter this is straight from the Lord Himself. If you live in and obey this book, the world will appear exactly as it is, a fading kingdom soon to be judged and renewed in righteousness just for the Bride of Christ and the saints of God.

> *And the Spirit and the bride say, Come. And let him that heareth say, Come. And let him that is athirst come. And whosoever will, let him take of the water of life freely* (Revelation 22:17).

The harvest of the precious fruits of the earth is never far from the heart of God. Right in the heart of Revelation, from chapter one to this transcending close of chapter twenty-two, "*there is a rainbow above the throne.*" It never gets so dark that something special does not appear to show the mercy extended to lost souls. This next statement is remarkable. *"The Holy Spirit says, Come."* The heart of the Holy Spirit's office is the wooing of the unsaved. *"Let him that heareth"* shows the obligation of every recipient of grace. No one can know of salvation without the obligation of telling it to others. *"Let him that is athirst come"* is a call that never ends until the last soul is saved or judged. *"Whosoever will"* is the invitation of Holy Scripture from Genesis to Revelation. No one has the right to tell even one soul that there is no hope. *"Whosoever will"* is the theme of the Bible.

> *For I testify unto every man that heareth the words of the prophecy of this book, If any man shall add unto these things, God shall add unto him the plagues that are written in this book: And if any man shall take away from the words of the book of this prophecy, God shall take away his part out of the book of life, and out of the holy city, and from the things which are written in this book* (Revelation 22:18-19).

The Word of God is forever settled in heaven. Before one word was ever given to any man to write, the Bible was complete. The Word of God is a heavenly book that has been given to the earthly church. The command has always been not to change or eliminate what the Spirit has given. He first warns us not to add to His revelations. We are warned that to add will be to receive the plagues written in this book. He then warns not to *"take away"* from the book. This warning comes with stated results. If we *"take away"* His words, He will take away our name from His Book of Life. These are awesome warnings.

> *He which testifieth these things saith, Surely I come quickly. Amen. Even so, come, Lord Jesus. The grace of our Lord Jesus Christ be with you all. Amen* (Revelation 22:20-21).

The parting words of our Lord as He closes His dialogue with John were beautiful. The elder speaks, *"He which testifieth these things saith,"* and then the elder gives the final words of the Lord, *"Surely I come quickly."* The elder added, *"Amen."* John then added by inspiration, *"Even so, come, Lord Jesus."* Maybe it was John that spoke the *"Amen,"* also. Either way this is a wonderful close to a heavenly vision. John then says to all the church that read these supernatural words, *"The grace of our Lord Jesus Christ be with you all. Amen."*

Conclusion

This chapter is a highlight of this great Masterpiece. To see the Garden of Eden reappear for the first time since Genesis chapter three is beautiful. Of course, it could not appear until redemption was complete. The entrance of sin had broken the great fellowship that men had with God. The Father's love demanded that a shadow of fellowship be restored, but the fellowship was always conducted with blood as its doorway. From the garden when coats were made by God the Father to this final revelation where a Lamb slain walks in every sentence, blood alone has been the Father's carefully laid plan. Now redemption is finished and God and His family are going to live together forever.

AND THE WORLD SAID, "AMEN"

This book began with the beautiful story of the glorified Christ and ended with the magnificent city of New Jerusalem. From the devil's scheme in the Garden of Eden to the final picture of his being cast into the Lake of Fire, the world is ready to say, *"Amen."* Global warming will never be discussed again. Right and wrong, debated by the religionist is forever settled. The God-haters have admitted that God is real, and the smorgasbord of gods has been assigned to the ash heap. The one God—Sovereign and Eternal—is in His temple, and there is none to challenge His Fatherhood. The world is at peace, and the "Amen" chorus echoes across a landscape of perfect beauty.

The only words fitting for the Book of Revelation is "The Masterpiece." There is no book of literature more filled with mysteries then this book; yet every mystery is a story in itself. The mysteries in this book are not meant to intrigue but to reveal. Every mystery has a background in one of the sixty-five books. It is the Bible itself that precedes this finish and helps unlock every great truth. The Lord Jesus Christ Himself gave this book to an angel, and the angel caused John to both hear and see the stories unveiled before him. There is no room to misread what the Lord said because He used these background mysteries to unlock every part of the story. Together, we have now learned it truly is a "masterpiece"

Christ's church is the focus of this book because she is absolutely

His "Sun-Clothed Woman." The wars of the last two thousand years have often centered on religion, sometimes the misguided in the church and sometimes hatred for the church. The church has had many competitors in the name of other acclaimed gods. This book has settled these arguments and established the grand truth of the identity of His chosen family.

Israel as a distinct culture and people were sidelined by the church age. Their ultimate rejection of Jesus Christ was a choice they made, but they remained very committed to their traditions during the two thousands years of church life. The God that chose them in the days of Abraham never forgot them. While the message of Jesus Christ in the church has been rejected by Israel, the Bible-believing church has not responded with the dismissal of Israel. Many in the more liberal church groups have preached Replacement Theology concerning these chosen people, but at the end of the Book of Revelation that theology was proven false and dangerous. At the end, Israel occupies the whole of the Abrahamic promise and Jesus Christ, Who has occupied the throne of David for one thousand years, now reigns in New Jerusalem.

Sin has finally been perfectly judged and the purifying of all things is complete. God's universe has no enemies left, no dark personalities seeking to defile and destroy, and all remembrance of those evil entities and their works are finished. Fallen angels, including the devil, are imprisoned within the Lake of Fire, along with every soul that has rejected the sacrifice of blood to redeem. The Bible proclaimed that every living being would confess that Jesus Christ was the Father's gift. That has now occurred, so the entire creation of angels and mankind have made the absolute confession that He alone saves.

New Jerusalem sits on the highest hill or clings to the lowest star. It is now the center of everything that exists. The Father has been exalted by His Son and is the everlasting love of all the heavens and the earth. The Garden of Eden, seen in the beginning of Genesis, has been replaced with a garden that touches the whole of His new earth, except for the center where Satanism reigned, which is called Babylon. The light of New Jerusalem will finally light the whole of the new heaven and the new earth. Nature has returned to its original perfection, so that all creation and all living matter are perfect in beauty and life-giving substance.

Music and singing will be the order of life just as Satan made it the order of vileness and destruction. Singing will be worship of the Creator and every expression of His holiness. The Tree of Life and the Water of Life will be available to all creation, and its supply will fill one and all with life everlasting. In the light of magnificent New Jerusalem, the universe will never quit proclaiming *"Amen, Amen, Amen."*

The glory of the Father, the Son, and the Holy Spirit will be unveiled to the glorified saints as it has always been to the angels. The cry of angels in His presence reflects nothing but a continuance of "Glory, glory, glory," because it is indeed indescribable glory. To be in God's presence and to look upon the awesome sight of His holiness is impossible to flesh and blood, but the bodies prepared for every saint will be fully prepared to share in His likeness. Scripture declares, *"... We shall be like him; for we shall see him as he is"* (1 John 3:2). Paul reminded the church at Corinth that our Creator has prepared and holds in hope for His creation our future eternal house or glorified body. *"For we know that if our earthly house of this tabernacle were dissolved, we have a building of God, an house not made with hands, eternal in the heavens."* (2 Corinthians 5:1).

The Father's throne was never far from any event in the Revelation story. Every great moment was a part of His design. The mysteries were present to keep unspiritual souls from their idle speculation. The dark deeds of Satan were allowed to provide the closing picture of the transgressions of angels and men. The story ends in the most spectacular fashion. Earthly riches that have seduced a multitude of lost souls are quickly visible as shadows of poverty. The new heaven and the new earth, resplendent in the lights of the Bridal city, become the eternal dwelling of all the Father's family. Every sound will be joyous, every smile will be natural, every song will be worship, and every soul perfectly satisfied. The universe is at peace and the Father is on His throne. Amen.

PAW CREEK MINISTRIES
5110 Tuckaseegee Road
Charlotte, NC 28208
704-391-0588
1-800-338-7884 (1-800-33TRUTH)

MINISTRIES:
Paw Creek Christian Academy
Two-Year Olds to Twelfth Grade
Organized 1974
A Beka Curriculum

Open Bible Dialogue
Sixty-Minute "LIVE" Talk Show Broadcast
Every Saturday 1:00 – 2:00 PM (EST)
Also Heard "LIVE" via Worldwide Internet with
Archives Accessible 7 days a week/24 hours a day

Website – http://www.pawcreek.org
Weekly Sermons
Articles on Hundreds of Bible Subjects

Campus and On-Line Bookstore

International Prophecy Publication
The End Times and Victorious Living